THE YORKISTS

The Yorkists
The History of a Dynasty

Anne Crawford

hambledon
continuum

Hambledon Continuum is an imprint of Continuum Books
Continuum UK, The Tower Building, 11 York Road, London SE1 7NX
Continuum US, 80 Maiden Lane, Suite 704, New York, NY 10038

www.continuumbooks.com

First published 2007

British Library Cataloguing-in-Publication Data
A catalogue record for this book is available from the British Library.

ISBN 978 1 85285 351 8

Typeset by Egan Reid Ltd, Auckland, New Zealand
Printed and bound by MPG Books Ltd, Cornwall, Great Britain

Contents

Illustrations

Between Pages 104 and 105

Family trees

Acknowledgements

In writing this study of the Yorkists, my biggest debt is to the late Professor Charles Ross, who first introduced me to fifteenth century research and was subsequently responsible for suggesting that I look in detail at the last medieval queens. I am very grateful to Professor Ralph Griffiths for suggesting that I be asked to write the Yorkist contribution to this series on medieval English dynasties and for his constructive comments on the early chapters which cover his own Lancastrian dynasty. Many thanks are due to our General Editor, Professor Nigel Saul, for his support and direction. Anyone writing on the history of late fifteenth century England owes much to a handful of scholars who have made the period their own and published so much on it, in particular Professor Tony Pollard, Professor Michael Hicks, Dr Michael K. Jones and Keith Dockray. Members of the Richard III Society have contributed enormous amounts of research to the study of their king and his contemporaries and their publications are a mine of information. Above all, my thanks are due to Dr James Ross, who read the text in draft and among many helpful comments, suggested its present structure.

Introduction

The fifteenth century was the most politically unstable period in English history and most modern readers' view of the period is heavily coloured by Shakespeare. He portrayed the bitter civil war known as the Wars of the Roses as divine punishment for the Lancastrian usurpation and the murder of Richard II, and in his portrayal of Richard III he created one of the most magnificent villains of the English stage. Shakespeare was certainly right to suppose that one cause of the war was the rivalry of two branches of the family of Edward III, but more immediately the war was a result of the incompetence of Henry VI's government rather than Yorkist ambition. Was he also right in his depiction of the last Yorkist king? Richard III is probably the most controversial king ever to sit on the English throne, forever overshadowed by the general belief that he murdered his nephews, the sons of Edward IV, in the Tower. Shakespeare was in no doubt about his guilt. Modern readers will wish to make up their own minds.

It is impossible to describe the rise of the Yorkists without studying the decline of the Lancastrians, since one was a direct result of the other. There was nothing inevitable about the accession of the Yorkist kings. For the first half of the fifteenth century, the family was only one of a number of similar ones, wealthy, descended from the royal house and active in royal service. Richard, duke of York, born in 1411, was the progenitor of the dynasty and for a while it appeared that he would take his rightful place among the ruling elite of Henry VI's government. Yet the king's lack of interest in ruling and the resulting rise of factions among those struggling to govern in his name led to York being excluded from the inner circle surrounding the king. He needed the repayment of large sums of money he had expended in previous royal service and his attempts to regain these and what he saw as his rightful position led to direct confrontation with the government. He also, unexpectedly, found that the role of reformer was thrust upon him by the commons. During the period of Henry's mental incapacity he was twice successful in being named Protector, but the insecurity of his position meant that his achievements were limited and he found himself drawn inexorably to challenge Henry for the throne itself. The armed struggle was not for the most part between two contenders for the throne but between two factions vying for control of the king and hence the government in his name. While York had the support of a number of peers in this, he had little or none in his attempt to dethrone Henry. The exception was his wife's family, the Nevills, specifically his brother-in-law, Richard, earl of Salisbury and his son, Richard, earl of Warwick. The deaths of York and Salisbury at Wakefield in 1460 led to a desperate gamble, masterminded by Warwick, to place York's eldest son, Edward, on the throne. The Yorkist dynasty had begun.

The young Edward IV held on to the throne by his military victory at Towton and spent the next few years mopping up pockets of Lancastrian resistance. To many it seemed that the 1460s were a decade when the Nevills, Warwick and his brothers, were the most powerful force in government, but this was to some extent a misconception. Edward was his own man, pursuing a pro-Burgundian policy abroad where Warwick favoured an alliance with France and crowning it with a match between his youngest sister, Margaret, and Charles, duke of Burgundy. The king's own marriage, contracted secretly to a Lancastrian widow with two sons, Elizabeth Woodville, Lady Grey, was a political blunder of the first magnitude which was to have unforeseen consequences for his dynasty. Warwick's alienation was completed by the king's refusal to permit a match between his brother George, duke of Clarence, his heir presumptive, and Warwick's elder daughter. The earl's decision to stage a *coup d'etat*, however, was indefensible. In his ambition, Warwick first tried to force Edward into a position where he might recover some of his lost influence, and failing that, to replace him with a more malleable king, his new son-in-law, George of Clarence. Clarence's disloyalty to his brother was the first indication of the internal rot which was to destroy the house of York. When Edward turned the tables on his cousin Warwick, the earl and Clarence were forced into exile, where Warwick performed a complete *volte-face* and allied himself with Queen Margaret of Anjou to restore Henry VI to the throne, thus earning himself the nickname of 'Kingmaker' by which he is known to history. The Re-adeption of Henry ended with Edward's return from exile, and his military victories at Barnet and Tewkesbury, culminating with the deaths of both Henry VI and his son, Prince Edward, ended the Lancastrian dynasty. Edward IV is the only English king to have successfully regained his throne after being dethroned, and one question to be addressed is why did Henry VI, so incompetent a king, hold on to his throne for so long, while Edward, able and popular, lost his after a decade?

The Yorkists were the shortest-lived dynasty to have occupied the English throne since the Norman Conquest, reigning between 1461 and 1485. They comprised only two kings in any real sense, Edward IV and his brother, Richard III; the boy king Edward V's brief reign was in essence only the prologue to that of his uncle, Richard. Countless books have been written on Richard III and his motives for replacing his nephew. All are agreed, however, on his loyalty to Edward during the king's lifetime. This loyalty, which contrasted starkly with the ambitions of their brother George of Clarence, was well rewarded, and combined with Richard's share of Warwick's inheritance through his wife, Anne Nevill, enabled him to become virtual ruler of the north of England. Edward's policy of delegating authority in the regions to a number of powerful magnates, of whom Richard was the leading example, worked well during his lifetime. The bond of trust on the king's side and loyalty on that of the magnates fell apart on Edward's death. Richard III's ruthless pursuit of the crown after Edward's death generated an atmosphere of unease and distrust, if not outright hostility, which he was unable to dispel during his brief reign. One reason for Richard's initial success in obtaining the office of Protector during Edward V's reign was the dislike many of the peers felt for the control the queen's family exerted over the young king. Edward IV's astonishing and ill-judged marriage to Elizabeth Woodville at least had the merit of providing him with a family of growing children and, in her own relatives, a group of supporters who relied totally on the king for advancement and in return offered complete loyalty. Edward compounded the error of his marriage by appointing the queen's brother, Anthony, Earl Rivers, as governor to the young Prince of Wales and by allowing the queen to ensure that many of those surrounding the boy were Woodville clients. No doubt if Edward IV had not died prematurely, his heir might have outgrown the Woodville influence, but in 1483 it was to prove fatal.

The Yorkists were the first post-Conquest dynasty which could claim to be entirely English. Edward IV's and Richard III's parents and grandparents were all English, and their queens were English also. Although foreign matches were proposed for both kings and other members of their family, only one, that of Margaret of York to Charles, duke of Burgundy, actually took place. In terms of medieval royal families this was unique, and would have been unlikely to continue had the dynasty lasted longer. While the dynasty is generally regarded as ending with the death of Richard III at Bosworth in 1485, this study seeks to look more closely at the role of the women of the family, and consequently the end of the Yorkist period is taken to be the death of Edward IV's daughter, Elizabeth of York, queen of Henry VII, in 1503. By this date it was clear that no scion of the house of York, real or pretended, would ever recapture the throne, and it was Elizabeth's surviving son, Henry VIII, who transmitted Yorkist blood down the line of English monarchs.

The origins of the Yorkist dynasty lie a hundred years or so earlier in the family of Edward III. Because of the nature of their claim to the throne through the line of two of Edward's sons, it is necessary to look at that line and how both it, and the rival Lancastrian line, developed. Not since the quarrelsome brood of Plantagenet sons borne by Eleanor of Aquitaine to Henry II had the English crown produced such a large royal family as that of Edward III and Philippa of Hainault. In the intervening two hundred years most kings had fathered an heir and a son to spare. This was regarded as essential for the safe passage of the crown from father to son, but too many sons created a good deal of trouble and expense. They had to be found heiress wives or settled with an appanage suitable for a royal son which then depleted the crown's land holdings, possibly permanently. From the accession of Henry II in 1154 until 1399 the English crown had passed from father to son except for John (a brother) and Richard II (a grandson). During that period there were also three noble houses descended from the younger sons of Henry III and Edward I, those of Lancaster, Norfolk and Kent. By the death of Edward III in 1377, Lancaster and Kent were represented only by women married into the royal family and Norfolk had also come down through the female line. At no time had any of the male representatives of these families posed a dynastic threat, while Edward III's own brother, John of Eltham, earl of Cornwall, had died childless, though married, at the age of twenty.

Edward III and Philippa, daughter of John, count of Hainault, had been married in January 1328, very soon after he came to the throne; Edward was sixteen and his bride a few months younger. Philippa became one of the English queens most beloved by her husband's subjects, and though not beautiful, she was generous, warm-hearted and physically hardy. She was deeply religious and brought up her children in the same spirit. Many young queens did not bear their first child until several years after marriage, but Philippa's first son was born in 1330, when she was sixteen. From that early start, Edward and Philippa went on to have twelve children, three of whom died in infancy. Their five surviving sons remained on good terms with each other, and more remarkably, with their father, in contrast to the sons of Henry II and their father. Much of the credit for this should go to Philippa and the loving and supportive atmosphere she created within the royal family.

However happy the family life of Edward, Philippa and their children, there remained the problem of how to provide for so many younger sons. The simplest solution was marriage to English heiresses of sufficient standing to provide more or less completely for the new family. Sometimes no suitable heiress of an appropriate rank was available and sometimes international politics required a foreign match, although this was generally reserved for the heir and for royal daughters. From the time of their children's births, Edward and Philippa were on the lookout for heiresses for their four younger sons, preferably ones with royal descent. The availability of an heiress dictated the time of a royal marriage; betrothal was an option, but never certain enough. This explains why Edward's second son, Lionel, was married in 1342 at the age of four to Elizabeth, only child and heiress of William de Burgh, earl of Ulster, as well as to a large part of the English estates of the de Clare earls of Gloucester through her mother; Elizabeth was ten. In 1361, when he was twenty-three, Edward III appointed Lionel viceroy of Ireland and shortly after created him duke of Clarence. When Lionel died in

1368 his heir was his only child, Philippa, married to Edmund Mortimer, earl of March.

The next substantial and suitable heiress to appear on the marriage market was Blanche, daughter of Henry, duke of Lancaster, a descendant of Edward I's younger brother. Blanche was snapped up as soon as she was twelve and legally old enough for marriage, as a bride for the king's third son, John of Gaunt; at the time of their marriage in 1359 the bridegroom was nineteen. When Blanche's father died in 1361, John was created duke of Lancaster and the couple came into the entire Lancaster inheritance. Duchess Blanche died in 1369, having borne a son, the future Henry IV, and two daughters, together with two sons who died in infancy. The widowed Lancaster then became available for a diplomatic marriage to Constance, daughter and co-heiress of Pedro the Cruel of Castile. Lancaster claimed the title of king of Castile in her right, but his military attempts to back up this claim ended in failure. In 1388 he resigned his claim in favour of Catherine, their only surviving child, who married the other claimant to the throne and became queen of Castile.

Gaunt's younger brother, Edmund of Langley, Edward III's fourth surviving son, was destined to live much of his life in the shadow of his elder brother. He was created earl of Cambridge on the same day that John was created duke of Lancaster but had to wait rather longer for a wife. After John married Constance of Castile, Edmund was married in 1372, to her younger sister and co-heiress, Isabella. Fifteen years later, and after they had two sons, Edward and Richard, Edmund was created duke of York, but, because he did not hold many lands in England, his new rank had to be supported with a grant from the crown of £1000 p.a. Thomas of Woodstock, the youngest of Edward III's children, was born in 1355, when his eldest brother, Edward, the Black Prince, was twenty-five. Created earl of Buckingham, with an annuity of £1000, when he was twenty, he received his dukedom of Gloucester on the same day that Edmund was made duke of York. The question of his marriage was settled early on when the two young daughters and co-heiresses of Humphrey de Bohun, earl of Hereford, came onto the marriage market on the earl's death in 1372. The elder, Eleanor, who was only seven, was marked out for young Prince Thomas, while her four-year-old sister Mary was betrothed to John of Gaunt's young son and heir, Henry.

Which, if any, of these marriages was a success is hard to judge after a period of more than six hundred years and any attempt to do so must be made on fourteenth-century terms and not those of today. No child born into a royal or aristocratic family (or indeed most other families of the time) would expect to make his or her own choice of a marriage partner. Marriage was a matter for the family in its widest sense. In the case of royal children that involved the realm, since their marriage could form part of a truce or peace treaty or be used to strengthen the loyalty of a vassal. For the English landed classes, marriage was a means of social advancement for family and individual, and its aim was the preservation of landed property and acquisition of further estates. Yet children could expect that the choice made by their parents and friends would fall upon one who was of the same class, and of similar age. The match of a young girl to a much older widower tended to occur only when she had little in the way of a dowry. Once married, the young couple would settle down to produce children and maintain and, if possible, extend the family estates, but that was by no means all that was involved. Romantic love was a well-known concept in the middle ages; it featured in songs and stories, and Geoffrey Chaucer, for instance, wrote The Boke of the Duchesse in memory of Duchess Blanche of Lancaster, relating the young John of Gaunt's courtship of her with great charm. But love was not something that most people expected to base anything as important as marriage upon. Love, they believed, if it came, was a result of marriage and not a prerequisite for it, and a newly married couple based their relationship initially on politeness and respect.

Yet there are plenty of well-documented examples of marriages made purely on the basis of the desires of the two people involved, some of them even in the royal family itself. Edward III and Queen Philippa were surprisingly indulgent towards their children, perhaps because of their own happy and loving marriage. Their eldest daughter, Isabella, was permitted to break off a foreign betrothal and remain at the English court, enjoying the income and estates equivalent to those of an English magnate until at the age of thirty-three she chose to marry a French hostage, Enguerrand de Coucy, whom the king created earl of Bedford. Isabella was undoubtedly her father's favourite; he described her as 'our very dear eldest daughter whom we have loved with a special affection'. A wilful daughter was one thing, but the king and queen were equally understanding with their eldest son. Perhaps because he had plenty of brothers, perhaps because no obvious bride appeared on the diplomatic scene, Edward the Black Prince was not betrothed as a child and entered his twenties unattached. He then fell in love with his cousin, Joan, the heiress of Edmund, earl of Kent, the youngest son of Edward I. Joan already had a somewhat chequered matrimonial career and was the widow of Sir Thomas Holand, with several children, when Prince Edward married her in 1361. The king and queen could not be anything other than unhappy at his choice, but wisely allowed the match to go ahead.

Most of the other marriages of interest here seem to have been reasonably contented, each couple producing children, administering estates, visiting court and fulfilling the religious and charitable duties expected of their class. One, however, seems to have been less successful, and that was the diplomatic match made for the widowed John of Gaunt. There is evidence that he was very attached to his young first wife and mourned deeply at her premature death, but throughout his second marriage to Constance of Castile he maintained a relationship with

Katherine Swynford, the widow of one of his household knights and governess to his daughters, which was clearly far more than a casual liaison and resulted in four children. The view of the Duchess Constance is unrecorded, but at least it was a situation she was familiar with from her father's court, since her own mother had played a role not unlike that of Katherine Swynford.

For a span of thirty years the royal family had cornered the market in eligible English heiresses; even the heir, Edward, Prince of Wales, broke with tradition and married one. All this was no doubt to the chagrin of the senior peerage, who would, under other circumstances, have been able to arrange such advantageous matches with their own heirs. It did, however, solve the crown's problem of providing for younger sons without the permanent alienation of crown lands, and only Edmund of York, with a penniless foreign wife, required a cash annuity to support himself and his family. As we have already seen, the policy continued in the next generation. Lancaster's heir married the Bohun co-heiress, while his cousin, Edward of York, had to be content with a lesser co-heiress, but a wealthy widow, in what turned out to be a childless marriage. Edward's younger brother Richard, created earl of Cambridge, did rather better, for he married Anne Mortimer, granddaughter and eventual heiress of Lionel of Clarence's daughter, Philippa, thus uniting the lines of the second and fourth sons of Edward III. Thomas of Woodstock's only son died young and unmarried, and Thomas's eventual heir was his eldest daughter Anne, who married into the Stafford family.

Thus, although the first generation of royal sons had to be provided for, childless marriages and those that produced only daughters in the second generation returned to the ranks of the senior nobility much of the inheritances they had missed out on in the first. Setting aside Edward III's heir, the Black Prince, whose son inherited the throne as Richard II, only two of the four younger sons, Lancaster and York, had sons of their own; the other two, Clarence and Gloucester, were succeeded by heiresses, who married English peers. The daughters of the royal dukes, with the exceptions of Lancaster's elder daughter, Philippa, who married John I of Portugal, and her half-sister, Catherine, who married Henry III of Castile, married Englishmen. Their sister Elizabeth, for instance, married John Holand, earl of Huntingdon, later made duke of Exeter, who was the son of Joan, Princess of Wales, by her first marriage. This network of royal marriages within the ranks of the senior peerage was later to have the important effect of providing a particularly supportive group of peers, like the Staffords and Holands, for the crown. The most important and influential family in this group, however, were the Beauforts.

The Beauforts were the three sons and one daughter born to John of Gaunt's mistress, the widowed Katherine Swynford. They were acknowledged by their father and given the name of one of his French possessions, but much more importantly, after the death of Duchess Constance, Lancaster married Katherine, and their children were legitimized with the assent of parliament in 1397. Exactly ten years later, the patent of legitimation was exemplified and confirmed by their half-brother, Henry IV, but with the additional clause, not in the original patent, 'excepta dignitate regali', barring them from the royal succession. This specific exclusion seemed of little importance in 1407, given the new king's family of stout sons. Once Henry IV became king, the Beauforts were rapidly advanced, partly because of their undoubted abilities, partly because Henry knew he could rely on their support. John of Gaunt's daughter, Joan, was almost as significant as her brothers. The childless widow of a knight at the time of her legitimization, she then married much higher, becoming the wife of Ralph Nevill, earl of Westmorland, a widower with a large family. That did not prevent him from having thirteen more children by Joan, a number of whom will feature prominently later in this story. In the fifteenth century the Beauforts were of major significance, not only because of their birth, but because of their power, ability and ambition.

During the lifetime of Edward III, the royal family was remarkable for its amity and co-operation, and there was never a suggestion of disloyalty to their father by any of Edward's sons. The size of Edward's family was to cause dynastic problems in the succeeding century, but none of this was apparent at the time. In 1376 the family was stricken by the death of the heir to the throne, Edward the Black Prince, but he left a healthy nine-year-old son behind him. This made John of Gaunt the senior active representative of the family during the king's declining years. The political problems with which he struggled then and, after 1377, during the minority of Richard II, led to his massive unpopularity, but there was never any serious suggestion that he wished to replace his nephew on the throne, while his younger brothers, Edmund and Thomas, did not play prominent roles in public affairs.

Serious dissatisfaction among the nobles with the extravagance and tyranny of Richard II's personal rule enabled Gaunt's son and heir, Henry of Derby, to usurp his cousin in 1399, soon after Gaunt's death. At that time, Henry was a widower, his young wife, the heiress Mary Bohun, having died at the age of twenty-five. By then they had four sons and two daughters, so the succession was secure and it did not matter that Henry had no further children by his queen, Joan of Navarre, the widowed duchess of Brittany. Fifty years later, in 1449, the picture was very different. Of the four Lancaster boys, Henry V had a single male child when he died prematurely in 1422 and none of his brothers, Thomas, duke of Clarence, John, duke of Bedford and Humphrey, duke of Gloucester, had a single legitimate child between them. Henry VI had married Margaret of Anjou in 1445, but that union had so far failed to produce a child. The king's nearest male relative was his second cousin, Henry Holand, duke of Exeter, the grandson of John of Gaunt's daughter, Elizabeth. Holand, however, was not next in line for the succession, for that position was held in 1449 by Richard, duke of York, grandson of Edmund of Langley. Thus the direct male line of Edward III and his five sons was reduced to two men by the mid-fifteenth century, while several noble families were representatives of the female line.

Richard, duke of York, was born in 1411 into the extended royal family. His father Richard, earl of Cambridge, was the younger son of Edmund, duke of York, fourth son of Edward III, and his mother was Anne Mortimer, great-grand-daughter of Lionel, duke of Clarence, Edward III's second son. Cambridge's elder brother, Edward, duke of York, was childless, so the prospects for his infant son were good. Anne died soon after her only son's birth (she had already borne a daughter, Isabel) and Richard's father swiftly married again but had no further children. In 1415 Cambridge was involved in the Southampton plot against Henry V, one of the aims of which was to place his former brother-in-law, Edmund Mortimer, earl of March, on the throne as heir general to Edward III.* March revealed the plot to the king and was pardoned, but Cambridge was attainted and executed. His infant son Richard was placed under the guardianship of Sir Robert Waterton, who remained with him until he was twelve, when his wardship and marriage were sold to Ralph Nevill, earl of Westmorland, for 3000 marks, to be paid over two years from 1423. At first sight this seems a very large sum to pay for the wardship of the boy, but in fact young Richard's prospects had been transformed in 1415, not by the death of his father, but a few months later by that of his childless uncle, Edward, duke of York, at Agincourt. Despite his father's attainder, the four-year-old Richard was allowed to inherit the dukedom.

Edward, duke of York, had enfeoffed trustees with a large proportion of his available lands to pay annuitants and to endow a college of priests at Fotheringhay, Northamptonshire, so only a modest number of lands reverted to the crown during his nephew's minority. In addition, there were two dowager duchesses holding dower and jointure from the York lands. Prior to their return, Richard had not initially inherited enough lands from his uncle to support a dukedom, but his situation changed radically in the early days of 1425 with the unexpected death of his maternal uncle, Edmund Mortimer, earl of March. March was childless, and his sister Anne, York's mother, was already dead. This meant that York was undisputed heir to all the Mortimer inheritance, largely situated in Wales and the Welsh borders and in Ireland. Again, the inheritance was encumbered, this time by two large fines that his uncle owed the crown and of which York was not pardoned until 1434. By that year, however, when he was only twenty-three, with the pardoning of the fines and the deaths of both dowager duchesses of York, Richard Plantagenet had fully come into a great inheritance,

---

* see family tree

which made him the wealthiest noble in the kingdom. The Mortimer inheritance also carried with it a less tangible benefit. By it York became the rightful heir of Richard II through the line of Lionel of Clarence, whose only child, Philippa, had married Edmund Mortimer, earl of March and whose son Roger, York's grandfather, had been Richard II's heir presumptive.* For many years both York and the Crown, in the form of the apparently secure Lancastrian dynasty, were content for this matter to lie dormant.

---

* see family tree

TABLE 1: YORK AND LANCASTER

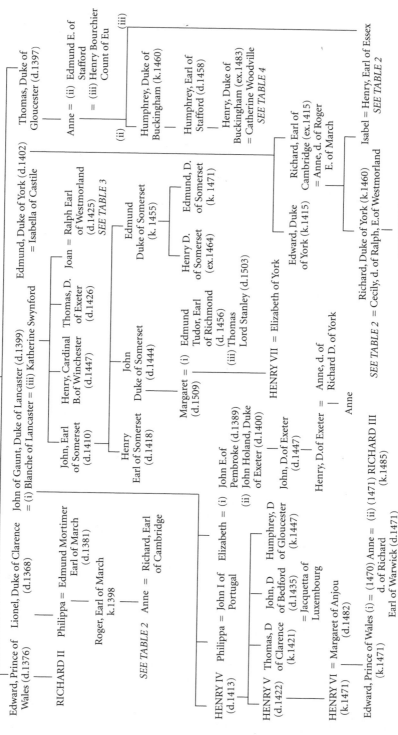

TABLE 2: THE HOUSE OF YORK

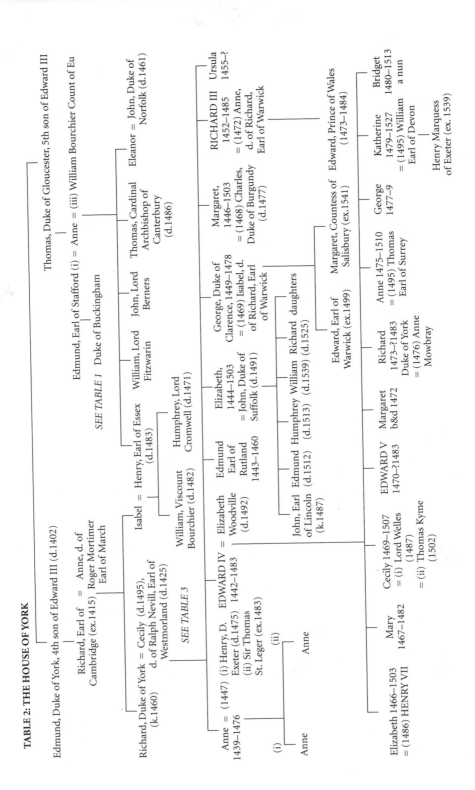

TABLE 3: THE NEVILLS

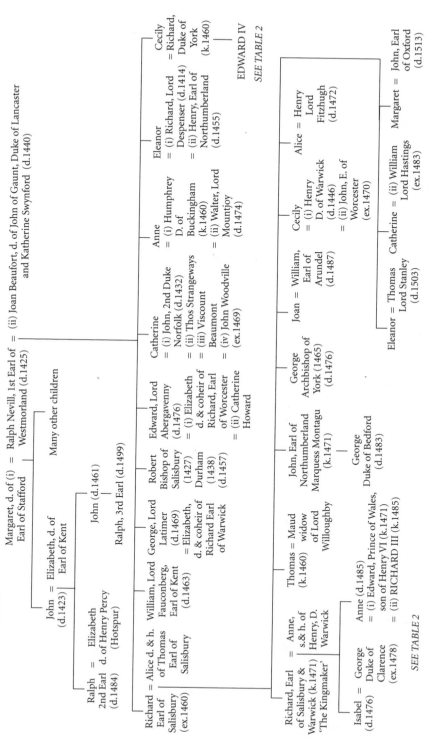

TABLE 4: THE WOODVILLES

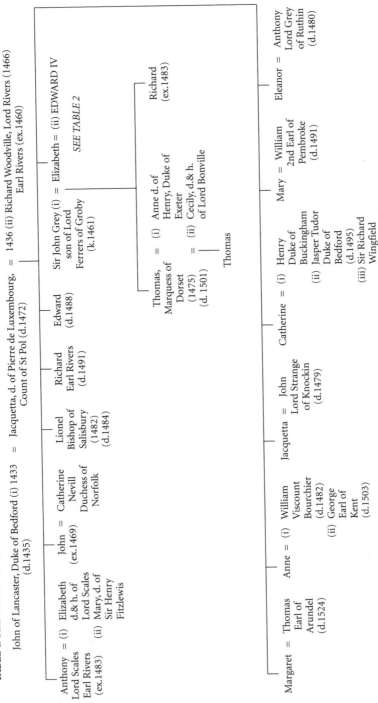

John of Lancaster, Duke of Bedford (i) 1433 = Jacquetta, d. of Pierre de Luxembourg, = 1436 (ii) Richard Woodville, Lord Rivers, = = 1436 (ii) Richard Woodville, Lord Rivers (1466)
(d.1435) Count of St Pol (d.1472) Earl Rivers (ex.1460)

Anthony = (i) Elizabeth
Lord Scales   d.& h. of
Earl Rivers   Lord Scales
(ex.1483)
         (ii) Mary, d. of
              Sir Henry
              Fitzlewis

John = Catherine
(ex.1469)   Nevill
         Duchess of
         Norfolk

Lionel
Bishop of
Salisbury
(1482)
(d.1484)

Richard
Earl Rivers
(d.1491)

Edward
(d.1488)

Sir John Grey (i) = Elizabeth = (ii) EDWARD IV
son of Lord
Ferrers of Groby
(k.1461)

SEE TABLE 2

Thomas,   = (i) Anne d. of   Richard
Marquess of   Henry, Duke of   (ex.1483)
Dorset   Exeter
(1475)   = (ii) Cecily, d.& h.
(d.1501)   of Lord Bonville

Thomas

Margaret = Thomas
Earl of
Arundel
(d.1524)

Anne = (i) William
Viscount
Bourchier
(d.1482)
     (ii) George
Earl of
Kent
(d.1503)

Jacquetta = John
Lord Strange
of Knockin
(d.1479)

Catherine = (i) Henry
Duke of
Buckingham
       (ii) Jasper Tudor
Duke of
Bedford
(d.1495)
       (iii) Sir Richard
Wingfield

Mary = William
2nd Earl of
Pembroke
(d.1491)

Eleanor = Anthony
Lord Grey
of Ruthin
(d.1480)

Richard of York

In many ways, medieval politics were family politics and at no time was this more true than in the mid-fifteenth century. All the senior figures who disputed with one another were related by blood or marriage. In England after 1399 much political opposition found expression in dynastic rivalry. In this respect Shakespeare was right in his interpretation. By the 1450s those disaffected with Lancaster looked to York and later those who were disaffected with York backed Henry Tudor, who had only the barest of Lancastrian claims. In the middle of the century England faced an unprecedented situation with Henry VI's failure to rule. Many turned to the man closest to him in royal descent, thinking that he should play the major role in government that his birth suggested. Richard, duke of York was a man in whose veins flowed the blood of two of Edward III's sons.

In 1423, when Ralph Nevill, earl of Westmorland, paid the sum of 3000 marks for Richard, duke of York's wardship he might not have anticipated the early arrival of the Mortimer inheritance, but it was inevitable that the young duke should be married off to one of his own large family of daughters. He had earlier paid the same sum for the wardship of the young John Mowbray, duke of Norfolk. He had been granted these two very lucrative wardships because of his Beaufort wife, Joan, and his own early support of the Lancastrian usurpation. Norfolk was married to Catherine, Westmorland's eldest daughter by Joan, and his youngest daughter was at a suitable age for York: Cecily was born in May 1415 and betrothed to Richard in 1424. A year later her father died and her mother inherited Richard's wardship. Joan and York moved to the royal household in 1428 and Cecily almost certainly went with them. Her mother was anxious that the marriage should take place as soon as legally possible, which was when Cecily was twelve, and they were certainly married before 1429, when a papal indult was granted for them jointly to choose a confessor. At that date, Cecily was fourteen, Richard four years older. As a young couple they were relatively lucky. They had grown up together, mostly at Westmorland's seat of Raby in county Durham, and their ages were compatible. After their marriage they probably lived in the king's household. Although, as far as we know, their first child, Anne, was not born until 1439, ten years after their marriage, they then proved very fertile. Cecily had eleven more children, of whom seven survived to adulthood, a total very similar to her mother's. This was in stark contrast to the size of York's own family; he had one sister, Isabel, married to Henry Bourchier, earl of Essex, and no cousins in the paternal line.

York's lands stretched from Pembroke to Lincoln, Yorkshire to Sussex, and into Ireland as well. They lay in eighteen counties and he was much the largest landowner in Wales. In the late 1420s, as far as can reasonably be calculated, the estates brought in an income of well over £4000 p.a. Because they were so widespread, they were grouped into nineteen receiverships, more than half of them in Wales and the Marches, with two main administrative centres, one at Ludlow and the other at Fotheringhay, which had been Edward, duke of York's chief seat and where, by his will, he had founded a college of priests. These in turn were to become the family's main residences and several of York's children were born at Fotheringhay.

While York had inherited great estates, when he reached his majority he had not inherited the service of men. His father had held no lands and his uncle York was long dead. March had been dead for only four years and a few of his men transferred their loyalties to York, but in essence he had to start afresh to build up a loyal following. Again he was lucky. The death of the king's uncle, John, duke of Bedford, without heirs in 1435, left a large group of men without a lord and most of them saw the benefits of transferring to York's service. This was to be a significant factor in York's career because these were men totally committed to maintaining the Lancastrian ascendency in France. Bedford's death also severely diminished the ranks of English commanders in France and left his younger brother, Humphrey, duke of Gloucester, as the young king Henry VI's heir presumptive.

Gloucester needed to remain in charge of the council in England and it was with some reluctance that the council appointed York as temporary lieutenant governor of France. He was twenty-five, completely untried, and his father had committed treason, but he was also England's premier duke after Gloucester and would be supported by Bedford's experienced commanders. The appointment was only for a year, and in 1437 York was replaced by the earl of Warwick, but he had done as well as might reasonably have been expected of him. Following Warwick's death in 1439 he was again appointed lieutenant governor, this time for a five-year term. During this second term a fierce debate was raging at home over the future of the English possessions in France. Cardinal Beaufort was the leader of those whose policy was to cede English sovereignty in return for the peace and security of Normandy and Gascony, for which the English king would do homage. He was strongly opposed by Humphrey of Gloucester, whose policy was never to cede any right or title of Henry VI and to reinvest in the war to secure control over those parts of France which had never accepted the Treaty of Troyes. Gloucester would have liked to take his brother Bedford's place in France, but although he knew he had to remain in England, he was very well informed about all that went on there. In York he found a willing ally.

In June 1441, at the beginning of his second term of office, York arrived at his headquarters at Rouen with a large retinue which included both Cecily and the wives of several of his other commanders. Cecily had given birth to their first son, Henry, at Hatfield the preceding February, but the baby had died soon after birth, almost certainly before the move to France, which in itself may have been a welcome distraction from their grief. After a few weeks in France, Cecily had conceived again and Edward was born at Rouen on 28 April 1442,* to be followed on 17 May 1443 by Edmund and on 27 April 1444 by Elizabeth. Their father, meanwhile, had been making a modest success of his appointment. Within weeks of arriving he had conducted a successful military campaign, and at Pontoise he put the French king and his army to flight and went on to restore effective authority in Normandy. He had sustained local confidence in a continued English presence, while his military commanders had continued a vigorous defence of the province.

York and all the commanders in Normandy were alienated by the decision of the council in England to finance an army for their assistance under Cecily's cousin, John Beaufort, earl of Somerset, who, to persuade him to undertake command, had been granted a dukedom and given powers which threatened York's supreme power as lieutenant governor. Somerset's expedition of 1443 was an expensive failure, which made it easier for York to be reconciled with those who had appointed him. It also encouraged the authorities in England to look at means to secure an accommodation with the French. Many of the English problems in France centred on Gascony rather than further north, and one solution proposed was a marriage between Henry VI and a daughter of one of the great southern French nobles. At the same time as negotiations were finalized for a match with Margaret of Anjou, daughter of Réné of Anjou, titular king of Naples, and the niece of Charles VII of France, the English raised the possibility of a marriage between York's young heir, Edward, and a daughter of King Charles. This was first broached during an embassy by the duke of Suffolk and was not at York's initiative, but York followed it up with a letter to the French king, who suggested his young daughter, Madeleine. The proposal indicates that Henry VI and his council were considering appointing York for a second term as governor, but the marriage itself was merely diplomatic manœuvring. It was hardly likely that either the king or the council would be prepared to accept York's son marrying a daughter of the king of France while Henry VI himself only married a niece, Margaret of Anjou. In any event, the death of the Dauphin Louis's wife meant that Charles turned his attentions from the marriage of a daughter to that

---

* For the controversy surrounding Edward's birth, see Appendix 1

of his heir. The suggestion of a York match was quietly dropped.

When Margaret of Anjou reached Rouen on her way to England, Cecily was one of the few English noblewomen present in Normandy. The two women seem to have established a rapport which lasted despite politics. It is likely that Cecily enjoyed her time in France, where she was, in effect, queen of a small kingdom. Certainly the French were impressed by the 'regal expenditure' of York and his wife. The duke may well have felt that the future of his family lay as much in France as in England, particularly with the possibility of a French royal match for young Edward. The negotiations about the match had continued for about two years before being broken off, although just how serious they were on the French side is open to speculation. The idea of creating an appanage consisting of all York's French lands for their second son, Edmund, was probably already in their parents' minds when they arranged a particularly grand christening for him in Rouen Cathedral, designed to impress the locals. Their heir, Edward, by contrast, had been christened in a small private chapel in Rouen Castle, although this might only indicate that he was not a robust baby and possibly premature.

York's term of office was due to expire in September 1445. He and his councillors travelled to London for a session of parliament and policy discussions. There is little doubt that the duke would have welcomed another term. One chronicler reported that the council thanked him for his successful efforts in Normandy and initially reappointed him for a further five years, but that Somerset, in collusion with Suffolk, engineered a reversal in his own favour. This, the chronicler declared, was the beginning of the bitter feud between York and the Beauforts.[1] In the event, York's commission was extended only for a year, but during that time relations between him and the government grew steadily worse. At home he had never been very highly regarded as a military commander, although he seems to have displayed considerable leadership and audacity in France, where he was valued by his men, and allies of the English. The Burgundian chronicler, Jean de Waurin judged that 'during his time in office, he governed admirably and had many honourable and notable successes over the French'.[2]

In London York's reputation as governor was tainted by rumours of embezzlement and malfeasance. The rumours about York were probably untrue (although the same cannot be said of some of his commanders). While he was criticized during a wide-ranging investigation, he was able to refute most of the charges and no further action was taken against him. The mere fact of the investigation is likely to have offended the duke – in one of his responses he says 'he feeleth him grieved, and his worship hurt', which may be described as a fair summary of York's relations with the Lancastrian government for years to come – but he may not have been totally surprised when his appointment was not renewed and he was replaced by Somerset's brother, Edmund Beaufort, marquess of Dorset, in December 1446. Somerset himself had died in 1444.

York was entitled to about £80,000 in payment for his four-year service in France and there was a steady flow of payments to him over the next two or three years, but the length of time and the fact that it was probably never fully repaid left him in financial difficulties. These were compounded by the fact that he had also advanced large sums to the crown by way of loans totalling some £26,000. York was the wealthiest man in England but even his income could not sustain unpaid debts on this scale and there is some evidence that, while his English income remained stable, in Wales, where he was much the largest landowner, the picture was rather different. Profits from justice, always a more important component of Welsh landed incomes, were dropping sharply, and this in turn must have had a serious effect on his general income. In the end he had to mortgage and even sell land. It was probably particularly galling to see Edmund Beaufort, elevated to the dukedom of Somerset, receiving first call upon what few funds were available. While poverty was not what drove York into opposition, it cannot be discounted as one of a complex series of motives.

York and Cecily settled into life in England and their daughter Margaret was born, probably at Fotheringhay, in May 1446. In the previous year they had agreed a match for their eldest daughter, Anne, then aged six, with Henry Holand, son of the duke of Exeter, who was nine years older. But while York's dynastic plans seemed to be progressing smoothly, the same could not be said of his political ones. In the five years that he had been away the political scene in England had changed substantially. Henry VI had been declared of age in 1437, when he was sixteen, but the intervening years had shown that he simply did not have the attributes required for a medieval king of England. He was not unintelligent, and when something caught his interest he could pursue it diligently, as his foundations of Eton and King's College, Cambridge, bear witness; but he was simply uninterested in the routine of government. This left an unprecedented vacuum at the heart of the kingdom: there had been kings who had ruled badly before, never one who had no wish to rule at all. Into the vacuum stepped William de la Pole, earl and, from 1448, duke, of Suffolk. With the assent of the leading magnates Suffolk was able to create a power base in the royal household from which he could exercise that authority which the king declined to wield, as if it were the royal will. In this he had the support of lords loyal to the memory of Henry V, who found it hard to believe that his son was a weak figure with no independent will for government.

Unlike earlier royal favourites, Suffolk's power rested on the acceptance by a large number of great men that through him Henry's personal rule could be made to function. To them it seemed there was no alternative, however costly it proved. And costly it was. Suffolk had to pay for what should have come freely to Henry VI, the loyalty of men. The distribution of Henry's patrimony among the men on whom the regime relied depleted the economic resources of the crown as well as its political capital. The weakness of the government under Suffolk and the council was twofold: it could not offer a comprehensive representation of interests as the crown under a competent king did, and so public authority was steadily undermined. Nor could it easily resolve differences among its own members. In trying to strike a balance by intermittently satisfying conflicting interests, it created those very divisions it was attempting to heal. While medieval kings did not govern by giving in to every demand made upon them, Suffolk could do very little else. The crown could not protect its agents and no lord embarked on a major military or government commission without long and detailed articles of service, by which they hoped to protect themselves. In struggling to keep the support of the lords, Suffolk was bound to neglect less obvious interests, including those of the realm at large: military success in France, law and order in the English regions and a level of taxation that seemed to most of the community appropriate. Neglecting these led slowly but inexorably to disaster.

The cession of Maine, agreed as part of the negotiations for the king's marriage, and accepted by most of the lords as essential, was nonetheless a matter of fierce regret to York and other former commanders in France. It is probably partly for this reason that, far from being reappointed as governor in France, York was sent as far away as possible in the other direction. In July 1447 he was made governor of Ireland for ten years at a fee of 4000 marks for the first year and 2000 annually thereafter. The length of the term made it quite clear that Suffolk and those around him had no intention of ever letting York return to France, but in other ways it was a highly suitable appointment. York was the greatest English landowner in Ireland and it was a post held by his forebear, Lionel of Clarence, and members of the Mortimer family. He could have chosen to be a non-resident governor, but although it took him nearly two years to make his preparations (as indeed it had done prior to his move to France), when he finally sailed in June 1449, Cecily went with him, indicating that he intended to stay there for some time. She was pregnant again and gave birth to a son, George, in Dublin. His new post gave York an opportunity to attend personally to his Irish estates, part of his Mortimer inheritance, but the promised funds from the crown were not forthcoming, since it had great difficulty funding the higher priority of the continuing military commitment in France. York's initiatives in Ireland were also ignored at home. He wrote to his brother-in-law, Salisbury, asking to have a letter published in parliament stating his position as an excuse against future accusations of neglect of duty. This should not have been necessary. That it was is an indication of the deteriorating situation in London.

It was becoming increasingly obvious that Henry VI would never take responsiblity for the government functioning in his name, and not only obvious to the lords, who had known it for some time, but to others as well. Complaints against the greed and corruption of his leading ministers, and the lack of respect for the law with which their followers (over whom they probably had less control than was assumed) oppressed the shires and evaded retribution, led directly to the impeachment of Suffolk by the Commons in March 1450 and, shortly afterwards, to his death. Even more dangerous was a popular uprising in the southeast led by Jack Cade that was essentially political in its nature. The rebel demand that the king should recall the greater nobility to his counsels made a particular point that this should include York because of his 'true blood of the realm'. A few years on, it became accepted government policy to declare that York had fomented Cade's rebellion and every popular uprising that followed it: a Chancery memorandum of July 1456 declared that 'from the time that Jack Cade or Mortimer, called captain of Kent, raised a rebellion in Kent, all disturbances are at the will of the duke of York, descended from the Mortimers'.[3] While this was almost certainly untrue, York would have been less than human if he had not taken advantage of popular support. The government survived both the fall of Suffolk and the rebellion, but in the autumn of the same year it faced another challenge, which was in the long term to be more serious. Richard of York returned from Ireland.

The reasons for York deserting his post and returning unannounced were almost certainly a mixture of the personal and the political, with the former dominant. Edmund Beaufort, now duke of Somerset, returned from France and took his place at the heart of government, which merely served to emphasize York's own exclusion from the royal councils, despite his close blood relationship with the king. York's view of Somerset was that he had been 'the means, consenter, occasioner, cause and mediator [of] the loss' of Normandy, and he was only one of many to feel outraged by the fact that such a man was now seeking political power at home.[4] As well as his personal hostility to Somerset and his own ambition, York was probably also motivated by his desire to act on behalf of the welfare of the realm. In terms of the latter he had popular expectations to fulfil and a leadership role if he so chose. That the government feared this is made clear by their immediate actions. When York landed at Beaumaris in north Wales, royal officials, presumably acting on orders that had gone out to all the ports in Wales, attempted to prevent him travelling on to Denbigh, one of his own lordships. He wrote to the king in protest. Why did the government fear him? Possibly because of rumours that he was in some way implicated in Cade's rebellion, possibly because it thought he was coming to claim a leading role in goverrnment that he felt was his due.

What York's exact plans were when he left Ireland we will never know, but the hostility he encountered on arrival played its part in pushing him towards an inevitable conclusion. He travelled on via his other Welsh estates and his important administrative base at Ludlow. When he arrived in London about three weeks later, he had a retinue of about five thousand armed men, almost certainly a defensive measure rather than an aggressive one. Once in London

York made a direct appeal to Henry VI. In the first of two bills he presented to the king, copies of which were widely available in London, he reiterated his loyalty to the crown and set out his more personal grievances: his exclusion from government despite his royal blood; the slow repayment of money expended on behalf of the crown; and the unjust accusation of treason made against him while he was in Ireland. The last may have been his most immediate concern, since a formal indictment against him, even if parliament found him not guilty, would have probably ruled out any question of him or a son being declared heir presumptive. Equally pressing was the question of the huge sums owed to him by the crown, both in repayment of sums expended during his service in Normandy and Ireland and additional loans he made to the crown. The failure to repay them was causing even the richest magnate in England severe financial difficulties. He was, he declared, forced 'to sell a great substance of my livelihood, to lie in pledge all my great jewels and the most part of my plate, not yet requited and therefore like to be lost and forfeited'.[5] No other servant of the crown was in such a position, and the contrast with which the crown honoured debts to the two Beaufort dukes of Somerset exacerbated York's feelings of grievance. Henry seems to have received York in a generous manner, acknowledging his allegiance and loyal service, but he was also well aware of the efforts of his household officers in charge of the government of north Wales to limit and control York's actions. The assurance by York of his complete loyalty to Henry, and a denial that suggestions or rumours that he should replace Henry on the throne emanated from him or his servants, was to remain a crucial part of his position for some time to come. Just how far he, or anyone else, believed them is open to speculation, but he was certainly concerned about the possibility of his own attainder for treason. His father's fate was probably never far from his thoughts. What is certain is that this was a period of unease and suspicion on both sides. Henry and his household were understandably jumpy after the murders of Suffolk and his closest associate, Bishop Moleyns, followed by Cade's rebellion and its championing of York, while York's fear of being indicted for treason and suffering the fate of the murdered Duke Humphrey of Gloucester was equally understandable.

York's discontent in 1450 was largely personal, based on defending his honour against rumours of treason and securing a remedy for the dire financial situation in which his service to the house of Lancaster had placed him. It would be wrong to credit him at this stage with any real kind of political vision for reform, but once parliament met, he filled the role of public spokesman allotted to him by the Commons. York's second bill, addressed to his fellow peers, was not a personal one like the first. It was a strong attack on the traitors, led by Somerset, who had surrounded the king and the need for them to face justice. He also proposed an Act of Resumption which would cancel some of the most lavish grants made to royal favourites and begin the process of repairing the royal finances. Henry, in an uncharacteristic show of firmness and bolstered by those who were closest to him and who would suffer most from the measure, refused what was demanded. While he conceded that he would employ a larger and more representative council, of which York would be a member, he refused to be advised by one man alone. In the autumn of 1450 a number of lesser peers and men of affairs had made overtures to York in the belief that he would be playing a more central role in government than heretofore, and, certainly at this stage, Somerset's elevation to fill Suffolk's pre-eminent role was by no means definite, but once the king made it clear that he would deny York the powers he needed for reform, all the duke was left with was the weapon of his popular support. This was demonstrated in the 1450–51 parliament, where his chamberlain, Sir William Oldhall was elected Speaker, but its limitations were clear when a petition that some twenty members of the household be dismissed was rejected out of hand by the king.

Under York's leadership a programme of reform began to be put into effect. He seems to have won the active support of some of his fellow peers, Norfolk, Salisbury, Warwick and Devon, all of them closely related to either York or his wife, and at least the acquiescence of the majority. Popular support in the Commons was all very well, but for York's attempt at government to be successful he needed more than that, and once parliament was in recess, he was unable to prevent a drift back to household government. Somerset was able to claw back enough support from the lords to enable him to regain control. The strength of loyalty to Henry should not be underestimated and gave authority to those who were acting in his name. The queen had also begun to play a major role; she had a good deal of influence over her husband and there is no doubt that she favoured Somerset. If the king, or those closest to him, wanted Somerset, then it was almost impossible for York to contest this by constitutional means. At this point, neither York nor anyone else realized that for him to get what he wanted, both for the good of the realm and for his own dynastic pretensions, he would have to be far more radical. But York was not a radical man, nor a natural leader. He seems to have been reserved and conservative, not the sort of man who could win people to his cause by force of personality. He was also, as we shall see, capable of serious misjudgement.

When parliament reassembled the following May, with one of York's council-lors, Thomas Young, as Speaker, it was because Henry and Somerset needed money for an expedition to Gascony. Under Young, the Commons presented a petition which linked the granting of money to recognition of York as heir presumptive. The Lancastrian dynasty was in dire straits by 1451. When Henry IV had come to the throne, he had four healthy, growing sons. The second, Thomas, duke of Clarence, died on the field of Baugé in 1421 and, although married, was childless. Henry V himself did not marry until 1420, at the advanced age of thirty-three, and had only a nine-month-old son when he died in 1422. His surviving brothers,

John, duke of Bedford, and Humphrey, duke of Gloucester, had no legitimate children, though each married twice and each had two bastards. When Bedford died in 1435, Humphrey became Henry VI's heir presumptive. While there could be no serious objection to the idea that he might one day succeed his nephew, it was clear that he had little likelihood of fathering a legitimate heir, and there was strong objection to the idea of his second wife becoming queen. Eleanor Cobham had been a lady-in-waiting to his first wife, Jacqueline of Hainault and his mistress before he discarded his wife in her favour. Humphrey had a number of serious enemies, who used Eleanor's interest in astrology and magic to charge her in 1441 with witchcraft and sorcery in trying to predict whether she and her husband would ever sit on the throne. She was found guilty of treason and was imprisoned for life and her marriage was annulled. While nothing could change Humphrey's position as heir presumptive, he was seriously discredited. At his death in 1447, and until Henry VI had a child by his queen, there was no obvious heir in the royal line.

In stark contrast to the Lancastrian line was the family of York, who, with Cecily, had produced four living sons by 1452. While Henry VI was descended from Edward III's third son, John of Gaunt, duke of Lancaster, York was descended from Edward's second son, Lionel of Clarence, in the female line, and his fourth, Edmund of York.* In addition, his maternal grandfather, Edmund Mortimer, had been regarded as a possible successor to Richard II. It could justifiably be argued that York's hereditary claim to the throne was stronger than Henry's own. This had not escaped the attention of Henry and his ministers in the 1440s. It led them to advance the families closest to the Lancastrian line, promoting the heads of the Beaufort and Stafford families to the dukedoms of Somerset and Buckingham respectively, while the head of the Holand family regained the dukedom of Exeter, forfeited in 1400. In the early 1450s, Henry's nearest male relative, Henry Holand, duke of Exeter, was excluded from the throne because parliamentary declarations of 1404 and 1406 had settled the throne on Henry IV's male heirs, thus excluding any rights of his sister Elizabeth, Exeter's grandmother. While this exclusion could have been set aside, nobody was pressing Holand's claim in 1451and there were in effect only two families to consider, that of York and that of Beaufort.

The Beauforts had been legitimized by Richard II, but an act under their half-brother, Henry IV, confirming the legitimization, inserted a clause specifically excluding them from the succession. This, too, could have been set aside by parliament, but the senior representative of the Beauforts was a girl, Margaret, daughter of John, duke of Somerset. Margaret's first marriage to the son of the duke of Suffolk was annulled and in early 1453 she was married to the king's half-brother, Edmund Tudor, who had been advanced to the earldom of

---

* see family tree

Richmond. Although Tudor had no claim whatsoever to the throne (he was the son of Queen Catherine and her second husband, Owen Tudor), the marrriage bolstered the royal family and he lost no time in getting his new twelve-year-old wife with child. The Staffords, descendants of Edward III's youngest son, Thomas of Woodstock, were obviously further from the throne than York's line, coming as it did via two of Thomas of Woodstock's older brothers, Lionel of Clarence and Edmund of Langley. The strong sense of dynasty present in all these families had led to a number of marriages amongst themselves, of which that of York's daughter, Anne, to Henry Holand was but one. Yet York could hardly fail to have felt snubbed, perhaps even threatened, by the advancement of the Lancastrian families. By 1450 there were numerous rumours and suggestions that Henry be deposed in his favour, some of which can be traced to the duke's own servants. This movement culminated in Young's demand in the Commons that York be formally recognized as heir presumptive. This was immediately dealt with – Young was sent to the Tower – but there was no escaping the sense of uncertainty surrounding the succession.

Having failed to take control of the government by constitutional means for any length of time in 1450–51, York resorted to force in 1452. Ignoring orders to come to a council meeting at Coventry, he set off to London, but his attempt to raise forces there, and later in Kent, led to an armed confrontation at Dartford, where his fellow lords would not support him. Having had his bluff called, he had no option but to surrender. As this failed *coup d'etat* illustrated, he had singularly failed to appreciate that the support he had among the lords when he attempted reform by constitutional methods would not materialize when he took up arms against an anointed king. He had no choice but to humble himself before the king and retire in disgrace to Ludlow. He avoided being charged with treason by the skin of his teeth, probably because Somerset could not be sure he would get the support of the lords for it. Yet the problem of the succession had not gone away. This was underlined in August 1453 when Henry became seriously mentally ill. In an impressive display of unity in the face of disaster, a great council comprising almost all the senior peers and bishops gathered in London to take an oath to uphold the law and act collectively against anyone who flouted the authority of the king and council. York's brother-in-law, the duke of Norfolk, made an outspoken attack on Somerset, who was removed to the Tower. Thereafter, a smaller group of councillors assumed the responsibility for exercising the king's powers of government during his incapacity. York and his associates had managed to seize the initiative, but only for a limited period.

The birth of a son to Margaret of Anjou in the following October, although solving the immediate problem of the succession, did nothing to settle the question of who should control the government during the king's incapacity. Indeed, it made matters worse, because the queen wanted to become regent on behalf of the baby Prince Edward. This did not find favour with the council, which preferred the solution of a protectorate similar to that established in 1422 on the death of Henry V. On that occasion there were two royal uncles, Bedford and Gloucester, to fill the role. Whoever was chosen this time would be in a strong position to be regarded as ultimate heir, should the direct royal line fail. The arguments raged throughout the winter and then in March 1454 Richard of York was appointed Protector. The wider community of peers had allowed natural justice to take its course, acknowledging not only his royal blood and his general competence, but also the isolation from power to which the government of Suffolk had subjected him. The council was fairly balanced and could not be described as particularly biased in York's favour; the other obvious candidate, Somerset, had been too closely linked to Suffolk, and had hardly covered himself with glory in France. Nobody wanted Exeter, described by a contemporary as 'fierce and cruel' and generally regarded as stupid to boot. This was seen as a time for unity and inclusion; to have rejected York would have led to a stark polarization and possibly violence.

York immediately made a public declaration of loyalty to the crown, agreeing to act until the king was himself again or until Prince Edward reached years of discretion and could take his place. As Protector, York tried to rule as justly as he could, through a broad-based administration and with a governing council similar to that in place during the king's minority. One of the major issues he faced was noble feuding, particularly in the north between the Nevills and the Percies, and while his attempt to exert government control and restore order was correct in principle, it was almost inevitable that in practice he would be seen as partisan. It was the Nevill family which won his support. Cecily's father, Ralph Nevill, earl of Westmorland, had been an early supporter of the Lancastrian line through the connections of his second wife, Joan Beaufort. He had been well rewarded for that support, the York wardship and marriage being among the benefits. Because of their Beaufort ties and the profitable results of such close court connections, the Nevills supported the government until the early 1450s. They changed their allegiance largely as a direct result of their feud with the Percy earls of Northumberland. In the first half of the century, the Percies had shared power with both branches of the Nevill family reasonably amicably, but the advancement of the Nevills in the 1440s, backed by their court ties, into areas that had previously been under Percy control, stirred the latter's resentment. The feud escalated into armed conflict which Henry's government was powerless to stop. The new earl of Warwick, Richard Nevill, also came into direct conflict with Somerset over the lordship of Glamorgan. Right was undoubtedly on Somerset's side, but that never stopped a Nevill. York's difficulties were compounded by his son-in-law, Exeter, who laid claim to the duchy of Lancaster while supporting the Percies and remaining loyal to the court faction.

When Henry recovered his senses, early in 1455, York's protectorate came automatically to an end. He had governed the country for almost a year with a fair degree of success and as one chronicler put it, then 'with great honour and the love of all, he resigned his office'.[6] It was inevitable that Somerset, who had never been formally convicted, should be released from custody, but the council's big mistake was to allow him to return to power. Given his bitter rivalry with York, the wisest move would have been to put the governing power in the more neutral hands of someone like the duke of Buckingham. Somerset would obviously try to eliminate York from all prospect of future power while Henry was well and he himself in control. A summons to appear before a great council at Leicester, which may have been intended to force from them an oath of submission similar to that extracted after Dartford, led York and the Nevills to retire north to raise their forces. This led directly to the first battle of St Albans. Whether this can truly be described as the first battle of a civil war is questionable. It was little more than a skirmish between the armed retinues of a number of lords. Its factional nature is clear from the fact that as soon as Somerset, Northumberland and their supporter, Lord Clifford, were dead, the fighting ceased. The great bonus for the triumphant York and his allies was possession of the person of the king, who had been slightly wounded in the fighting and captured. This led to a short-lived second term of York's protectorate.

York worked hard for a form of reconciliation, not only with the king, who pardoned him and his allies for taking up arms against him, but with his fellow members of the council. One of the most significant actions of the newly called parliament was the rehabilitation of Humphrey, duke of Gloucester, declaring him to have been a true liegeman of the king until the day of his death. While this may not have had any apparent relevance to the current troubles, as far as York was concerned it had a two-fold symbolism: it associated him with a man who had struggled against Suffolk's disastrous policies, particularly in France and it linked York in the popular mind with Henry VI's last undoubted heir presumptive. The king's health seems to have deteriorated somewhat in the autumn of 1455. This time, although Henry was ill, he seems not to have lost his wits and occasionally was capable of transacting business. Almost certainly at York's instigation, a delegation from the Commons pressed for York to be given a second term as protector; with a certain amount of reluctance, the lords agreed. York's reasons probably sprang first from self-preservation, and second from a continuing desire to see more of the debt owed him by the crown repaid. The protectorate did not give him unassailable authority, because it could be terminated at the king's pleasure on the advice of the lords.

One of the major tasks facing York, and one of the reasons he was given the protectorate, was the Courtenay and Bonville feud in Devon, where the Courtenay family was using armed force and acting in a totally lawless manner.

Although the head of the family, the earl of Devon, had been one of the few peers to support York at Dartford, he seems later to have turned against him. York was preparing to go west, but the Courtenays submitted before he did so; a commission of oyer and terminer was set up, but in the end they were granted a royal pardon for everything, even murder. A second task was the chronic state of the country's finances. In this area, one of York's most significant achievements was to raise enough money to pay the Calais garrison and secure the installation of his wife's nephew, Richard Nevill, earl of Warwick, as captain. Warwick held this post for the rest of the reign. Without possession of Calais, the Yorkist claim to the throne might never have been made good. It was clear to York that the only way to rectify royal finances as a whole was by a large-scale act of resumption, taking back to the crown most of the grants made during the king's reign. The Commons thought so, too, but it is hardly surprising that even with many compromises, and promises of exemption, too many of the lords had vested interests in opposing it, and York's power was terminated in the spring of 1456. Only a strong king could have imposed such an act; a Protector lacking real authority had little chance of success.

When York was relieved of the protectorate by the king in parliament, it was rumoured that Henry would have kept him as chief councillor, but the queen was determined that this should not happen. For the next three years there was an uneasy peace, while everyone involved tried to create a sense of normality. Far from the country dividing into two armed camps, most members of the nobility were anxiously doing their best to avoid civil war. In this they were aided by the king's own peacekeeping efforts, ably seconded by the duke of Buckingham, as wealthy, influential and as royal-blooded as York himself. All the peers had taken repeated oaths of loyalty to Henry, who was their anointed king, however inadequate, and to break such oaths was simply treason. They were certainly not about to take up arms on behalf of York. While they were willing to work with him when he held the legitimate power they were responsible for granting him during the protectorates, he was never to receive widespread support for his claim that his royal blood gave him the right to determine who should give counsel to the king.

What, then, brought about the renewal of fighting in the autumn of 1459? For this, the primary responsibility must lie with the queen. In the preceding four years, Margaret of Anjou had signally increased her influence over her husband, partly driven by her determination to protect the inheritance of her son, but partly as a result of the absence of a strong councillor such as Suffolk and Somerset. She withdrew the court from London for much of the time, settling in the midlands, close to the crown lands of the duchy of Lancaster and the earldom of Chester, whose resources allowed her to build up support. While this policy was understandable, what was less acceptable was her association with known enemies of York, including the sons of the three lords killed at St Albans, and the earls of Shrewsbury and Wiltshire. Margaret never learned that in England, successful royal government entailed the crown being above faction, dealing more or less even-handledly with all comers.

In Margaret's fierce defence of the rights of her husband and son, she continued where Somerset had left off. York was an enemy who could no longer be left to live quietly; as a dynastic threat to the house of Lancaster, he had to be destroyed by force. The queen, a chronicler noted, 'greatly loathed' both York and Warwick.[7] A great council was summoned to meet at Coventry in June 1459, to which York and his friends were not invited. Believing, probably correctly, that they would face a series of indictments from the council, York gathered his people at Ludlow, planning a display of force which would gain them a hearing from the king. The queen forestalled him, and the earl of Salisbury, on his way to Ludlow, was met by a royalist force at Blore Heath in Shropshire. The encounter was indecisive and Salisbury continued to Ludlow. There, faced with an army led, at least nominally, by Henry VI in person, the soldiers of the Calais garrison under Warwick's command, who formed a substantial part of Salisbury's forces, refused to fight. With generous offers of pardon, York's rank and file slipped away. The 'Rout of Ludford' as it is known, in October 1459, finally left York convinced that he would never now be given a renewal of his protectorate, nor see his line acknowledged as holding the ultimate succession to the throne.

York and his closest supporters decided they had little choice but to flee. Duke Richard and his second son, Edmund, earl of Rutland, sailed for Ireland, where he had supporters. The Nevills, Salisbury and Warwick, sailed with York's eldest son, Edward, now earl of March, prudently separated from his father and brothers in case the worst befell. It is possible that they, too, were heading for Ireland, but, wherever they were planning to go, they made landfall in Guernsey (which had formerly been in Warwick's possession and whose governor was a trusted retainer) and from there moved on to Calais. Warwick had been captain of Calais for four years, defying attempts by the government to remove him. Duchess Cecily remained temporarily at Ludlow with her younger children. This was certainly not a case of abandonment. She had no serious reason to fear any personal threat to her safety and her continued residence maintained a Yorkist presence in England. In November 1459 a parliament, held at Coventry, attainted the Yorkist lords. Cecily went to Coventry herself and submitted. With the lives, lands and goods of the Yorkists forfeited to the crown, she received a grant of 1000 marks p.a. for 'the relief of her and her infants who had not offended against the king'. She was not personally attainted like her sister-in-law, the countess of Salisbury, and may have owed this to her former friendship with the queen. She was initially placed in the custody of her sister Anne, duchess of Buckingham, whose husband was a loyal Lancastrian, killed six months later fighting Warwick,

Salisbury and Edward of March at the battle of Northampton. Cecily then moved to London with her younger children, staying in Sir John Fastolf's town house in Southwark, to await events.

Since York could no longer hope for a renewed protectorate, his only way back was at the head of an army. In the spring of 1460 Warwick journeyed to Ireland, to confer with York on the best way to return to England. They had borrowed heavily in order to fit out a proper war fleet, which had dispersed a Lancastrian fleet off Sandwich in January 1460. Part of it remained to guard Calais, where Edward of March, at this stage seventeen years old, was left in comparative safety. York, in Ireland, was in a strong position; he was still technically lieutenant and enjoyed considerable Anglo-Irish support, but Ireland was much further away and any force arriving from that direction would be countered by the royal forces in Wales and the midlands. Any armed invasion would have to come from Calais and reach London quickly. The Lancastrians' retreat to the midlands had led to a falling off of support from the capital and the southern counties, which were still smarting over the harsh suppression of Cade's rebellion, and might turn in the Yorkists' favour. Warwick, who was now the driving force, overshadowing his father, Salisbury, returned to Calais to make preparations and to embark on a major propaganda campaign on the Yorkists' behalf. The issue in June of a letter of grievance, the main points of which were drawn up in Dublin, set out their view of the errors of the government. This followed the usual pattern: the list of grievances, for which the king was not to blame, was the fault of evil councillors, namely Shrewsbury, Wiltshire and Lord Beaumont, who were responsible for the attainder of great lords (the Yorkists). The accusations were well known and allowed the Yorkists to present themselves as potential saviours of the realm. What is slightly more problematical is exactly what the Yorkists intended to do if they made a successful return, but it seems possible that the plan hatched in Dublin involved deposing Henry and crowning York.

The Yorkist earls landed at Sandwich and reached London with little opposition. The capital, after a little hesitancy, opened its gates and its Lancastrian garrison retreated to the Tower. To hold the capital was a great asset to the invaders, but for any permanent success they knew they would have to defeat the queen's forces. Within a few days they left London and marched north, where they met and defeated the Lancastrians at Northampton. Buckingham, Shrewsbury and Beaumont were killed and the king captured, but the queen and Prince Edward were safe further north. King Henry had now been present at two defeats, where, if the will had been there, he could have 'died of his wounds'. While this was something that even the Nevills drew back from, there was in reality no alternative. If the king's deposition in favour of York was planned in Dublin, this is given credence by the fact that, after he landed at Chester and journeyed south, York's behaviour was that of a rightful king. He bore the arms of Lionel of Clarence to emphasize his superior claim to the throne, and failed to use the king's regnal year in charters he issued. When he landed, Cecily and the younger children were in London, but he sent for her to meet him at Hereford so that she could make a triumphal entry into London with him. Once there he proceeded to the assembled parliament which the Yorkists had summoned to reverse the acts of attainder passed at Coventry,

> with 700 horse and men harnessed at 10 of the clock, and entered the palace [of Westminster] with his sword borne upright before him through the hall and parliament chamber. And there under the cloth of estate standing he gave them knowledge that he purposed not to lay down his sword but to challenge his right, and so took his lodgings in the queen's chamber ... and took upon him the rule of all manner of offices of that place and purposed no man should have denied the crown from his head.[8]

Yet the king was still alive, the queen and the prince in the north, and there was no popular acclamation of York by parliament. It would seem that the manner of his arrival had upset Londoners, who protested to Warwick, who was himself beginning to rethink the idea of Henry's deposition. The Yorkists might now control the government, but their writ ran only in the south east, and Duke Richard's behaviour embarrassed them. He had again misjudged the situation, believing that sympathy for his position would extend to support for an attempt on the throne. It was Warwick who had the task of telling him that the plan to depose the king was unacceptable both to the lords and the people. The key figure here was the archbishop of Canterbury, Thomas Bourchier, who refused point blank to go along with a deposition, despite his own family's Yorkist loyalties; without his support, a valid coronation was out of the question.

Edward II and Richard II had personal failings which led to their depositions. Henry had none. His personal conduct was beyond reproach and too many oaths of loyalty had been sworn to him. It may have been Warwick who devised the compromise plan accepted by parliament: that Henry should rule for his lifetime, but that York and his line should succeed him, thus disinheriting Prince Edward. This mirror image of the settlement of the French throne by the treaty of Troyes in 1420 left York dangerously exposed, since even the Nevills were content with the power they had achieved by holding the person of the king. York controlled a very narrowly based government centred on Calais and London and his own estates. Elsewhere local factions were settling scores, and York and Warwick had no means of restoring order quickly and no money for patronage.

It was hardly likely that the queen would acquiesce in the disinheriting of her son; in fact it made her all the more determined to destroy the man who held her husband. With the Lancastrian forces massing in the north, York marched to face them, sending his heir to Ludlow to prevent the Welsh Lancastrians under Jasper Tudor, earl of Pembroke, the king's half-brother, joining the queen, and leaving

Warwick to defend the capital. At Wakefield York made his final misjudgement, leaving the safety of Sandal Castle to challenge the queen's army. He was killed in the rout that followed, as was his son Edmund; Salisbury was captured and executed. York had earned himself a respectable military reputation during his time in France, but in England he failed miserably when he took to the field.

It is not hard to feel some sympathy with Richard of York. He was a reasonably competent peer, whose pedigree should have ensured him a place in royal councils. At the beginning of his career, in France, it looked as though he would indeed have a prominent role in service to the crown. The hostility of first Suffolk and later Somerset, and his gradual exclusion from public affairs forced him into opposition and then rebellion, but for most of the time he was only reacting against the treatment meted out to him by the Lancastrian government. So confident was he in the justice of his cause that he seems never to have regarded his actions as treasonable. Given the opportunity of the two protectorates, he tried hard to improve the quality of government, but the radical solutions necessary could never be achieved without the full authority of the king. The breakdown of law and order in the country, typified by the violent family feuds like the one between the Nevills and Percies in Yorkshire and that between the Courtenays and Bonvilles in Devon, led inevitably to the larger battles, with local disputes often determining which side peers fought on in the wider conflict.

York could not rise above faction, nor did he have the insight to see that most of his fellow peers were not prepared to see him depose Henry. Indeed, one of the most astonishing features of the period is most peers' abiding loyalty to the person of Henry VI. This was due in part to the enduring myth of Henry V as a national hero, triumphant in war and wise in government. Ancient Roman texts were becoming increasingly available – the most popular writer on warfare was Vegetius – and Henry V embodied the Roman values. He had bequeathed to his son a relatively peaceful and stable kingdom in England and a new realm in France, and subjects who were developing a sense of national feeling. While he was a deeply pious man, Henry V was a king who saw that religion should be made to serve the state and that heresy was a divisive force which had to be stamped out. These secular, expansionist values appealed to the governing classes, but they could not find them in Henry VI, whose religion was personal and private, and who had no interest in military affairs, or even in government. This did not matter so much while Bedford remained to embody his brother's values, but in the 1440s Henry's withdrawn and melancholic nature, and his peaceful policy, followed by his mental collapse, seemed to symbolize the sickness of the body politic. York in many ways was Bedford's successor in his belief in English rule in France and the need for a strong, just government at home to accommodate it.

After York's death, Queen Margaret was to declare to the citizens of London that York 'of extreme malice long hid under colours, plotted by many ways and means the destruction of my lord's [Henry's] good grace'.[9] While her own 'malice' is clear, many would have agreed with her. With hindsight, it is possible to exonerate York from long-term plotting to seize the throne, but he was pushed inexorably towards it by the particular circumstances of Henry's reign. If York was not the greedy, self-seeking villain of Lancastrian propaganda, neither was he the altruistic defender of the common good as portrayed by the Yorkists. He broke his oath of allegiance to his crowned king, refused to accept his authority and spurned any olive branch offered him, and finally resorted to force. His motives were undoubtedly mixed: he was competent, unimaginative and often lacking in judgement, while his family pride made him determined to seek a role fitting his status, from which he felt he was being deliberately excluded. Exactly when he began to see his role as that of an alternative king will never be known for certain, but if Henry VI had been half the man his father was, the Yorkist claim to the throne would never have arisen. As it was, York put forward his claim to the throne in October 1460 in the following words, 'To Richard duke of York as son to Anne, daughter to Roger Mortimer earl of March, son and heir to Philippa, daughter and heir to Lionel, third [but second surviving] son of King Edward III, the right, title, royal dignity and estate of the crowns of the realms of England and France, and the lordship of Ireland, of right, law and custom appertains and belongs, before any issue of John of Gaunt, fourth son of the same King Edward'.[10]

Edward IV's First Reign

With the death of York and Salisbury at Wakefield on 30 December 1460 it seemed as if the Lancastrians had triumphed and the Yorkist cause had been annihilated. Yet within three months there was a Yorkist king upon the throne. The events of 1460/1 are a perfect illustration of the medieval concept of the 'wheel of fortune' – the idea that a person or a family could be triumphant one minute and in the next utterly cast down, and conversely that someone at the very nadir of their fortunes might suddenly begin to rise again. Edward IV, with the help of his Nevill cousins, spent most of the 1460s dealing with continuing Lancastrian resistance, particularly in the north. By the late 1460s it looked as if he had been successful and that any challenge to his throne had been overcome. The threat, when it came, was from a direction he had not anticipated – members of his own family. With another turn of the wheel, the king found himself in exile and the Lancastrians re-established. How was it that Henry VI had held on to the throne for so long and Edward lost his so soon?

At Wakefield, Duchess Cecily had lost her husband, a son and a brother in a single day. To make matters even worse for the Yorkist cause, Queen Margaret's army scored another victory on the way south to London, defeating the earl of Warwick at St Albans and rescuing the feeble Henry VI. This removed the final justification for the Yorkists to govern in Henry's name. In desperation, Cecily despatched her two youngest sons to the safety of Utrecht and the protection of the duke of Burgundy, but stayed in London herself. The city authorities were reluctant to admit the royal army, full of marauding northerners of whom fearful tales were being spread, and they hesitated long enough for the queen to make her own major error and withdraw her forces northwards. The only glimmer of hope for Cecily and the Yorkists in London was a victory by her eighteen-year-old son, Edward, at Mortimer's Cross over Jasper Tudor, earl of Pembroke, and the Welsh Lancastrians. Edward arrived at the family's London home, Baynard's Castle, at the head of a force drawn from his father's Welsh and Marcher estates. With Henry VI in the queen's hands to give legitimacy to her actions, the Yorkists now had no choice but to take a bold step. On 3 March 1461 a great council was hurriedly convened in London and, with many absentees, endorsed the claim of Edward of March, the new duke of York, to the throne. The following day, to popular acclaim, Edward went though a series of solemn ceremonies in

Westminster Hall and in the Abbey designed to be as close to the coronation rituals as time permitted. A full coronation had to wait upon military success.

The council that endorsed Edward's claim to be king was, of course, both unrepresentative and partisan. For him to be king anywhere outside London would require a military victory over the queen's forces at a time when the very act of usurpation was likely to drive many lords from passive acceptance of Henry into more active loyalty. It is quite clear that it was Edward's decision to assume the crown and that the young king was very far from being a puppet in the hands of his older cousin, Warwick. He already knew his own mind and he and his army were fresh from their victory at Mortimer's Cross, while Warwick had been humiliated by his defeat at St Albans. The idea that it was Warwick who was responsible for putting Edward on the throne seems to have emanated from continental sources, always prone to exaggerate the earl's influence because he was so well known to them. If Warwick, unable to read the signs that Edward was very much his own man, thought he could control the king, then that would be his political downfall.

The king moved swiftly and energetically to advance his forces northwards and the subsequent battle of Towton on Palm Sunday, 29 March 1461, was an overwhelming victory for the Yorkists. Fought in a snowstorm, it was the largest and most bloody battle of the civil war, and it has been reasonably estimated that over 50,000 men were engaged and at least three quarters of noble families had at least one member present. The official figure given at the time of those who died was 28,000, but it has been calculated that a more realistic figure was about 9000. This is a large figure by any standards for a single day's fighting; to put it in perspective, it was the equivalent of nearly a quarter of the population of London, then reckoned to be about 40,000. Equally significant was that large numbers of northern peers and gentry either died on the field supporting the Lancastrians or were captured and immediately executed. Although Henry VI and Queen Margaret escaped after Towton to Scotland, the Lancastrian power in the north was reduced to minor activity in the far north east and the great estates of the Percy family were divided between Warwick, his brother John, Lord Montagu, and the king's brother George, duke of Clarence. A few months after Towton, Edward was secure on his throne and largely in control of his kingdom. Largely, but for the first decade of his reign, never completely. For a start, Henry VI remained an alternative king, and his diehard supporters, particularly in the north, did not see their defeat as final. Much time, military effort and hard-to-come-by cash had to be spent containing rebels.

At the time of Edward's accession, Warwick was seen as the director of the Yorkist regime, certainly abroad and probably at home as well; although his influence may, in fact, have peaked in 1460, this was not apparent at the time. The earl was fourteen years older than his cousin the king, and he had been a commanding, glamorous and successful figure throughout Edward's most impressionable years. It was small wonder that Edward was content to leave many issues in Warwick's capable hands. To Englishmen and foreigners alike, the dominance of the Nevill family was the key factor in politics. Warwick relied on a close network of relatives and retainers. His brother George, bishop of Exeter, was translated to the archbishopric of York as soon as it fell vacant in 1465, and was chancellor until 1467. His uncle William, Lord Fauconberg, was created earl of Kent and given large swathes of confiscated land in the west country; he remained his nephew's loyal lieutenant in the north and at sea until his death in 1463, when he was replaced by Warwick's younger brother, John. John Nevill, whom Edward created Lord Montagu in 1461, was advanced to the forfeited earldom of Northumberland in 1464 and thus took over the great Percy powerbase in the northeast.

With Warwick's own control of the Nevill lands and their brother George at York, the Nevills were truly lords of the north. In the next few years they had to work hard to keep it that way. Warwick himself was frequently on the Scottish border dealing with the last remnants of Lancastrian support for the exiled Henry VI and Queen Margaret. When he was absent, his brother John was an able deputy, certainly earning his elevation to the Percy earldom. After Towton, Edward was content to leave the pacification of the north to the Nevills. Warwick's good lordship was eagerly sought by anyone anxious for success, since he was the primary conduit of royal favour and patronage; it is perhaps not surprising that many at home and abroad formed the impression that he was the real ruler. Edward was a very young man who wanted to enjoy the pleasures of being king. Although he could take decisive military action when matters in the north looked as if they were getting out of hand, he was content for his cousin to deal with many of the more tedious aspects of government. That did not mean, however, that he would always accept his direction and control, and the gradual erosion of Warwick's influence was very difficult for the earl to accept. While allowing Warwick to become all-powerful in the north, Edward refused to allow the expansion of Nevill family power in south Wales, and instead advanced his own man, William Herbert, later to be made earl of Pembroke.

One of the major foreign policy issues for the new Yorkist government was that of selecting a suitable bride for the king. Although Edward was apparently extremely eligible, foreign rulers tended to be wary of bestowing their daughters on usurpers who might not last on their newly won thrones. The matter was not as urgent as it might have been because the king had two young brothers, George and Richard, whom he had created dukes of Clarence and Gloucester respectively. The marriages of the boys and their only unmarried sister, Margaret, were also available for diplomatic use. The two leading powers across the Channel, France and Burgundy, had supported different sides in the recent

English upheavals: France had backed the Lancastrians, while Burgundy had supported York. In the early years of Edward's reign, it was clear that if French support for the Lancastrian activity in Northumberland could be cut off, then the Lancastrians would effectively be finished. Both Edward and Warwick, therefore, recognized that intense diplomatic negotiations were in order. Louis XI of France, whose centralizing policy had brought him into sharp conflict with the semi-autonomous states of Burgundy and Brittany and who was nothing if not wily, recognized in turn that if he rejected Yorkist overtures, the only effect would be to thrust England closer into alliance with his enemy, Burgundy. In October 1463 Louis agreed to a truce and renounced all future aid to Henry VI, and the Scottish government followed suit. Much of the English negotiation was done by Warwick and it would be difficult to overestimate the importance with which the French regarded him. Their chronicler, Philippe de Commynes, says he 'could almost be called the king's father as a result of the services and education he had given him'.[1] With John Nevill's final rout of the Lancastrian forces in the north in 1464, the Yorkist triumph was complete. Henceforth the rule of York could only be defeated by internal divisions.

One aspect of the peace with France was the proposal of a French marriage for the king. Louis' own daughter was still an infant but he offered his sister-in-law, Bona, daughter of the duke of Savoy, and stepped up his campaign of flattering Warwick into supporting the match. Just before a conference planned at St Omer in 1464 to discuss the marriage and alliance, Edward stunned his councillors by announcing that he had already married a Lancastrian widow, Elizabeth, Lady Grey. If their view of his political judgement took a severe blow, it did not, in fact, damage the plans for a French alliance, and Warwick and Louis continued to work towards that end. Edward, however, had other ideas. He was slowly moving in favour of a much closer link with Burgundy, a crucial trading partner. In this he was more in tune with popular feeling in his kingdom than Warwick. During 1467 both France and Burgundy competed for an English alliance, and Burgundy won. Treaties of commercial intercourse were followed by a proposal from the Burgundians that their newly widowed Duke Charles should wed Edward's sister, Margaret, and his only child, Mary, should wed Edward's heir presumptive, his brother George, duke of Clarence.

In 1468 Margaret of York became Charles of Burgundy's third wife in a marriage ceremony of unparalleled splendour. In the view of the Crowland Chronicler, one of the better informed of his kind, it was this match which was 'the real cause of dissension between the king and the earl rather than the marriage between the king and Queen Elizabeth',[2] but it almost certainly simply compounded the alienation Warwick had felt from 1464 onwards. Edward had demonstrated to Warwick that when they diverged, it was his own views which would prevail. Warwick took the loss of influence hard and, perhaps equally importantly, he felt he had lost face, both at home and abroad. In addition, he can hardly have relished negotiating for a match for George of Clarence, whom he hoped to marry to his own elder daughter and co-heiress, Isabel. The Burgundians were not seriously interested in George, but Edward made it quite clear that he would not countenance a Nevill match for his brother. A further blow to the Nevills was the dismissal of Archbishop George Nevill from the chancellorship in favour of Robert Stillington, bishop of Bath and Wells, in the summer of 1467. The reign of the Nevills was effectively over.

Warwick retreated to his estates and, sulking like Achilles in his tent, refused to have anything to do with the preparations for the Burgundian marriage. Nonetheless, there was a rapprochement with the king. Edward made no attempt to humiliate the earl, the flow of favours continued and eventually Warwick reappeared at court, but nothing was ever the same again. In early 1469 Edward agreed in principle to the marriage of George, son of John Nevill, now earl of Northumberland, to his eldest daughter, Elizabeth. Warwick, however, was not to be placated. The outbreak of civil war which followed occurred solely because Warwick refused to accept that his influence over the king, and hence real political power, had largely vanished. In the words of a contemporary, 'his insatiable mind could not be content and yet there was none in England of half the possessions that he had'.[3] He was still of immense importance, the richest and most popular man in the kingdom, laden with offices and the acknowledged leader of English embassies abroad, but for Warwick that was not enough. However sincerely he may have believed that the king's foreign policy was wrong, that hardly excuses the fact that by the end of 1468 he was planning a *coup d'etat* based largely on his own self-interest.

What Warwick wanted was a return to influence over Edward, or, failing that, over a more pliable Yorkist king, namely George, duke of Clarence. Edward's relationship with his brother is discussed later, but here it is sufficient to say that Warwick's actions in 1469–70 would have been impossible without Clarence's complicity.* The latter had been the earl's preferred candidate as a husband for his elder daughter for some time, possibly since the beginning of the reign and certainly since the marriage of the only available non-royal duke, Buckingham, to the queen's sister in 1465. The king, as we have seen, had other ideas. His brother's marriage was a diplomatic asset which he was unwilling to lose. He refused Warwick's proposal, to the displeasure of both the earl and Clarence himself, who clearly had an eye on half the Warwick inheritance and who preferred to stay in England rather than go into matrimonial exile abroad. Whether at the same time Warwick was considering the king's younger brother, Richard of Gloucester, for his second daughter, Anne, is not clear. What was apparent was that Warwick

---

* see below, pp. 92–93

wanted his daughters, two great heiresses, matched to men of rank as high as his own, if not higher, and of equal fortune. Having failed to obtain Clarence, Isabel was not married elsewhere. As Warwick grew more disaffected in 1468 he reverted to the discarded marriage plans, with the full support of Clarence. Since George and Isabel were closely related, no marriage could take place in any event without a papal dispensation, and this was sought without the king's knowledge.

In theory, the match might have brought about a reconciliation with the king, but Warwick now wanted revenge, not reconciliation, and in Clarence he had a willing tool. In addition there were continuing Lancastrian conspiracies, none successful, but enough to keep the government on edge. Warwick and his brother George, archbishop of York, and until recently chancellor, continued to be active at court and in council, and on the surface it looked as though they had accepted the loss of some of their influence. In fact they were merely biding their time, while fomenting popular, local disturbances. Then, in the summer of 1469 Warwick and his brother-in-law, the earl of Oxford, crossed to Calais, where Archbishop George conducted Clarence's marriage to Isabel. Clarence had repeated his brother's error, marrying where he chose without regard to the political consequences; he was, after all, still the king's heir presumptive.

While Warwick and Clarence were in Calais a series of popular risings broke out in northern England, the major one under a leader known as 'Robin of Redesdale'. Although probably inspired by Warwick's agents, and consisting of a hard core of Nevill tenants, the rebellion did attract popular support, but it is not easy to judge how much of it was fomented by Warwick and how much he was simply making use of general discontent. Warwick had always been a master of propaganda and the Yorkist regime's failure to remedy many of the grievances against Henry VI's government meant successful recruitment to a movement which protested its loyalty but demanded redress of those grievances. The charges were all substantially true: the new king had not provided financial solvency for the crown despite heavy taxation (Henry VI's debts had not been paid and new ones had been incurred); there had been little improvement in law and order in the localities; his foreign policy had not been noticeably successful; and old corrupt favourites had simply been replaced by new ones. In short, there was general disillusionment with the Yorkist regime, and Warwick was able to capitalize on it. Despite being so closely identified with King Edward's rule, the earl had been able to maintain his prestige with the common people by reason of his open-handed generosity, something that can hardly have endeared him to the king. For Warwick himself, it was the failure of the king's anti-French, pro-Burgundian foreign policy which was the catalyst. Louis of France had simply outmanoeuvred Edward, coming to terms with all his former allies, including Brittany and Burgundy, and leaving England isolated. Warwick's own consistent pro-French attitude now appeared vindicated in the eyes of his countrymen. So, too, did the distance he had conspicuously maintained between himself and the king's new favourites.

Edward himself was understandably slow to recognize the degree of deceit that existed behind the Nevills' behaviour, but the treason of his cousin and brother appears to have taken him by surprise. On their way to deal with the north country rebels, the forces of his chief lieutenants, the earls of Pembroke and Devon, were defeated by Warwick's forces at the battle of Edgecote. Warwick had the two earls, together with earl Rivers and John Woodville, the queen's father and brother, all executed. Edward's support evaporated and soon he, too, was in Warwick's hands. At first Warwick attempted to continue government in Edward's name. An Italian observer noted that 'the earl of Warwick, as astute a man as ever was Ulysses, is at the king's side and from what they say the king is not at liberty to go where he wishes'.[4]

This experiment in control proved a failure, for while many of the leading men of the kingdom may have welcomed the fall of unpopular favourites, they were not prepared to rally round Warwick while the king was in custody. History was in danger of repeating itself. A Lancastrian rising in the north, however, required the king's own authority to deal with it and Warwick was forced to release Edward. Once free, Edward naturally began to rebuild his own support while undermining Warwick's, but first there had to be a formal reconciliation between the two. What form these delicate negotiations took is unrecorded, but the result was a declaration of peace before the lords in Parliament. As the Crowland Chronicler noted astutely, 'It is likely, however, that there remained a sense of outraged majesty, deep in the heart, on the one side and on the other a guilty mind conscious of an over-daring deed'.[5] Warwick had failed but he had not been defeated.

The psychological strain on Edward during this period was surely considerable. In addition to coming to terms with his own failure as king, he had to acknowledge the treachery of two family members whom he had trusted completely and, in addition, handle the grief and anger of his wife over the execution of her father and brother. And that was not all. In what was almost certainly a cynical attempt to boost Clarence's position, rumours began to circulate suggesting that the king was a bastard – not the son of Richard of York but of a Rouen archer – and it is noteworthy that the rumours first appeared on the Continent among Warwick's allies.

One of the king's first moves when he regained control of his kingdom was to place the responsibility for controlling Wales that had been Pembroke's, on the shoulders of his younger brother, Richard of Gloucester, who had never wavered in his loyalty to Edward, despite having spent much of the time since 1461 growing up in Warwick's own household. In the north of England, Edward faced a dilemma: he needed to resurrect the power of the Percies to counter-balance

that of the Nevills, but to do so without alienating John Nevill, whose military
capabilities were considerable and who had, rather surprisingly, remained loyal
to the king. He did this by removing the earldom of Northumberland from Nevill
and restoring it to the Percy heir. At the same time, early in 1470, he raised Nevill
to a marquessate, and compensated him with lands in the west country; these
were all that were available, but quite apart from being so far from John Nevill's
area of influence, they hardly matched the Percy earldom. In the previous year the
king had agreed in principle to a marriage between his eldest daughter, Elizabeth,
and Nevill's son George; now a formal betrothal took place, and George was
created duke of Bedford. A dukedom had not been forthcoming for Warwick,
but it was for the king's potential son-in-law, who was about nine, and therefore
unlikely to cause any problems for a few years to come.

Despite their apparent reconciliation with the king, Warwick and Clarence
were clearly implicated when a local feud in Lincolnshire erupted into a rebellion.
Edward had no difficulty in putting it down, but although he declared the two of
them traitors, he failed to capture them, and they took ship for Calais. For once,
Calais let Warwick down. His deputy there, Lord Wenlock, though sympathetic,
told them it was unsafe to enter and they were forced to flee further south to the
protection of Louis XI. Edward's vigilance and speed of action in 1470 contrasted
strongly with his slowness the year before, but his success owed much to the fact
that none of the nobles were willing to support such blatant self-interest as that
displayed by Warwick and Clarence; the earl could not even rely on his brother,
for the newly created Marquess Montagu continued in his loyalty to the king.
What support they could muster seems to have come largely from substantial
gentry with strong Lancastrian tendencies. Yet within a year Edward was in
exile and Warwick in command of the royal government. This extraordinary
turnaround had come about through the agency of Louis XI.

The arrival of Warwick and Clarence in France was a golden opportunity
for Louis, the arch-diplomatist. He engineered what, on the face of it, appeared
impossible: a rapprochement between Warwick and Margaret of Anjou. He
brought them together at Amboise and, according to the Milanese ambassador,
'the same evening the king presented him [Warwick] to the queen. With great
reverence Warwick went on his knees and asked her pardon for the injuries and
wrongs done to her in the past. She graciously forgave him and he afterwards did
homage and fealty there'.[6] How far the reconciliation was Louis' plan and how far
Warwick's is open to question. The suggestion that the reconciliation should be
celebrated by a marriage between Edward, the Lancastrian Prince of Wales, and
Warwick's younger daughter Anne was almost certainly Warwick's. The chance
to set his daughter on the throne of England would have been hard for him to
resist. In her turn, however much Queen Margaret loathed Warwick, she was
realistic enough to know that the only way her husband could be restored to the

throne was with French help, and if that could only be achieved by an alliance with her old enemy and a match between her beloved only son and that enemy's daughter, then she would swallow her pride and agree. But she insisted that the marriage should not take place until Warwick had regained her husband's kingdom for him. If the scheme was successful, then Warwick would be back in London, controlling the government of a far more malleable king than Edward. But what of Clarence? He was now redundant, though he was probably fobbed off with the promise of either the reversion of the crown should Henry VI's line fail or the duchy of York. Not only that, but a Lancastrian restoration would strip him of many of his lands, once held by Lancastrians, who would undoubtedly demand them back. In the enterprise that followed, the twenty-one-year-old Clarence was a lukewarm partner.

With the aid of the long-term Lancastrian exile, Henry VI's half-brother, Jasper Tudor, earl of Pembroke, and Warwick's brother-in-law, the earl of Oxford, preparations for an invasion continued all through the summer of 1470. Well aware of what was going on, Edward strengthened Calais and made use of Warwick's fleet, now under his control, to bolster his own naval forces. He had learned from Warwick the value of sea power, and, with the aid of a Burgundian fleet, he set about blockading the French coast. In view of this it is somewhat surprising, certainly to contemporaries like Sir John Paston, that he went north himself to deal with a pro-Nevill rising in Yorkshire led by another of Warwick's brothers-in-law, Lord Fitzhugh, and then lingered in the north after the rebellion had collapsed instead of moving rapidly south again. It was the wrong decision, and he was still in Yorkshire when news of Warwick's landing came. The Channel fleet had been scattered by autumn gales, allowing Warwick and Clarence to cross unhindered to Devon.

In a proclamation of breathtaking effrontery the invaders described Edward as 'late earl of March, usurper, oppressor and destroyer of our sovereign lord [Henry VI] and of the noble blood of this realm'. They declared they had come 'into this realm for the reformation thereof, and in especial for the common weal of all the realm [and to] deliver our sovereign lord out of his great captivity [and to] amend all the great and mischievous oppressions and all other inordinate abuses, now reigning in the realm'.[7] In the southwest, where Clarence held extensive property and where there were still strong Lancastrian sympathies, they had no difficulty recruiting supporters, and when they reached Bristol, they were joined by Lord Stanley and the earl of Shrewsbury, while Pembroke went off to gather forces in Wales. Up north, Warwick's brothers, Archbishop Nevill and Marquess Montagu had been informed of his plans. Montagu had stayed loyal to Edward last time, but, despite the dukedom for his son and his own compensatory lands and title, he did not feel he had been treated well over the return of the earldom of Northumberland to the Percies. The Nevills' old rivals were now back vying with him for hegemony in the north, and he had not been granted Warwick's lands when they had been confiscated, which, as his male heir, he might have hoped for. Both Edward and Montagu deserve sympathy here. The king could not fail to have some suspicion of Montagu, given the treachery of his brother, and did not dare leave him in total control of the north, while Montagu felt the injustice of Edward mistrusting him despite his loyalty. He would not remain loyal a second time. As the king headed south he waited for Montagu and the troops he had been assembling, only to learn that Montagu had defected and was in pursuit.

At this juncture, it seemed to the king that his only safety lay in flight. Why this should have been so is open to question, since he still had a considerable force with him, but there were reports of substantial defections and there is little doubt that popular sympathy had swung once again and was now in Warwick's favour. Edward was in the north, where the Nevills' strongest support lay, so with a few loyal lords, including his brother Gloucester, brother-in-law Rivers and his closest friend Hastings, he escaped and took ship from King's Lynn, an area where Rivers's influence was still effective. Landing in Holland, they were kindly and generously received by Charles of Burgundy's governor of Holland, Louis de Gruthuyse, who knew Edward personally, having served on several embassies to England. There was little Edward's other supporters at home could do except acquiesce in the change of government, while the queen and her three young daughters took sanctuary in Westminster Abbey.

Soon after Warwick, Clarence, Shrewsbury, Stanley and Archbishop Nevill arrived in London, the frail Henry VI was removed from his imprisonment in the Tower and conveyed to Westminster. Contemporary evidence suggests that there was still sympathy and respect for the former king: 'all his good lovers were full glad and the more part of the people', but as he was led to Westminster, the frail and dazed king, dressed in a less than impressive blue gown, 'not honourably arrayed as a prince and not so cleanly kept as should be such a prince' was hardly likely to provoke much enthusiasm from the citizens of his capital.[8] The Re-adeption of Henry VI had begun, but it depended on a shaky coalition between Warwick and Clarence, with their personal followers, and the body of long-standing Lancastrians, as well as on the acquiescence of moderate Yorkists, who formed the majority of the peers. A redistribution of land, always a way of bolstering support, was beyond Warwick's powers, since he could not afford to offend Yorkists by restoring Lancastrians to their former estates. Indeed, the person who suffered most was Clarence, many of whose estates had come from the holdings of Queen Margaret and Prince Edward and now had to be returned, while the only block of land available for redistribution was the dower of Queen Elizabeth, most of which went to Queen Margaret. Yet Warwick's main problem was in many ways foreign policy.

When Louis XI had financed the invasion, his price for support was England's active co-operation in a war against Burgundy. Warwick was perfectly willing to go along with this in policy terms, but the practical difficulties were legion. The government was bereft of funds, and war with Burgundy would outrage the mercantile community, who were the best source of loans. Above all it would lead to Charles of Burgundy's active support of his brother-in-law, Edward. Charles, never very fond of either England or his wife's family, initially maintained a strict neutrality; he ignored Edward's presence on his soil and left all hospitality to Louis de Gruthuyse, not even meeting the king for two months. The prospect of an Anglo-French alliance against him changed his attitude, but his help with money and ships remained covert. Edward, meanwhile, had been in contact with potential supporters in England, including Northumberland, who feared the reinstatement of Montagu into his earldom, and Clarence, whom Edward hoped to persuade to return his true allegiance. He appealed to Duke Francis of Brittany for aid and entered into negotiations with the Hanseatic League of north German towns for ships in return for future trading concessions.

After four months in exile, Edward could not really afford to delay much longer, and on 11 March 1471 he set sail from Flushing with a force of about 1200 men, part English, part Flemish. His plan was to make for East Anglia, where he could look for support from his allies, the dukes of Norfolk and Suffolk. Warwick's preparations had been effective both at sea and on land, and the exiles' first landing at Cromer was brief in the extreme; both dukes were in custody and Oxford had the entire area under his own control. Edward was forced further north, his fleet being scattered by storms. Eventually he landed at Ravenspur on the Humber, where Henry of Bolingbroke, duke of Lancaster, had arrived on a similar quest over seventy years previously. Since Yorkshire was essentially hostile territory, Edward took another leaf out of Bolingbroke's book, declaring he had only come for his own ducal inheritance and pledging loyalty to Henry VI. Even so 'came some folks unto him, but not so many as he supposed would come'.[9] On this occasion popular support was not important; what mattered was the attitude of local peers and gentry. Crucially, neither Montagu, torn by conflicting loyalties, nor Northumberland, grateful for the restoration of his earldom in the previous year, moved against him, giving Edward a brief respite and allowing his supporters to join him as he moved south. This was the crucial period. Edward had to move safely south towards the midlands where his support lay. The longer he avoided confrontation, the more he attracted support and the less need there was for the pretence that he had only come for his father's dukedom.

Montagu finally set off in pursuit and, to the east, the forces of Oxford and the duke of Exeter lay between Edward and the safety of the east coast, though they avoided conflict by moving south to join Warwick in the midlands. Warwick, meanwhile, was learning who his true friends were and discovering they were not numerous. Shrewsbury and Stanley remained inactive, while Somerset and the earl of Devon stayed in the south west awaiting the arrival of Queen Margaret. Warwick, who was at Coventry raising forces, retreated behind the town walls, probably awaiting reinforcements from his brother Montagu and from Clarence, and would neither fight nor surrender, so Edward and his forces pressed on to London, always Yorkist in sympathy. Clarence, who had been awaiting his moment, anxious not to back the wrong horse, finally accepted the mediation of his mother and sisters and, throwing himself on Edward's mercy, was welcomed back into the Yorkist fold.

Gathering other supporters who had arrived in the city, Edward turned back to face Warwick's forces. The battle of Barnet was fought in heavy mist on Easter Sunday morning, 1471, and by the end Warwick and Montagu were dead. Warkworth relates that Montagu had an agreement with Edward and put on his livery, but was killed by one of Warwick's men for such treachery, while Warwick himself was killed fleeing the field.[10] Exeter, severely wounded, but still Edward's brother-in-law, was conveyed to the Tower, while Oxford escaped back into exile. On the evening of the defeat at Barnet, Queen Margaret finally arrived on English soil. The forces of the Lancastrians from the southwest were formidable, but Edward defeated them at Tewkesbury as comprehensively as he had beaten the Nevills at Barnet. Prince Edward and the earl of Devon were killed on the field and Somerset and several other leaders executed immediately afterwards. Queen Margaret, who had taken refuge at a nearby religious house, was taken prisoner. With the smashing of a pro-Nevill uprising in the southeast, Edward was able to enter his capital in triumph.

There was one last obstacle to complete Yorkist victory. During his son's lifetime, there was little point in the death of Henry VI, but after Tewkesbury it surprised very few that Henry met a violent end on the night of Edward's return to London. 'King Harry, being inward in prison in the Tower of London, was put to death, the 21st of May, on a Tuesday night, between 11 and 12 o'clock, being then in the Tower the Duke of Gloucester, brother to King Edward, and many others'.[11] His body was carried on a bier through Cheapside to St Paul's, so that all might see that he was indeed dead. Finally, there was no Lancastrian competitor for the throne and the Yorkist dynasty was safe. Edward's joy was completed by his first meeting with the son the queen had borne him during her period of sanctuary in Westminster Abbey, and who had been christened Edward after his exiled father. A contemporary poem depicted the scene in the following words:

> The king comforted the queen and other ladies eke;
> His sweet baby full tenderly he did kiss;
> The young prince he beheld, and in his arms did bear.
> Thus his bale turned him to bliss
> After sorrow joy,

The course of the world is.
The site of his baby released part of his woe;
Thus the will of God in every thing done.[12]

3

Edward IV's Second Reign

The twelve years of Edward's second reign were internally peaceful, giving the king a chance to undertake some reforms, particularly of royal finance, which he had begun to tackle earlier. His attempt to solve the chronic problem of law and order met with rather more mixed success. The most serious domestic event of the second part of the reign was the death of George, duke of Clarence.[1] Peace at home, of course, did not preclude the possibility of military action overseas. Edward was a successful general and knew perfectly well that campaigns abroad helped to maintain domestic peace. His foreign policy in the first part of his reign had been largely determined by domestic affairs and the need to find support for the new dynasty and ensure that the Lancastrian exiles were not backed in any serious attempt to regain the throne. After 1471 that view of foreign affairs changed. The king's policies began to be dominated by the desire to establish the house of York firmly on the European stage and to arrange the most advantageous marriages possible for his growing family.

Edward was well aware of the need for a king to live in a style which would impress not only his own subjects but foreign visitors with the magnificence of his court. If, however, he wished to pursue an ambitious building programme, collect expensive books, ensure the splendour of his person and provide sumptuous ceremonies, where was the money for it all to come from? One of the major reasons for the decline and collapse of Lancastrian government had been its worsening financial predicament. The effects of a major economic slump in the middle years of the fifteenth century were exacerbated by the costs of trying to maintain English possessions in France. Real revenue fell from approximately £90,000 p.a. under Henry IV to less than £24,000 p.a. in the last five years of Henry VI's reign. Crown debts were £372,000 by 1450, and the government found it increasingly difficult to raise loans, even at ruinous rates of interest. Parliamentary taxation could only be used for 'extraordinary' expenses such as defence and military expeditions, and the crown had to rely for its regular income on the profits of royal lands and customs duties. The latter were badly depressed because of war and continuing bad relations with England's neighbours, and did not seriously improve until the trading treaties and other alliances of the 1470s created better trading conditions. At best, customs brought in a little over half the annual sum of £50,000 which, it has been calculated, was required for the crown's annual expenditure on the expenses of the royal household, the wages of royal officials, the wardenships of the Scottish marches, the garrison of Calais, diplomacy, and the support of a much larger royal family than that of Henry VI. The rest of the royal revenue came from its estates, swollen in 1461 by large numbers of lands forfeited by Lancastrians.

In addition to the crown revenue, Edward also had the income from his own large paternal inheritance to call upon, although this was to some extent cancelled out by the need to provide an appanage for each of his two younger brothers. Many of the confiscated Lancastrian holdings were granted out again fairly quickly, either to reward Edward's own supporters, to whom he was generous, or given back to the men who had forfeited them once they had submitted to the new regime. Only a very few families like the Courtneys and the Cliffords failed to regain what they had lost during his reign. The narrowness of Edward's support in 1461 meant that he had to do all in his power to win over Lancastrian adherents, but it also accorded with the king's own spirit of magnanimity. That did not prevent him from executing men who submitted and then turned traitor, like the duke of Somerset and Sir Ralph Percy, but it meant that on the whole lesser men were spared or fined.

Edward introduced a much more efficient form of administration for the crown estates, based on the practice of his own and other great estates. Where formerly the crown had farmed out property for a fixed rent, with the tenant retaining any profit, Edward placed the estates under the direct control of royal receivers and stewards who were instructed to pay the income direct to the king's chamber in the household rather than to the exchequer. It is perhaps unsurprising that Edward brought to the royal estates practices in which he had been trained in the private estate sector. Whether he did so because it was a system to which he was accustomed or as part of a long-term vision of reform is immaterial. The upshot was that crown finance was brought directly under the personal control of the king, an innovation for a long time attributed to the early Tudors.[2] It would, however, be true to say that it was the ruthless application by Henry VII which eliminated the considerable degree of inefficiency and financial laxity that remained even after Edward's reforms. Despite his efforts, Edward was to suffer from chronic lack of funds for almost all his reign.

The improvement in both trade and royal administration took time to become effective. In the meantime the king was obliged to take less praiseworthy steps to find the money he needed. In 1464 the king and his council levied what was in effect a 25 per cent annual tax on every grant of land, annuity, fee or office which he made, ostensibly to help pay the military costs of subduing the Lancastrian resistance in the north. Shortly afterwards the coinage was revalued, officially because of the shortage of gold and silver in the realm but in reality because it offered the king a splendid opportunity for profit. The recoinage introduced a new gold coinage, with the rose noble worth 10s., together with a half noble and a quarter noble, while the king increased the minting charge from 3s. 4d. to 47s. 8d. for gold and 3d. to 3s. 4d. for silver, which brought him a profit of at least £17,500 in the two years 1464–66 and lesser amounts thereafter.

Because the crown at last seemed to be in capable financial hands, it found it much easier to raise loans from London or Calais merchants and alien bankers, particularly the Florentines. In addition Edward undertook personal trading ventures to help improve his finances, which seem to have been successful. The expedition of 1475 was paid for largely by taxes granted by parliament, but Edward raised further sums by the financial expedient known as the 'benevolence'. These were supposedly free gifts in lieu of military service and they were extracted remarkably painlessly by the king exercising his considerable personal charm. Despite all his efforts, it was not until the mid 1470s, and in particular the receipt of the French pension after 1475, that the crown even approached solvency. The Crowland Chronicler says, 'all these particulars in the course of a very few years rendered him an extremely wealthy prince',[3] but probably this was not so much true, as what Edward wanted everyone to believe was true.

To have rescued the crown from much of the morass of debt and financial ineptitude of the Lancastrians was a considerable achievement, which Edward capped by his behaviour in 1475. The French expedition was paid for largely by his subjects by way of taxes and gifts, but by allowing himself to be bought off by Louis rather than be dragged into a money-draining military campaign, the king pulled off the difficult feat of making war profitable. He did so, however, at considerable cost to his popularity at home; the very high levels of taxation paid by his subjects, particularly in view of the French pensions received by the king and his leading councillors, meant that Edward would have had great difficulty in asking for taxation in the future. The French pension, however, together with the ransom paid for Margaret of Anjou, helped him to rule without recourse to parliamentary taxation for the rest of his reign. The king took a number of other financial measures. He extended his personal trading ventures; the Crowland Chronicler says that, 'having equipped merchant ships and loaded them with the finest wool, cloth, tin and other commodities of the kingdom, [he] exchanges merchandise for merchandise with both Italians and Greeks by means of his agents, just like a private individual earning his living by trade'.[4] As soon as parliament assembled, an act of resumption took back a large number of royal grants, no matter to whom they had been made. Also, although the king did not dare to levy general taxation, he was able to bully the clergy into the payment of frequent tenths. It is hardly surprising, therefore, that in his later years Edward gained a reputation for avarice both at home and, because of his attitude to the financing of his children's marriages, abroad as well. He paid for the Scottish war in the early 1480s largely from his own resources, however, which meant that at his death the royal coffers were depleted, and he bequeathed to his son much less than might have been expected.

When Edward declared to parliament in June 1467 that 'I propose to live upon mine own [ordinary revenue] and not charge my subjects except in great and urgent causes', he was not only fulfilling his subjects' expectations, he was laying down a considerable financial challenge to himself. It was one he successfully met, though not in time to deflect the rebels' claims in 1469 that he had not only failed to discharge the debts of the Lancastrian Crown, but had laid up more of his own. Another charge made by the rebels related to the second major challenge to any medieval king, the maintenance of law and order. One of the reasons for the collapse of Lancastrian kingship had been its inability to provide at least relatively unpartisan justice and prevent the increasing violence and disorder of local society. Edward might say to parliament in 1468 that 'justice was the true ground and root of all prosperity, peace and politic rule in every realm', and there is no doubt that he aimed to provide impartial law. He declared in a message to John Paston that 'he would be your good lord therein as he would be to the poorest man in England ... and as for favour he will not be understood that he shall show favour more to one man than to another, not to one in England'.[5] Despite his laudable aims, did he do any better than Henry VI's government? Here, an open verdict should probably be returned. It would be fair to say that during his reign disorder never reached the levels of the 1450s.

Late medieval kings ruled the regions through delegation of power to the largest landowners, and one of the major results of a regime change such as that in 1461 was to alter the personnel at the top. Edward had firstly to reward men who had been loyal to him and his father. Chief beneficiaries in the north were, of course, the Nevills, John Nevill fully earning his succession to the Percies. In Wales William Herbert, later advanced to the earldom of Pembroke, was initially given responsibility in south Wales, but later was permitted to extend his authority into north Wales as well. In the second reign, after Herbert's death, authority in Wales passed to Earl Rivers in the name of Prince Edward. In the north west, the Stanley family was powerful enough for the king to recognize the status quo, but by making Lord Stanley steward of his household, he hoped to convince them that their interests ran in tandem with those of the regime. The king's friend, William, Lord Hastings, was granted extensive estates in the east midlands, which countered those of Clarence in the west of the region, and, although he was essentially based at court, his relationship with Edward was such that he became the principal influence there. In the north the hegemony of the Nevills was taken over and extended by the king's brother, Richard of Gloucester, though the Percies remained in control of Northumberland. In East Anglia, control was shared by his queen's duchy of Lancaster officials and the duke of Norfolk and later, John, Lord Howard; in the southwest the Yorkist regime was represented first by Humphrey Stafford, earl of Devon, and later John, Lord Dinham.

This policy of delegation was not so much planned by the king but rather an extension of a system that had been in place for generations and which in some cases was driven by the nobles concerned and approved by the king rather than initiated by him. These men wielded large amounts of power and authority, but they were expected to do so in the king's name. Beneath these leaders, the local network relied upon a large number of gentry acting as justices of the peace, many of whom also held minor royal offices. How far these men were able to provide swift and impartial justice is open to question. Much of the evidence suggests that it was still essential to have the support of a influential lord to be successful at law, and those in power naturally ensured that matters fell out as they wished. The king did not necessarily agree with everything that was done in his name, but in general the system served his purpose. On occasion, Edward was willing to accompany his judges on their perambulations, particularly after civil disturbances. Such was the unrest after the outcome of the French expedition that he felt compelled to do so again, rigorously enforcing justice, even against members of his own household. It is probably fair to say that Edward tried hard to impose the rule of law on his subjects and succeeded to a degree, but he also undermined his cause by his own behaviour. Very early in his reign, for example, a law had been passed forbidding retaining, but the king was willing to overlook breaches of that law if it suited him or his closest lieutenants.

An unlikely ally in Edward IV's search for financial stability proved to be the French king. Louis XI's support for the Lancastrians and Warwick had been deeply resented by Edward and when his old allies of Burgundy and Brittany began to put together an offensive alliance against France, the king was of a mind to support them. A campaign against France had definite attractions for Edward. Apart from paying off old scores and helping allies who had supported him in exile, the chance of regaining Normandy for the English crown would earn the king fame indeed. However, both Brittany and Burgundy were fickle partners; Brittany backed down in the face of a possible French invasion and Duke Charles of Burgundy was distracted by his scheme for imperial advancement in the east. Plans for an English invasion army, for which Edward had, with some difficulty, raised the money from parliament, were postponed in 1473 and finally went ahead two years later, after he had pinned Duke Charles down; even Brittany returned timidly to the alliance. If the war was successful, the agreement with Burgundy included the duke gaining all the French lands which lay between the north and south parts of his divided duchy, together with the lands of his enemy, the count of St Pol. England needed Duke Charles's active cooperation, for the Burgundian army was undoubtedly a strong and well-equipped one.

In planning to invade France, Edward also had to ensure the safety of his own backyard. An agreement with Scotland was easily reached in 1474 and concluded with the betrothal of James III's infant son James, born in 1473, and Edward's third daughter, Cecily, who was four years older. The marriage was to take place within six months of their reaching marriageable age, but in the event of either of their deaths beforehand, other suitable offspring were to be substituted. Edward agreed to pay a dowry of 20,000 crowns payable over seventeen years commencing immediately. Finally, in early 1475, everything seemed to be in place for the invasion of France.

The army that the king assembled that spring was described as 'the finest, largest and best appointed force that has ever left England' by an Italian visitor, who also remarked on the personal interest Edward took in his ordnance and pronounced that his siege and artillery train was even finer than Burgundy's.[6] Edward himself told the Milanese ambassador to Burgundy that the army numbered about 20,000 men, nearly twice the number Henry V took to France, while Commynes reckoned that 'All the great English lords, without a single exception, were there. They probably had more than 1500 men-at-arms, a great number for the English, all of whom were very well-equipped and accompanied. There were 14,000 mounted archers, all of whom carried bows and arrows, and plenty of other people on foot serving in their army'.[7] The support among the nobility that the king could now command was noted by the shrewd Commynes, and is indicated by the fact that almost every peer except the aged and infirm had brought his force in person to join the army. The need to secure the safety of the Channel and transport so many men across it taxed the English mercantile marine to its limits and necessitated hiring additional ships from Burgundy's provinces of Holland and Zeeland. It was a major feat of logistical organization to raise, assemble and transport such a large army, with all its supplies, equipment and support services, across the Channel and the king and his officers deserve considerable credit for it.

Despite his formidable force, it was clear that Edward needed Burgundy's active cooperation if the campaign were to be a success, but his brother-in-law proved as unreliable as ever. In the early summer, he was single-mindedly pursuing a struggle with the archbishopric of Cologne and was bogged down in a siege of Neuss in the Rhineland. Neither the entreaties of the Duchess Margaret, nor a personal visit by Earl Rivers could recall him to the duty of his treaty obligations. The amount of time, effort and money Edward had already expended meant that, in terms of prestige alone, he could not back down from the invasion, but even before his army landed his diplomats were seeking an accommodation with Louis and a way out of the impasse. The wisdom of this approach was made clear after the king reached Calais. Instead of being joined by a Burgundian army, Duke Charles arrived late, with only a bodyguard in attendance; he was nearly bankrupt and his army was a mere shadow of its former self. He pursuaded Edward into some half-hearted campaigning, but Brittany made no move and Burgundy would not even allow the English entry into the duke's own towns. With winter coming on, the prospect of fighting the French alone did not appeal to the English leaders, who were not the hardened campaigners of a previous generation, and they had no scruples about entering into serious negotiations with Louis.

The story of what happened next is told in detail by Philippe de Commynes, who was personally involved. Having made discreet contact with Louis, Edward's instructions to his delegates, witnessed by his brothers and most of the leading members of his army, were hard-headed and explicit. He would take his army peacefully out of France and abandon claims to Normandy and Guienne in return for an immediate payment of £15,000 and an annual payment of 50,000 crowns (£10,000) as long as both kings lived. The dauphin was to marry either Edward's eldest daughter, Elizabeth, or her next sister, Mary, without a dowry, and provide her with a jointure of £60,000 p.a. (fifteen times that paid to her mother, the queen). This would be a serious dynastic coup for Edward; despite three daughters of French kings becoming queens of England, no English princess had yet married a French king. A private agreement between the kings to come to each other's aid against rebellious subjects was balanced by a public truce for seven years and free trade for each other's merchants. Louis agreed immediately to the terms, anxious to have things settled before Charles of Burgundy reappeared.

The treaty was sealed by a meeting between the two kings on 29 August 1475. It took place at Picquigny, on a bridge over the River Somme, with all the appropriate pomp and ceremony. However, the memory of the assassination of a duke of Burgundy on a bridge at a similar sort of meeting ensured that there was a secure barrier between the two sides. At the meeting Edward IV appeared a truly regal figure ... When he was within four or five feet of the barrier

> he raised his hat and bowed to within six inches of the ground. The king [Louis], who was already leaning on the barrier, returned his greeting with as much politeness. They began to embrace each other through the holes and the king of England made another even deeper bow. The king began conversation and said to him: 'My lord, my cousin, you are very welcome. There is nobody in the world whom I would want to meet more than you. And God be praised that we have met here for this good purpose'. The King of England replied to this in quite good French.[8]

Leaving hostages behind, Edward retired to Calais and within a month was back in London, taking his army home with him. His Burgundian brother-in-law had been furious on his return to the English camp when he found out what had gone on behind his back. Edward considered that Charles had brought it on himself by his behaviour, but told him he could be included in the truce, an offer rejected by the offended duke as he took himself off. Louis lavished generous gifts and pensions on most of the influential English lords, and Commynes says that even those, like Richard of Gloucester, who were opposed to the peace, became reconciled to it. Among the expedition's leaders, it was considered an honourable peace, but the rank and file of the English army viewed it rather differently, feeling somewhat disgraced, their martial pride injured and their hopes of plunder dashed amid the jeers of the French. A Gascon in the service of Earl Rivers told Commynes that Edward had won nine victories and only lost one battle, the present one; and that the shame of returning to England in these circumstances outweighed the honour he had gained from the other nine. Edward's previous military successes just about rescued him from accusations of cowardice, but he was hard put to explain the waste of money. Luckily, Louis's pension enabled him to remit most of the next round of taxes that were due and remain largely independent of parliamentary taxation for the rest of his reign. He could also argue, with justice, that the trade elements of the treaty provided substantial benefits for his subjects. One final financial benefit to the crown was that Louis agreed to ransom the imprisoned Margaret of Anjou for the sum of £10,000. She was returned to France but, in order to enjoy any liberty, she had to surrender to Louis all claims on the inheritance of her parents in return for a small pension, on which she lived in retirement until her death in 1482.

Historians have long been divided over Edward's motives and actions in the French expedition. Did he ever intend a serious campaign in France to restore the lost province of Normandy to the English crown? It seems plausible that he certainly began with that intention. He had a strong desire for revenge on Louis after the latter's support for Margaret and Warwick in 1470–1, and the influence of his father's views and his own early years in Rouen cannot be overlooked. The image of himself in the heroic, martial mould of Henry V is one that would have appealed to any medieval king and Edward had already proved himself a more than capable soldier. He worked extremely hard to set up the necessary alliances and neutralize any threats. The fact that parliament, usually reluctant to grant money, was willing to provide him with a large amount, though not as much as the king required, suggests not only Edward's powers of persuasion, but perhaps that some Englishmen still dreamed of restoring English rule in northern France. Whether that could have been achieved by the type of short hard campaign that was Edward's forte is another matter, but a campaign ending in another Crecy or Agincourt would have seriously enhanced his standing in Europe, and if he had so chosen, would have been a strong start to a long-term conquest.

Whether either the king or his subjects would have been able to sustain the long, grinding and expensive undertaking that would have been the reality of conquest of Normandy is open to question. Commynes certainly did not think Edward was cut out to endure all that was necessary for a king of England to make conquests in France. Edward was a pragmatist and, however sincere he may have been in his desire to emulate Henry V, he was well aware that any campaign in France required a solid military alliance with Brittany and Burgundy. It was only when he began to have doubts about the reliability of Burgundy's support that he started to look for alternatives before his army got bogged down in campaigning. Once the decision to pull out without fighting had been made, the king acted decisively. He knew exactly what he wanted, and the likelihood that he would get it was strong. In fact, Louis barely quibbled, so anxious was he to get rid of the English force, so Edward emerged richer, if not covered with military glory. Only those among the English leaders who saw little further than the military ignominy could fail to see the advantages of what he had achieved. This included not only financial solvency under the treaty with France, but the extended truce with Scotland and the prospect of crowns for two of his daughters. The views of the majority of Edward's subjects were less sanguine; they resented the waste of their taxes and what they saw as a national humiliation.

In the years following the French expedition, Edward and Elizabeth were deeply involved in schemes for suitable marriages for their children. Only the two youngest, Catherine (born 1479) and Bridget (born 1480), were too young to be considered as serious marriage prospects. Any usurping dynasty was viewed with a certain degree of suspicion by more established reigning families, and Edward's loss of the throne in 1469–70 confirmed these reservations. Despite the Yorkists' ultimate success in 1471, it was never going to be easy to make suitable diplomatic alliances, a difficulty compounded by Edward's lack of money to provide suitable dowries for his daughters. The two matches arranged in 1474 and 1475 therefore were a triumph for Edward.

Buoyed up by this, he turned his attention to finding a suitable bride for the Prince of Wales, young as he was. In the winter of 1476 tentative negotiations had begun with the court of Spain for the hand of the Infanta Isabella, daughter of Ferdinand of Aragon and Isabella of Castile. These were still active in 1478, but Edward was beginning to turn his attention elsewhere. Maximilian of Austria, son and heir of the Emperor Frederick III, proposed a match with his sister, but Edward was more inclined to favour a match with a daughter of the duke of Milan, famed for his wealth. The duke had been murdered in 1476, but his widow was Bona of Savoy, who, having been jilted by Edward in favour of an English widow in 1464, rejected the proposals. One of the shrewd Italian observers, this time the Milanese ambassador to France, reported home that 'the chief difficulty which they speak of will be owing to the great quantity of money which the king of England will want ... for the dowry and presents, as they say he knows you have a great treasure, and he proposes in this way to obtain a good share of it, as being in any case one who tends to accumulate treasure'.[9] What was regarded as unseemly greed, but was more likely to be Edward's constant lack of money, was once more in evidence during the more serious proposals for Prince Edward to marry the elder daughter and eventual heiress of Duke Francis of Brittany, a family with a long history of marriage with members of the English royal family. In 1481 agreement was reached that Anne of Brittany, then aged four, should marry Edward as soon as she reached the age of twelve. Her dowry was to be 100,000 crowns, but this was to double if in the interim the duke had a son; and if a son was born after the marriage, then he was to marry a daughter of Edward's. This was not unreasonable, but Edward then over-reached himself by stipulating that, in the latter event, Duke Francis would provide the dowry of 100,000 crowns for Edward's own daughter.

At the same time as the Breton negotiations were taking place, Edward's second daughter, Mary, who had been held in reserve to replace her elder sister, Elizabeth, in the French match, was betrothed to King Frederick I of Denmark, but she died on 23 May 1482, aged fourteen. Her next uncommitted sister, Anne, was only seven and too young to be a substitute, so the opportunity of a Danish match was lost. Throughout the late 1470s Edward IV was in a strong diplomatic position, with both Burgundy and France bidding for his support. At one time Louis had offered him Holland and Zeeland if he would join the dismemberment of the duchy, but Edward would not be drawn and continued to remain neutral in the French and Burgundian struggle.

Duke Charles of Burgundy died early in 1477, leaving an only daughter, Mary, who thus became the greatest heiress of Europe. Her stepmother, Margaret of York, is said to have urged Edward to allow his brother Clarence (widowed a few months previously) to marry her. Edward would not countenance the match because the house of Burgundy had a claim to the English throne through the Portuguese mother of Duke Charles, who was a granddaughter of John of Gaunt. Nor did he trust Clarence, with all the resources of Burgundy at his disposal, not to attempt a coup in England. Margaret and Mary would undoubtedly have welcomed an English alliance, but Clarence was the only suitable candidate available and a suggestion that Earl Rivers be considered was rejected by Burgundy because he was not royal. Edward was seriously torn between not wanting to see Louis destroy the state of Burgundy and not wanting to lose his daughter Elizabeth's match and his own pension. In the end he did nothing and the Duchess Mary went on to marry Archduke Maximilian of Austria, who took up the struggle with France on behalf of his bride.

In August 1478 Edward raised with Louis the point that, at thirteen, Elizabeth was of marriageable age, and that a formal betrothal should now take place and she should begin to receive her large jointure. Louis, who was far less committed to the match than Edward, prevaricated, not entirely unreasonably, on the grounds that the dauphin was still only eight and jointure depended on the consummation of a marriage. There was a growing mood of irritation with France in England, but Louis conceded enough to keep things going, offering a partial payment for Elizabeth's maintenance. Edward rejected this, demanding full payment, but he was aware that time was not on his side, and if Louis could not be pinned down at a time when Maximilian was successful in Burgundy – in August 1479 he had won a victory over the French – and France needed English support, then if the tables were ever turned, the marriage was doomed. If Edward continued to deprive Maximilian and Mary of English support, then either France would overwhelm Burgundy, or they would be forced to come to an agreement with Louis. Either way, England would be left out in the cold.

As Edward began to consider seriously moving in Burgundy's direction, his sister, Margaret of York, once again acted as intermediary in an attempt to gain Burgundy an offensive alliance with England against France, proposing a marriage between Edward's fourth daughter, Anne, and Maximilian and Mary's only son Philip, born in 1478. Edward was not averse to this prospect, except that Maximilian wanted a dowry of 200,000 crowns with Anne; Edward, after all, was marrying her to one of the wealthiest heirs in Europe. Once again the king drove a very hard bargain, regarding a dowry-free match as part of the price Burgundy would have to pay for the alliance. He also insisted that Burgundy would have to replace his French pension of 50,000 crowns, which he would inevitably lose. He was, however, prepared to remit the first year's payment of the latter in lieu of a dowry, and the agreement was signed in August 1480.

Maximilian's weak position meant that all he got in return was the promise of 6000 English archers, provided he paid for them and Edward's undertaking that, if his own mediation between France and Burgundy was not successful, he would openly declare for Burgundy. At the same time, negotiations with Brittany over the marriage of the Prince of Wales included a treaty of mutual aid, with English archers coming to the duke's aid if Brittany was invaded by France. Edward encouraged a formal alliance between Brittany and Burgundy, but he was reluctant to make it a triple alliance. One result of England's treaty with Burgundy was that Louis refused to pay the instalment of Edward's pension due in September 1480, rejected Edward's offer to mediate and made an attempt to stir up the Scots against England.

Since the treaty of 1474, Anglo-Scottish relations had been amicable. Despite his reluctance to spend money, Edward regularly paid the instalments of Cecily's dowry and in 1478 the alliance was further strengthened by James III's offer of his sister Margaret as a bride for Earl Rivers. Arrangements for the marriage were virtually complete and a date and time fixed when serious breaches of the truce occurred on the borders. While James had little real control over his more bellicose nobles, his government does seem to have condoned the raids. There is also little doubt that the English government over-reacted and threatened war if reparations were not immediate. Suspecting Louis of meddling, Edward brushed aside James's overtures and in November 1480 decided on a military expedition to teach the Scots a lesson, which he planned to lead himself the following summer. Preparations were, needless to say, expensive.

A naval force under Lord Howard successfully raided the Firth of Forth in June 1481, burning towns and shipping, but the land army never reached the border. After months of vacillation, the king decided he needed to stay south where he could easily monitor what was happening in France and the Low Countries, and because he did not go north, the forces of his main courtiers probably did not move either. His brother, Gloucester, and the earl of Northumberland were left to take care of things on the border, and while this was by no means beyond their powers, the uncertainty of the king's actions was not helpful. With troops committed to Brittany and Maximilian pressing for active English support against France, Edward found himself overstretched. He could either send an army against Scotland or he could give substantial aid to Burgundy, but he could not do both.

Amid the shifting sands of European diplomacy, Edward decided that a rapprochement with France was in order. The difficulty of persuading Parliament to grant money and the unpopularity of the outcome of the 1475 expedition meant that realistically there was no likelihood of a major campaign against France. Despite all Louis' machinations, Edward still seriously hoped he could pull off the French marriage for Elizabeth and the avarice for which he was becoming renowned made him extremely reluctant to lose any final chance of restoring his French pension. He made an offer to Louis that he would turn the great army being assembled against the Scots, thus effectively ending any possibility of active support for Maximilian; in return he expected a renewal of the truce, firm arrangements for the marriage, and the restoration of the pension. It seems these terms were immediately accepted by Louis. In response to Maximilian's pleas for help and the fulfilment of their agreement, Edward gave only evasive answers, which suggests that he had either entered into a truce with France or was waiting for the death of the seriously ill Louis, who had already suffered two strokes in the course of 1481.

The campaign against Scotland, planned for the summer of 1482, was given an unexpected boost by the arrival in England of Alexander, duke of Albany, the disaffected brother of King James. His plotting had already led him to flee to France, but he now provided an alternative claimant to the Scottish throne with which to threaten James. He accompanied Gloucester north with an army which encountered little resistance after discontented nobles took James prisoner, and which entered Edinburgh as the Scots retired to Haddington and sued for peace. Albany immediately changed his allegiance, but this made little difference to the outcome. The Scots offered a peace treaty and the renewal of former agreements, including the marriage of Cecily and the future James IV. While disclaiming any authority from the king to make peace, Gloucester demanded the surrender of

Berwick Castle to the English and the return of money so far paid for Cecily's dowry. However, he made no attempt to seek instructions from Edward, and, having got Scots acquiescence to his demands, abandoned his occupation of Edinburgh, withdrew to Berwick and disbanded most of his army. The very expensive expedition, from a position of great advantage, had achieved only the retaking of Berwick-upon-Tweed (in Scottish hands since 1461) for the English crown; a mixed blessing because its defence was a constant drain on royal finances. In October 1482 Edward finally called off the marriage of Cecily to James III's heir and that of Rivers to Princess Margaret. He demanded the return of his dowry payments and did not renew the short truce, probably with a view to renewing the war in the following summer.

The aggressive attitude Edward showed towards Scotland, where a little diplomacy would have achieved all he wanted, was in marked contrast to his reluctance to become embroiled in military activity on the Continent when support of Maximilian was required to counter Louis. The outcome was the same in both cases – the failure of the king's policies. Mary of Burgundy died in a riding accident in March 1482 and her Flemish subjects, never very enthusiastic about her husband, took charge of her children and opened peace negotiations with Louis. This opened up the exciting possibility of a marriage between the dauphin and Mary's baby daughter, Margaret, who might bring with her a substantial slice of territory to the north of France. Just to ensure that Edward would not at the last minute come to Maximilian's aid, Louis published the terms of the secret treaty he had agreed with England the previous autumn. Maximilian had no choice but to come to terms with France and in December 1482 the treaty of Arras agreed the marriage between the dauphin and Margaret, whose dowry was to be the counties of Arras and Burgundy.

England, together with Brittany, was excluded from the Franco-Burgundian truce, which meant that Edward lost not only the long-desired French marriage but the pension which had kept him independent of parliamentary taxes. By the end of 1482 much of what Edward had worked for on the diplomatic front for the previous ten years had been destroyed; his daughters Elizabeth and Cecily had both lost the prospect of foreign crowns, and the death of their sister Mary deprived Denmark of an English queen. Both English and continental observers believed that the king's reaction to the treaty of Arras was one of the causes of his death in April 1483, but, if he had lived, it is entirely possible that Edward would have been capable of restoring his diplomatic position after the death of Louis, who had outsmarted and out-manoeuvred everybody, a few months later. In this period, royal marriages could change the face of Europe. If Edward had lived long enough to maintain the match of his son Edward with the heiress Anne of Brittany, then the union of Brittany with France by her eventual marriage to Louis' son, Charles VII, would not have occurred. Likewise if Edward's daughter

Anne had indeed married Philip, the son of Mary and Maximilian, then Philip would not have been united with the Spanish Infanta Joanna, and the great Hapsburg empire would not have been created.

When Edward IV was taken sick at the beginning of April 1483, initially none of those around him had any reason to suppose that his illness would prove fatal. There had been signs in the preceding years that his health was not all it might have been and, given his lifestyle, that was not surprising, but the exact cause of his death can only be guessed at. Mancini reported that it resulted from a chill contracted while fishing, Polydore Virgil simply blamed an unknown disease, which the Crowland Chronicler supports, saying that Edward at forty was unaffected by old age or any known disease, while Philippe de Commynes attributed it to an apoplexy brought on by his grief and rage at the failure of his foreign policy which had culminated in the treaty of Arras a few months earlier. Given his self-indulgent lifestyle and the increasing girth noted by contemporaries, it is possible that Commynes' diagnosis of a stroke is the most likely explanation. The king seems to have been ill for about ten days or so, and after the first few days aware of approaching death. The stroke, if that is what it was, or pneumonia did not incapacitate him mentally because he added several codicils to the will he had drawn up in 1475, made a serious attempt to heal the quarrel between Hastings and Dorset and repented sincerely of his sins. He died on Wednesday 9 April 1483 and his body lay in state in Westminster Hall until his funeral cortege set out with fitting splendour for Windsor for burial in the king's chapel of St George. Edward had left detailed instructions for the design of the tomb he wished built but, in the upheavals which followed his death many of them were simply not carried out. For centuries his tomb remained unmarked.

4

Edward the King

Edward IV is the only king to have gained, lost and regained a throne in the history of England. Henry VI's brief readeption was as a mere puppet, and although, like Edward, Charles II spent time in exile, this was before he was crowned. While early modern historians rarely look back, there are, in fact, some strong similarities between Edward and Charles. Both were sensual cynics, intelligent but lazy, and both were prepared to take large financials handouts from France to maintain their thrones and their independence from taxation. While the parallels between Edward and Charles were in character, the physical likeness between Edward and his grandson, Henry VIII, as young men has long been noted. Both Edward and Henry came to the throne as teenagers on a tide of popularity and hope for the future. The Milanese correspondent in London wrote of the king after he had been on the throne a month: 'King Edward has become master and governor of the whole realm. Words fail me to relate how well the commons love and adore him, as if he were their God. The entire kingdom keeps holiday for the event [the battle of Towton], which seems a boon from above.'[1] When he became king Edward was only eighteen, but he was already a seasoned and successful soldier, one of the major necessary attributes of a medieval king. In his father's lifetime, Yorkist propaganda had already been singing his praises, describing him as the 'Rose of Rouen', – his mother Cecily had been dubbed the 'Rose of Raby' for her beauty – 'manly-hede', 'trew in euery tryall'. One chronicler describing the arrival of the young earl of March in London early in 1461, mourning his father and brother, wrote 'then all the city was glad, and thanked God [and said], "Let us walk in a new vineyard and let us make a gay garden in the month of March with this fair white rose and herb, the earl of March"';[2] the white rose was a Mortimer badge.

Another point made firmly by his supporters was that he was 'comyn of blode ryall'. This was crucial. Edward was descended from three of Edward III's four eldest sons, Lionel of Clarence, John of Gaunt and Edmund of Langley, while Henry VI descended only from John of Gaunt. In addition, Edward's Mortimer and Clare inheritances made him a descendant of both King John and Edward I as well as Llewellyn the Great, Prince of Gwynedd, which in terms of myth and legend linked him to the pre-Saxon inhabitants of the British Isles, the time of Arthur and Merlin. Merlin's prophecy of the defeat of the Saxons by the Welsh looked as if it might be fulfilled in Edward. The potency of myth and legend on the fifteenth century attitudes should not be overlooked, however sceptical the modern mind, and however hard-headed and pragmatic many medieval political players seem to have been. If Edward had a sense of destiny, it was almost certainly reinforced by the appearance of three suns, a natural phenomenon known as 'parelia' that occurred just before the battle of Mortimer's Cross. He presented it to his appalled troops as a portent of victory, and, when victory was achieved, he took his future badge, 'the sun in splendour' from it; the sun already had the advantage of being another Mortimer badge. The contrast between the rising sun of York and the waning moon of Lancaster was hard to ignore. In contrast to the far from regal figure of the ageing Henry VI, Edward looked like a king. Henry was described in his youth as tall and slender – he was about 5 feet 10 inches – but Edward was a true Plantagenet, very tall (when his coffin was opened in 1789, his skeleton showed him to have been 6 feet 3 inches) and, by all contemporary accounts, extremely handsome; something it is rather hard to reconcile with the broad, bland and wooden face which stares out from his portraits. Sir Thomas More described him as 'of goodly personage and vey princely to behold, of visage lovely, of body mighty, strong and clean made'.[3] He had already proved his military credentials and he seems to have been possessed of that vital characteristic, the common touch, quite unlike his father, who was never able to persuade men to love and follow him. Richard of York had been smaller and dark, much less physically impressive, and Edward presumably inherited his looks from his mother. The Plantagenet genes were Edward's inheritance from both his parents. The question of Edward's possible illegitimacy, first raised on the Continent as a piece of political propaganda by Warwick, has long been dismissed by historians, despite a recent attempt to substantiate the theory; such charges were not uncommon against a royal son born abroad.

The young man who somewhat unexpectedly found himself king in 1461 was in many ways a typical product of his age and class. Although he was the eldest surviving son of a great landowner, much less is known of his upbringing and education than that of a king's son. In his earliest years his name is often coupled with that of his next brother, Edmund, both of them born in Normandy during their father's governorship. Their nurse was a Norman, Anne of Caux, and Edward seems to have had fond memories of her care, because much later, in 1474, he granted her the substantial pension of £20 p.a. When the York household returned to England, the two boys were probably set up in a household of their own at Ludlow, one of the York administrative centres, and where Edward was later to base the household of his own son. The boys would have been under the care of a governor, but although he has sometimes been identified as Sir Richard Croft, an obscure Herefordshire gentleman who later became a successful royal servant, the identification is almost certainly wrong, since Croft was not much older than Edward himself. It rests on a complaint by the boys in a letter to their father dated 3 June 1454 against the 'odious rule and demeaning' of Croft and his brother. The most likely explanation is that the Croft boys were also members of the household and, being somewhat older, bullied the young lords.

Little more is known of Edward's education. The customary schooling in manners, riding, hawking, hunting and the martial arts undoubtedly played a major part in it, but well-born children in the fifteenth century were also expected to perform creditably at music and dancing, at languages and, above all, to take their faith seriously. This was underpinned by a strong element of book-learning. Edward and his brother learned Latin and could speak and read French, while the study of law as it affected the management of estates was essential for a landowner. That Edward and Edmund were expected to do well at their studies is evident from the same letter to their father in the summer of 1454, when Edward was twelve:

> And where ye command us by your said letters to attend especially to our learning in our young age, that should cause us to grow to honour and worship in our old age, please it your highness to wit that we have attended our learning sith we came hither, and shall hereafter; by the which we trust to God, your goodlordship and good fatherhood shall be pleased.[4]

The letter was written from Ludlow, though not, of course, by either of the boys. That was the job of a clerk, but they added their signatures at the end. If Edward received the education and training required for a man of affairs in the late fifteenth century, what he did not receive was any training in the role and duties of a king. He had no opportunity to watch and learn from a royal father as would any Prince of Wales.

Although much of his time as a youth was spent at Ludlow, Edward had begun to be noted on the national scene as early as 1452, when he was ten. The London Chronicles report that after York's attempt at a *coup d'etat* ended in disaster at Dartford, the duke was briefly imprisoned, but was soon released from custody because his son Edward was marching on London with ten thousand men from the Marches, many of them York's experienced soldiers from France. Even if this story is not true, young Edward accompanied his father to London in January 1454 at the head of their household force, and he probably learned early on that in politics a large force of armed men strengthened an argument considerably. This lesson was reinforced by his father's defeat at the rout of Ludford. When York escaped to Ireland, taking his son Edmund with him, Edward chose to go with his uncle Salisbury and cousin Warwick to France. From then on, at seventeen, he was an independent figure.

It was with another force from his father's western estates that Edward won the crucial battle of Mortimer's Cross, which enabled him to enter London and seize the throne. Having then confirmed his military prowess by a stunning victory at Towton, however, it is perhaps not surprising that Edward was more than willing to allow Warwick to control the more tedious aspects of government, while he enjoyed the lighter side of kingship with his friends. His behaviour was understandable, but it was less than wise. It was Warwick and his circle of supporters who dealt with the day to day business of government and leading the earl to believe that he was in control of the government and that the king would allow himself to be led whither Warwick chose. Edward could act decisively when military affairs demanded it, but back at court, like his descendant Charles II, he enjoyed spending his time feasting, hunting and, particularly, enjoying the company of ladies. Edward had gained a reputation for licentiousness by the time he was in his early twenties. Sir Thomas More commented that 'he was of youth greatly given to fleshly wantonness ... this fault not greatly grieved the people'.[5] It was after all to be expected of a young, unmarried man. The Crowland Chronicler commented on his subjects' astonishment that he was able to combine a grasp of business with 'conviviality, vanity, drunkeness, extravagance and passion',[6] while the shrewd and worldly Italian observer, Mancini, agreed with More that 'he was licentious in the extreme ... he pursued with no discrimination the married and the unmarried, the noble and lowly: however, he took none by force. He overcame all by money and promises, and having conquered them, he dismissed them'.[7] Mancini was referring to the king in his later years, but early in his reign the young, tall and handsome king was probably well-nigh irresistible to his female subjects.

Edward IV was intelligent and witty and, because he had not grown up with the trappings of royalty and had suffered the vicissitudes of fortune by the time he was twenty, he was able to communicate easily with ordinary people in a way not given to many kings. This showed in his amicable dealings with the city of London, and in the ease with which he could persuade people to part with their money to his benefit. He also seems to have had the gift of friendship. All the surviving evidence credits him with a particular friendship with William Hastings. The latter was more than ten years Edward's senior, and had been a loyal supporter of his father. He was knighted at Towton and very soon after created a baron. He went on to receive numerous grants of lands and offices, of which the most significant was probably that of chamberlain. This appointment gave Hastings control over who had access to the king, which, together with his intimacy with Edward, meant that he was recognized very early in the reign as having a great deal of influence. In 1462 he was given large grants of forfeited land in Leicestershire, Lincolnshire and Rutland, turning a formerly Lancastrian area into one the king knew he could rely on. This proved the case in 1471 when Hastings produced a large number of men to reinforce Edward as soon as he made a bid to regain the crown. After his restoration, Edward made Hastings captain of Calais, and his significance in the Yorkist hierarchy was recognized by Louis XI, who paid Hastings the largest pension of any of the English save the king in 1475. Charles of Burgundy was already paying him a substantial annuity as well. Despite the level of rewards he received from the king, and the acknowledged influence he had with him, very few of the chroniclers have bad things to say of Hastings. The only criticism is that he was one of Edward's companions in his debauches, 'the accomplice and partner of his privy pleasures', as Mancini puts it.[8]

Edward's womanizing was another aspect of his charm of manner and ease with people outside his court circle. Although the names of most of his mistresses are not known, there is little indication that any of them had any influence over him, an impression underlined by the fact that he remained on good terms with his wife. The probable mother of his two bastards was a gentlewoman, Elizabeth Wayte, Lady Lucy. Like the queen, she seems to have been a young Lancastrian widow, and her liaison with the king began well before his marriage. Her daughter, Elizabeth, was born early in the reign, but her son, Arthur, was almost certainly born after the king's marriage. Both children were acknowledged by their father, but the king did not do anything for them. Arthur was subsequently recognized by Henry VII, probably at the urging of his half-sister, the queen, and he was given an heiress for a wife and created Viscount Lisle in her right.

Elizabeth Lucy died before Edward, perhaps as early as the late 1460s, since Edward's relationship with the best-known of his mistresses seems to have begun about 1470. She was Elizabeth Shore, often referred to erroneously as Jane, who was the wife of a London merchant. Her name has come down to us because she was known to Sir Thomas More at the time he was writing his history. Like her royal lover, she seems to have been possessed of charm, intelligence and wit, as well as beauty. The king called her the merriest harlot in his kingdom, and More says that while 'many he had, but her he loved, whose favour to say truth she never abused to any man's hurt'.[9]

It was only after the king's death that the name of a third significant lady, Eleanor Talbot, Lady Butler, surfaced. Eleanor Talbot was the daughter of John, earl of Shrewsbury, and in about 1449, aged fourteen or so, had been married to Sir Thomas Butler, son and heir of Ralph, Lord Sudeley. Her sister Elizabeth had made a somewhat grander marriage to John Mowbray, duke of Norfolk, while her mother's half-sister was the countess of Warwick. In other words, her birth and connections were every bit as good, if not better, than those of Elizabeth Woodville. Sir Thomas Butler died in 1461, though whether in the fighting is not known; if so, it is likely to have been on the Lancastrian side, since his father remained a convinced Lancastrian. Eleanor was therefore yet another Lancastrian widow to come to the new young king's notice. In chronological terms, she came after Elizabeth Lucy and before Elizabeth Woodville. Her significance was only to emerge after the king's death, when a charge that the king had contracted to marry her was used to cast doubt on the legitimacy of his marriage to the queen.*

In late medieval society the splendour of a king's court was a direct illustration of his wealth and power. His household and style of living had to set him above his nobles, and when he came to the throne, Edward was, in a sense, setting himself to outdisplay Warwick, not a cheap or easy thing to do. It was one of Edward's great achievements that he managed to give the impression of wealth while being almost continually hard-pressed for money. A royal style meant rich robes and jewels, furs, fine linen, new or refurnished buildings, plate and vestments for his chapel. Since Duchess Cecily's court in Rouen had befitted that of the governor of English Normandy, it was probably a lesson Edward learned at his mother's knee. In marked contrast to the modest Henry VI, Edward found it easy to look like a king. As well as being good-looking, he had a magnificent figure to set off the trappings of royalty – even at the end of his life, when his addiction to feasting meant he had grown fat, he appeared at the Christmas court of 1482 'clad in a great variety of most costly garments, of quite a different cut to those which had usually been seen hitherto in our kingdom'.[10]

Edward clearly loved clothes and it would be interesting to know where, or from whom, the inspiration for the new cut had come. The great wardrobe accounts for 1480 list his personal clothing as twenty-six gowns, doubtlets and jackets in rich materials such as blue cloth-of-gold upon a figured satin background and lined with green satin, black velvet lined with purple, white damask furred with sable, purple cloth-of-gold upon a satin ground furred with ermine. There were several dozen pairs of boots, shoes and slippers, hats, bonnets and other clothing, including forty-eight handkerchiefs. The last item suggests a degree of refinement at the Yorkist court which is underlined by the king's enjoyment of bathing. It was seen as a sociable occasion and a mark of favour to be asked to join the king. When his Burgundian host, Louis of Gruthuyse, visited England in 1472 to receive the earldom of Winchester in token of the king's gratitude, William, Lord Hastings, who was acting as his immediate companion, shared his bath at the end of a state banquet, in rooms hung and decorated with white silk and linen. The beds had fine sheets from Rennes in Brittany, counterpanes of cloth of gold furred with ermine and curtains in fine white silk.

The royal palaces were all furnished in an equally lavish scale, hung with the finest arras and displaying costly plate. Expenditure on the latter was not quite as profligate as it sounds, because plate and jewellery could easily be pawned or used as security for loans. They were also used for diplomatic purposes. On his 1472 visit, Edward gave Louis de Gruthuyse 'a cuppe of Golde garnished with perle' in

---

* see Appendix 2.

the middle of which was a great piece of unicorn horn and it had a cover crowned with sapphire (which was believed to be an antidote against drunkenness). Quite apart from being a present to a friend to whom he was indebted, Edward's gift was an indication of his own wealth and taste and a compliment to Louis' lord, Duke Charles. Despite all his lavish purchases, it is doubtful whether Edward spent as much as his successor; between 1491 and 1509, Henry VII spent £200,000 on plate and jewels, belying his reputation for miserliness.

Despite being short of money in his early years on the throne Edward knew the political importance of impressive ceremonial, particularly for a new king who had not been born to the throne. At his belated coronation in June 1461, he authorized the spending of £1000 for 'ready money necessary for our coronation'.[11] By 1466 a Bohemian visitor, Gabriel Tetzel, accompanying his master, Leo of Rozmital, to England, could conclude that Edward had the 'most splendid court that could be found in all Christendom'.[12] Admittedly the visitors had just attended the splendid ceremony arranged to celebrate the churching of Queen Elizabeth after the birth of her first child, the Princess Elizabeth, but the Bohemians had come straight from Burgundy, long regarded as the epitome of courtly magnificence. There were equally lavish ceremonies to welcome the Bastard of Burgundy on his visit in 1467, and when the king's sister Margaret crossed to Burgundy to marry the duke, Edward was prepared to borrow several thousand pounds from Italian bankers and pawn some of the royal jewels to have her escorted by a suitably equipped entourage. Court spending had the added advantage of being very good for trade and prosperity, particularly in London, and it is worth noting that the city was always far more supportive of the Yorkists than their rivals.

The splendid trappings of courtly life, however, were pointless without appropriate settings, and Edward was undoubtedly a great builder. His interest was evident even in the impoverished first half of his reign, but in the 1470s peace and growing affluence allowed him indulge his passion to the full. Despite being a successful soldier, he was not primarily a military builder. He was prepared to spend heavily on the defences of Calais, where expenditure averaged between £1000 and £2000 a year throughout the reign, and his remodelling of the castle of Guines made it one of the first fortresses to be adapted fully for artillery. This second interest of the king's was also reflected in the work put in train at the Tower of London, but at Nottingham, the great royal fortress of central England, the works were purely residential. His visit to Bruges in 1470 had shown Edward the beauty and comfort of Louis de Gruthuyse's new house and he wanted to do even better in England, developing an English style rather than simply emulating the Burgundian. For most of the second, peaceful, half of his reign, the court remained in the Thames valley, travelling between the various royal palaces of Greenwich, Eltham, Westminster, Sheen and Windsor, and it was on these that money was lavished, enlarging and improving, particularly at Eltham, where by his death a magnificent new hall had been completed, and at Windsor.

Just as Edward was not primarily a military builder, nor was he a religious one. Yet at Windsor, in St George's Chapel, he was responsible for one of the greatest glories of late English Gothic architecture. He is said to have been very attached to Windsor as a residence, and to have taken a particular interest in the Order of the Garter, for which the chapel was the spiritual home. Edward used membership of the old and prestigious Order as a personal tool, granting it to friends before more important peers, offering it to foreign rulers as part of diplomatic negotiations, and keeping the feast of St George, which fell a few days before his own birthday, at Windsor whenever he could. He almost doubled the size of the college of priests and choristers which served the chapel, and which was one of the three Chapels Royal from which England derived its considerable reputation for music and musicians. The culmination of the king's vision for Windsor was the complete rebuilding of the chapel, which by the mid 1470s he intended as a monument to his dynasty and for his own mausoleum. Though not finished by the time of his death, it was sufficiently ready to receive his body in April 1483, rather earlier than intended.

His exile in Bruges in 1470 influenced Edward in another area of conspicuous consumption. Louis of Gruthuyse had an extensive library and soon after he regained his throne, the king began to commission a series of lavishly illuminated manuscripts from Flemish scribes and artists, many copies of works he had seen in Louis' collection. Thereafter he developed a book collection based on his own taste; Edward read for pleasure in French and English, but not in Latin, and his tastes were strictly conventional. His book collection was largely confined to histories and chivalric romances and, unlike several of his lords, lay and clerical, he had no interest in contemporary humanism. When William Caxton set up his printing press in Westminster in 1477, he had moved from Bruges, where the king's sister, Margaret, duchess of Burgundy was already a sympathetic patron. In London he found a supporter in Anthony, Earl Rivers, the king's brother-in-law, and several other members of Edward's family and court were patrons of Caxton, but the king was not. Edward's lack of interest in Caxton's work is slightly surprising because the books he was producing were designed to appeal to the tastes and interests of his aristocratic supporters, which were also those of Edward himself. Caxton tried to obtain royal patronage, dedicating two of his works to the king and asking him to receive a copy 'and not to destayne to take it of me so poure and ignoraunt & symple a person'.[13] Although he graciously deigned to receive such copies, and by his death his library did contain a number of printed books, it is clear that Edward never directly commissioned work from him. In dedicating his *Life of Jason* to the young Prince of Wales, Caxton says it was 'to thentente that he may begynne to lerne rede English', and that he would not present it to the king, 'for asmoch as I doubte not his good grace hath it in frensh, which he well understandeth'.[14] The king liked his books to be beautiful, not utilitarian, and continued to commission richly illuminated manuscripts from Bruges, which he then had lavishly bound in silk and velvet with gold clasps. If Edward can be condemned for not appreciating the importance of print, he must be given credit for being the first English king to establish a permanent royal library, which by his death numbered about forty books in English or French. Both Henry V and Henry VI had large book collections of a more learned nature than Edward's, but they were largely dispersed by gift or will. Relatively few religious works appear in the collection that Edward bequeathed to the nation, but then he left all the books of his chapel to the queen in his will.

The royal couple followed the customary pattern whereby a wife was expected to display greater religious devotion than her husband. There is no evidence that Edward, unlike his mother or youngest sister, was ever anything more than conventionally pious. His religious patronage was usually connected with the royal residences, as at Windsor. At Sheen he and the queen patronized the Carthusian monastery founded by Henry V; at Greenwich he was responsible for introducing the continental order of Observant Friars, probably at the urging of his sister, Duchess Margaret, and for offering them a site for a house next to the palace. Further up the Thames, the royal couple had a particular devotion to the Brigitine abbey of Syon, another foundation of Henry V.

Far from London, at his parents' favourite residence of Fotheringhay, Edward pursued family, as much as religious, piety. In the early years of the reign, its church seemed likely to become the mausoleum of the house of York. A college of priests had been founded by Edward, duke of York, in 1412, and the church contained his tomb. Richard of York continued building and may have expressed his own wish to be buried there. After the battle of Wakefield, however, his dismembered body was buried at Pontefract, along with that of his son, Edmund. In 1462 Edward refounded the college at Fotheringhay, almost certainly with the intention of transferring the bodies of his father and brother there, and asked for prayers for himself, his parents, his brother Edmund and his grandparents, in addition to those already being said for the founder and his parents. As soon as he became king, Edward celebrated obsequies for his father at St Paul's and obits and anniversaries continued while plans for the reburial at Fotheringhay were made. The Nevills reinterred the remains of the head of their family, Richard, earl of Salisbury, at Bisham Abbey, Berkshire, early in 1463, in a ceremony of great splendour, where the York family were represented by George, duke of Clarence, and his sister, Elizabeth, duchess of Suffolk. A similar reburial of York was essential to the image of the reigning house, and although politics provided major reasons for its delay, the fact that it did not take place until 1476 cannot really be explained except by the king's lack of funds earlier.

In the spring of 1469, at the king's request, Duchess Cecily surrendered Fotheringhay, held as part of her dower, to her son in exchange for the more convenient castle of Berkhamsted in Hertfordshire. This was almost certainly part of the plan to turn the former into a mausoleum rather than a family home. The upheavals of the next few years put the plans on hold again, but the early 1470s saw a major re-glazing project in the chapel. By late 1475 the new glass was all in place and planning for the very belated reburial of York and his son could begin. The bodies of Richard and Edmund were finally exhumed on Sunday 21 July 1476 and began their solemn and splendid journey south. Each church where the bodies rested overnight was supplied with a new hearse, richly furnished, which remained to enrich the church after the cortege had moved on. A life-size effigy of the duke was at the centre of all the ceremonial; only kings, queens and bishops were permitted funeral effigies, and to underline the point, the duke's was dressed in a gown of dark blue, the mourning colour of kings. An angel held a crown over his head in token that he was king by right. In the normal course of events, the effigy represented the royal dignity until the interment, and the king's successor only briefly attended the burial ceremonies because of the ambiguity of his position. It was presumably for this reason that Richard, duke of Gloucester, based in Yorkshire, was the chief mourner in the journey south, attended by several noblemen from the region. At Fotheringhay, he was met by the king, senior members of his family and a large number of prelates. The burial ceremony itself was attended only by men, and the king remained separate and secluded. The feast that followed was served to 1500 people in vast tents put up for the occasion and this did not include the royal household or the great numbers of the poor who were charitably fed on the leftovers. There are references to the presence of the queen, her two eldest daughters and Margaret Beaufort, countess of Richmond, at the ceremony, but none to the dead man's widow. We do not even know whether Cecily attended, and, if she did, whether she remained, like her son, separate. The difficulties of precedence may have played a part. In such a formal ceremony she should have played the role of dowager queen, but she had never been queen and this left her daughter-in-law taking undisputed precedence, something that Cecily may not have been able to bear on this particular occasion. On her death Cecily was buried with her husband, but even by the time of his father's reinterment the king had abandoned the idea of Fotheringhay as the family mausoleum in preference for Windsor. The memorial to Richard, Cecily and Edmund was desecrated in the sixteenth century but in 1573 their descendant, Queen Elizabeth, ordered the existing one to be erected in its place.

In the reburial of his father and brother, Edward was displaying a strong sense of family which manifested itself in other ways as well. His brothers, for example, were endowed much more generously than either the sons of Edward III or the brothers of Henry V. Even though the crown could ill-afford it, Edward felt it proper to ensure that they were not just dukes, but the wealthiest of his subjects, and duchy of Lancaster estates were alienated in their favour. By the time of the king's death, plans were well advanced for his younger son, Richard, to be equally well-provided for. Dukedoms were reserved for members of the royal family, and George Nevill was only created duke of Bedford expressly on his betrothal to the king's eldest daugher. The queen's family had also to be advanced as befitted its new connection with the crown. It was appropriate that her sisters' husbands should be not only loyal Yorkists, and preferably already with royal connections, but at least of comital rank, and if they were not, then they or their fathers were advanced to earldoms. No less could be done for the queen's father or her elder son, who received first an earldom and then a marquessate.

Just as he lacked the piety of the Lancastrian kings, so Edward displayed little of their concern for learning and scholarship. As councillors and servants, he had many churchmen who were both learned and patrons of learning, but not only did the king show no interest in following Henry VI's example of founding educational establishments, he very nearly wrecked the latter's foundations of Eton and King's College, Cambridge. The estates of King's were confiscated in 1461 and, while some were restored the following year, much of Henry's endowment was permanently lost and the number of fellows had to be substantially reduced. Eton was very nearly suppressed altogether and annexed to nearby St George's Windsor; in 1465 its bells, jewels and furniture were removed to Windsor, but in the end the king softened and restored some of its lands. After 1471 he even gave it a little inexpensive patronage and permitted his queen to give rather more. His only real educational benefaction was to found a free lectureship in divinity at the university of Oxford in 1481, after he had been magnificently entertained by Bishop Wayneflete of Winchester at his new college of Magdalen, when the company had included his mother-in-law, the duchess of Bedford, and his sister, Elizabeth, duchess of Suffolk, together with three bishops and several lords.

Edward IV's ease and charm of manner were in many ways as useful in dealing with men as they were in conquering women. The way in which a medieval king controlled his nobles and other powerful men in his realm was one of the measures of competent kingship. It was an area in which Henry VI had conspicuously failed and the various noble feuds, in many places leading to a virtual breakdown of law and order, were one of the underlying causes of the civil war. It would not have been difficult for Edward to have improved on his predecessor, but that is not to underestimate the task he faced on his accession. He had come to the throne with the backing of only a faction of the peerage, mostly related by blood or marriage to his mother, and after his success at Towton, he had to win over as many of his opponents as possible. The king was by nature magnanimous and did not bear grudges. In many cases he was happy to pardon men who had fought him, or in cases where they were dead, allow the rehabilitation of their sons.

This was a policy that was largely successful, even if it meant grumbling from those who had always supported the Yorkists, that former Lancastrians like Earl Rivers were receiving too much favour. There were, however, a few undoubted failures. Early in the reign, Edward faced the rebellion of the earl of Oxford and his eldest son, and while they were executed, the second son, John, was permitted to succeed to his father's honours when he came of age. The young earl was never to forgive Edward for the deaths of his father and brother, first joining his brother-in-law, Warwick, in opposition to the king and then in the 1470s continuing to fight a forlorn rearguard action until he was captured and imprisoned at Hammes. Edward's policy of placing the regions under the broad authority of his most loyal supporters, though in the first instance a pragmatic response to a problem rather than a long-term vision of local government, was a solution that worked well during his lifetime because of the personal loyalty the great magnates felt for the king. By and large they ensured that peace was maintained in the regions and that the law was administered, if not totally impartially, then at least reasonably fairly. In one area, however, their efforts were undermined by the king himself.

Laws relating to the inheritance and the descent of property were among those closest to the hearts of his subjects, not just the great lords but every landowner in the country, no matter how small his holding. Where members of his family were concerned, Edward was prepared to set such laws aside. Warwick's widow, herself a considerable heiress, was denied her right to her own lands after his death, so that her inheritance could be divided between her two sons-in-law, Clarence and Gloucester, as though she were dead. Here the driving force was the demands of his brothers. Since Edward did not command the resources to enable him to endow them to the level they expected, he was prepared to stand aside and let them despoil the aged countess. The situation repeated itself when the widowed countess of Oxford was stripped of her lands in return for a modest annuity in a similar manner to the benefit of Richard of Gloucester in 1472–3. When the last Mowbray duke of Norfolk died in 1476, leaving only a four-year-old daughter, Anne, and no brother or cousin as heir male, the king took the initiative and rapidly married the child to his younger son, Richard, creating him duke of Norfolk and ensuring by two acts of parliament that, in the event of her death without children, York would retain her lands at the expense of her heirs at law. The Holand inheritance of the dukes of Exeter was likewise manipulated with the intention of benefiting the queen's son, Thomas Grey. All these actions, while cloaked with a degree of legality, were deeply offensive to Edward's subjects. The fact that he and his brothers could act in this way with impunity is one indication of how much authority Edward had over his kingdom and its nobles during his second reign.

In 1461 Edward IV became king with the support of only a faction, but by his death he had established his dynasty firmly upon the throne. Despite being toppled from that throne, he had regained it decisively, destroying any hope of future Lancastrian restoration. The dynasty was recognized by continental powers, and if he had failed to get the better of Louis XI, he was certainly not alone in that. By the end of his reign, the country was peaceful, the authority of the crown re-established and, if justice was not impartial, at least the rule of law was in place. The finances of the crown had been restored and the king could usually persuade parliament to grant the taxes he needed. Despite his financial depredations and single-minded pursuit of his own best interests in a way which had become increasingly tyrannical, there seems to have been real grief as well as shock in the country at his sudden death on 9 April 1483 after an illness which lasted only about ten days.

5

The King's Mother and the Queen

Edward IV owed his throne to the support his mother's family gave to Richard of York, and Duchess Cecily was a figure of considerable influence even before her son's accession. In the years immediately afterwards, Cecily took what she regarded as her rightful place as first lady in the kingdom. With the death of her husband, she could never become queen, so her queenship had to be exercised through motherhood. She began to style herself 'the king's mother, the duchess of York', and early in the reign, the Irish bishop of Elphin, representative of the papal legate, Cardinal Coppini, commented 'she can rule the king as she pleases'.[1] It was his mother whom Edward recommended to the mayor and assembled Londoners as his representative when he went north to Towton. A few months later, he formally granted to his 'most beloved mother' his father's town house of Baynard's Castle and the family home of Fotheringhay as part of the 5000 marks' worth of lands in full recompense of her jointure, and he paid £1700 for her household expenses at Baynard's Castle while he was in the north. Even this was insufficient to cover the gifts and rewards the duchess deemed it necessary to make; economy had never been her strong point.

In the next few years, Cecily spent a good deal of time in the king's company and his subjects regarded her as the queen dowager. This was not a role which could be played cheaply and Edward continued to grant her other lands formerly held by his father and added to her income with annual payments from the customs to help her cover the heavy expenditure on rich clothes, vestments, plate, books and jewellery which she considered essential to her position. It was almost certainly from his mother that Edward learned the importance of looking like a king. Cecily's status was bound to be affected when her son came to take a wife, but she would probably have found little difficulty in playing second fiddle to a foreign royal bride. To be supplanted by a Lancastrian widow of lower rank than her own was almost insupportable. His mother was perhaps the only person who could tell Edward exactly what she thought of his behaviour, condemning his sexual self-indulgence and hole-in-the-corner marriage as utterly unworthy of the inheritance his father had bequeathed him. Whatever happened between the king and his mother, however, there is no contemporary report of it. It is very likely that Duchess Cecily had a blazing row with her son and words were spoken that neither found it easy to forgive or forget, but there is no reason to take as the literal truth the highly circumstantial account written fifty years later by Sir Thomas More, supposedly using the king's mistress, Jane Shore, as a source, nor Mancini's report that Cecily fell into such a frenzy of rage that she declared her son illegitimate.* What is clear is that the duchess could not bring herself to attend the new queen's coronation and it is difficult not to believe that her other children took their mother's view of the king's new wife. Despite their disapproval, however, the marriage was an accomplished fact and all that could be done was to put as good a gloss on the situation as possible.

The birth of grandchildren may have softened Duchess Cecily's attitude to her daughter-in-law and she could not have wished to remain estranged from her son, but the inevitable result of Edward's marriage was his mother's gradual retirement from court. This was the normal procedure for a queen dowager making way for her successor, but Cecily still retained her apartment in one of the royal palaces, because Edward built a new one for his wife. Cecily enjoyed developing her title and seals, which grew ever more elaborate, and most often described herself as 'Cecily, the king's mother, and late wife unto Richard in right king of England and of France and lord of Ireland'. She might not have borne the title of queen, but she undoubtedly regarded herself as 'queen by right' and the York family matriarch. While it is not easy to judge her relationship with the king after his marriage, her development of titles and seals does suggests that it was done with his knowledge and approval. She was present at many major family events, standing as godmother to her granddaughters, Elizabeth and Bridget, and probably also to her namesake Cecily, and she attended the marriage of her grandson, Richard of York, and the founding of the Luton guild of Holy Trinity, all occasions when the queen would have taken precedence.

When her nephew, Warwick, and her younger son, George of Clarence, first began to defy the king over Clarence's marriage to Isabel, Cecily pursued them to Sandwich. It is difficult to analyse her motives, but she returned the next day to Canterbury, so the visit may well have been a failed attempt to recall them to their duty. It was not long afterwards that Warwick was responsible for circulating the rumours on the continent that Edward was illegitimate. It was a common political tactic, used against every king who had been born abroad, but Cecily was probably deeply offended by having her honour impugned in such a way by her nephew. Later, in March 1470, she invited both Edward and Clarence to stay at Baynard's Castle, hoping to reconcile them and drive a wedge between Warwick and Clarence. Again she failed, but she did not give up and, with her daughters, was finally successful in drawing Clarence back into the Yorkist fold after Warwick allied himself to the Lancastrians. She remained in London throughout the Re-adeption, and it was to his mother's house that Edward brought his wife

* see Appendix 1

and new-born son from sanctuary in Westminster Abbey when he returned to his capital.

Baynard's Castle was Cecily's London residence and seems to have remained a focal point for the family throughout her life, but she also held Kennington, a country manor just south of the Thames, where she built a new chapel in 1472. In 1469 Edward asked his mother to surrender Fotheringhay to him so that he might turn it into a mausoleum for his father and brother. Fotheringhay formed part of the dower of Duchess Cecily and had long been one of her chief residences and it was the birthplace of several of her children, but there is no evidence that she spent much time there after her husband's death. It is thought that she was responsible in the 1460s for the major re-glazing of the church and the cloister and hall of the college, which featured saints for whom the house of York felt a special devotion, including St George, St Bridget and St Erasmus, and heraldic devices of the family and many of their closest connections. Cecily agreed to the king's request to surrender Fotheringhay and in exchange was given the more convenient castle of Berkhamsted in Hertfordshire.

It has been suggested that this was an indication of Edward's displeasure at his mother's attitude to his wife, but this is unlikely because, although Berkhamsted was not in a good state of repair, it had frequently been a home of queen dowagers and it was fitting for Cecily to have it. She presumably brought it up to her own exacting standards as she turned it into one of her main residences. Unlike Fotheringhay, it was on the court circuit, being closer to London. It was therefore much easier for the king and her other children to visit her there. In a letter written to her son Richard, probably in 1474, she said, 'Son, we trusted you should have been at Berkhamsted with my lord my son [Edward] at his last being there with us, and if it had pleased you to come at that time, you should have been right heartily welcome. And so you shall be whensoever you shall do the same.'[2] This hardly suggests that she was not on good terms with the king. Her name, however, is conspicuous by its absence from accounts of the reburial of her husband and son at Fotheringhay in 1476, an absence which nobody is able to account for. Nor do we know what her reaction was to Edward's final loss of patience with his brother Clarence and the latter's trial and execution. Whether or not Clarence had repeated the charge of bastardy against the king since their reconciliation in 1471, Edward certainly took the opportunity to refute the accusation in public, calling it 'the falsest and most unnatural coloured pretense that man might imagine'.[3] There is no reason to believe the charge, but for Edward and Cecily, the most hurtful thing was that it had been circulated by two of their closest relatives.

In 1480 Cecily's youngest daughter, Margaret, duchess of Burgundy, made a state visit to England and Edward, in a gracious gesture, gave a banquet in honour of his mother and sister at Greenwich at which Cecily's four surviving children were present. In her later years, the king's mother became noted for her piety, her life becoming monastic in all save vows. She had seen great fluctuations of fortune in her life, and was drawn to the mystical form of contemplative piety exemplified by St Catherine of Siena and St Bridget of Sweden. The great Bridgettine abbey of Syon, just outside London, had been founded by Henry V, but Cecily and her family made it the centre of their religious life. Edward IV, not a particularly pious man, was regarded as its second founder and, tellingly, he named his youngest daughter Bridget, a name almost unknown in England at that date. Her grandmother, who was also her godmother, may have hoped that he would be willing for this child to become a nun, as after her father's death indeed she did. A second granddaughter, Anne de la Pole, entered Syon and eventually became its abbess. There is a strong echo here of Queen Eleanor of Provence, the only post-Conquest widowed queen to become a nun, who ensured that one of the daughters of her son, Edward I, took vows in her abbey of Amesbury, along with a second granddaughter, Eleanor of Brittany. Cecily was also closely involved with the college of secular priests established at Stoke-by-Clare; the York family were the heirs of the Clares and Edward had granted her the honour of Clare in 1461. Cecily's piety did not, however, mean that she neglected her business interests, and the dean of the college, William Wolflete, received a sharp reminder of his duty as surveyor of her lands in Suffolk, Essex, Cambridge, Huntingdon and Hertford:

> we, putting our trust in you in that behalf, considering you to be our surveyor and great officer in that country, charge you therefore straightly, as you will have our good ladyship, to put you in faithful and true devoir to see it amended. And that you fail not hereof as you will avoid the awful peril that may ensue with our great displeasure and heavy ladyship.[4]

Duchess Cecily may never have been crowned queen, but she presided over her family and the country as queen dowager, much as her friend and successor, Margaret Beaufort, was to do in the future. A great deal has been made of her anger at Edward's marriage, and she may never have been totally reconciled to it, but there is little evidence that she and the king were estranged for any length of time. The final word on her relationship with Edward should perhaps go to Elizabeth Stonor, a gentlewoman who describes a meeting between the two in October 1476:

> I have been with my lady of Suffolk [Cecily's daughter, Elizabeth] as on Thursday last was, and waited upon her to my lady the King's Mother and hers, by her commandment. And also on Saturday last was I waited on her thither again, and also from thence she waited upon my lady her mother and brought her to Greenwich to the King's good grace and the queen's; and there I saw the meeting between the King and my lady his Mother. And truly me thought it was a very good sight.[5]

When Edward IV took the reckless step of marrying Elizabeth Woodville in secret her family was unlikely to have been uppermost in his mind, but it was to become a major factor in the history of his reign. Elizabeth, the widowed Lady Grey, was a few years Edward's senior, since she was probably born in Grafton, Northamptonshire, in 1437. Her father, Sir Richard Woodville, came from a line of respectable Northamptonshire gentry, but his father had been a younger son, who had made his own way in Lancastrian service, rising to become seneschal of Normandy. This enabled Richard to enter the service of John, duke of Bedford. On the latter's death he soon married his young widow, Jacquetta, daughter of Pierre de Luxembourg, count of St Pol. There are plenty of examples of noble widows taking simple knights as second or third husbands, but Jacquetta was the second lady in the kingdom and the couple had to pay a stiff fine for their temerity. Jacquetta had had no children by Bedford, but she and Richard settled down to produce a large family, of whom Elizabeth was the eldest. The couple found favour with the new French queen, Margaret of Anjou, to whom Jacquetta was related by marriage, and Richard was created a baron. The new Lord Rivers became a respected crown servant under the Lancastrians and spent a considerable period, like his father, serving in France, some of the time under Richard, duke of York. When Rivers and his eldest son were captured in a surprise attack at Sandwich in 1460, they were mustering forces against the Yorkist lords at Calais. They were taken across the Channel to Calais, where, according to a Paston witness, they were subjected to a humiliating verbal attack on their inferior birth and false loyalties by Salisbury, Warwick and the young Edward, earl of March.

Despite the views of the Yorkist leaders, the Woodvilles' social advancement under Henry VI had already enabled them to make a match for Elizabeth with John, the heir of Sir Edward Grey and his wife, Elizabeth, who held the barony of Ferrers in her own right, and she went as a child to be brought up in the Grey household. She later served in the queen's household, an indication of the favour in which her parents were held. When of age the young couple married and had two sons, Thomas and Richard, before John Grey was killed at the second battle of St Albans, and Elizabeth's father and eldest brother were captured at Towton. The latter were soon pardoned since they were not large landowners who might continue to pose a Lancastrian threat but useful royal officials. Edward had little choice but to win over as many of their kind as he could. Elizabeth was not so lucky: a dispute over her dower with her mother-in-law and her second husband led the young widow to apply for help and support to William, Lord Hastings, the friend and chamberlain of the new king and newly become the most powerful influence in the midlands. Hastings seized the opportunity to drive a hard financial bargain and to arrange a marriage between her son Thomas, heir to the Ferrers barony, and a daughter of his own, as yet unborn. Almost immediately after the agreement was completed, Elizabeth married the king. It is inconceivable that Hastings was by this time unaware of his king's interest in Elizabeth; but, if he had had any inkling of an intended marriage, it is unlikely that he would have taken financial advantage of his future queen.

Exactly when and where Edward and Elizabeth's relationship began is unknown. In the relatively small world of English noble life, they may well have been acquainted for years. The traditional story is that she waylaid him while hunting, holding her sons by the hand and pleading for his support in her dispute with the Grey family. We also do not know exactly how that relationship developed, but given Edward's habits it was inevitable that he attempted to make her his mistress, only to be thwarted by the lady's virtue. If credence is given to a story current on the Continent three or four years later, she resisted him even when he placed a dagger at her throat. The king was not accustomed to rejection, and it was perhaps inevitable that the more she refused him, the more his passion for her grew: so much so that he made the greatest mistake of his career and married her. On his way north to deal with a Lancastrian threat in 1464, he stopped at Stony Stratford. Then, early in the morning of 1 May, he slipped away to Grafton where he and Elizabeth were wed. One account has it that at the ceremony there 'were no persons present but the spouse, the spousess, the Duchess of Bedford her mother, the priest, two gentlewomen and a young man to help the priest sing. After which spousals ended he went to bed and so tarried there three or four hours and after departed and rode again to Stony Stratford and came as though he had been hunting, and there went to bed again'.[6] While the marriage was undoubtedly a secret one, it is difficult to accept that Edward, surrounded by attendants as he presumably was, had managed to disappear for hours on end with his whereabouts unaccounted for.

There were other secret meetings until September, when Edward was forced to admit what he had done to his assembled council, which was pressing him to consider the match offered him with Bona of Savoy. The council were understandably shocked. Edward had completely abandoned any sense of royal duty, thrown away the opportunity of a dynastic match with a European ally and a substantial dowry, all for the sake of a former Lancastrian widow several years older than he and encumbered with two sons. The king had compounded his difficulties by refusing to face up to what he had done. Assessing the likely long-term effects of his actions was not Edward's strongpoint. If it had been, he would have anticipated the doubts thrown on the legality of his secret marriage, and after allowing a space for any ecclesiastical objections, would have gone through a public ceremony that nobody could have challenged. As it was, during the intervening five months between May and September, the negotiations for a French match had advanced considerably and the news left Warwick understandably angry at his loss of face. If the king had hoped in September to soften the blow of his marriage with the news that his wife was already pregnant, he was disappointed, since their eldest child, Elizabeth, was not conceived until the following year, although it is not impossible that Elizabeth had an earlier pregnancy which ended with a miscarriage. The Burgundian chronicler, John de Waurin, though obviously not present, reported the council's reaction in words that exactly summed up the situation:

> They told him that she was not his match; however good and fair she might be, he must know well that she was no wife for so high a prince as himself; she was not the daughter of a duke or earl, but her mother, the duchess of Bedford, had married a simple knight. Therefore, although she was the daughter of the duchess of Bedford and the niece of the count of St Pol, she was not, all things considered, a suitable wife for him, nor a woman of the kind who ought to belong to such a prince'.[7]

Foreign opinions, written immediately after the event, all stress the unpopularity of the king's action.

Elizabeth was crowned in May 1465, a year after her marriage. The delay between the king announcing that he had married her and the new queen's coronation was almost certainly due to the king's wish to ensure that her uncle, St Pol, attended, thus emphasizing his wife's links to European nobility. The coronation was a public statement of their marriage in the eyes of the church and an affirmation of her status as queen. Elizabeth did have some assets other than her continental family connections. She was beautiful and had already proved fertile, while her situation was not unprecedented. Edward the Black Prince had married an English widow, his cousin Joan of Kent, for love, and only his premature death had prevented her being queen. Joan had proved extremely popular with the English people, who did not always take kindly to foreign queens. It is quite likely that most of Edward IV's subjects were more pleased with his marriage than those at court.

Elizabeth brought very little to the marriage and she had to be provided with an appropriate dower. This was much more modest than that provided for her Lancastrian predecessors, which had been the unusually generous sum of 10,000 marks (£6666) per annum. Elizabeth was given a similar endowment to the fourteenth century queens, worth £4500 per annum, largely secured on royal lands. It is possible that while serving Queen Margaret she saw at first hand the difficulty of collecting income from customs, fee farms or exchequer grants and had learned her lesson from her financially embarrassed predecessor. If it was she who persuaded her husband to secure her own income from land, then she had already developed into a sound businesswoman. She managed to live within her income, employing a household of about a hundred persons, about a third less than Margaret, and paying them smaller salaries. Elizabeth, for instance, managed with seven ladies-in-waiting, whereas Margaret had needed ten; Elizabeth made do with two attornies-at-law, Margaret had five. Elizabeth did spend lavishly when the occasion demanded, on plate, furs, jewels and cloth, but in general she was far less extravagant. In many cases when the largest sums of expenditure in the accounts of the two queens are compared, Margaret's spending was almost double. Several members of Elizabeth's family held positions in her household, but always in established posts and never for higher than usual salaries. Her brother John was master of her horse, her sister Anne one of her ladies, amongst whom were also numbered her sister-in-law, Lady Scales, and Alice, Lady Fogge, the wife of a cousin. It was a useful way of helping her family without giving offence to anyone, or expense to the king.

A medieval queen's first duty was to provide for the succession. Edward is said to have told his mother that 'Elizabeth is a widow and hath already children, by God's Blessed Lady I am a bachelor and have some too: and so each of us hath a proof that neither of us is like to be barren'.[8] This comment was hardly likely to have mollified Duchess Cecily, but the king was right. Elizabeth did indeed proceed to do her duty. Their first child, Elizabeth, was born on 11 February 1466, to be followed by two more daughters, Mary and Cecily, in 1467 and 1469 respectively. The lack of a son was unfortunate, but not disastrous, since Edward had two brothers to follow him in the Yorkist succession. The king was thirty and in exile when his elder son was born in the sanctuary at Westminster, where the queen had taken refuge with her daughters. Christened Edward, the new Prince of Wales was given a younger brother, Richard, two years later; a third son, George, lived less than two years. There were four more daughters, Margaret, who lived only a few months, Anne, Catherine and the last child, Bridget, born in 1480, when the queen was forty-three. She had borne twelve living children and raised ten of them, an impressive tally by any standard. While the king was certainly not faithful to her, Elizabeth was secure in her position and presumably able to turn a blind eye to his behaviour with some degree of equanimity. The fact that she continued to bear his children suggests that their union remained affectionate.

Elizabeth fulfilled her role admirably in other ways besides her motherhood. She ran her household economically, providing dependable support for her husband's attempt to make the royal household efficient and solvent and yet impressive in appearance and style. Although her income was more securely based on land than that of her predecessor, Margaret of Anjou, it is nonetheless clear that Elizabeth was able to live within her means because of her own efforts. Many of the dower lands granted her were those held by Margaret, including a number of duchy of Lancaster manors south of the Trent, and since a considerable number of the duchy officials served both queens, it is clear that it was as much the queen's personality as the efficiency of her officials which determined the financial state of her household. The queen was the only married woman in the kingdom who was legally permitted to administer her dower lands during her marriage herself as if she were a *femme sole*. The income from those lands was intended to support her household during the king's lifetime and to provide for her financial independence upon widowhood. The extent and value of her dower lands made the queen one of the leading landowners in the country, and it was in the administration of those estates that most of her husband's subjects outside London became aware of her. In East Anglia, for instance, where many of her duchy lands lay, Elizabeth was regarded as the main instrument of royal authority there by the end of her husband's reign.

The queen, like her predecessors, had a council to assist her in the administration of her lands. This comprised senior officials such as her chamberlain, treasurer and stewards, some of whom were also duchy officials, and the style and procedures of the queen's council were similar to those of the duchy council. The council dealt with an infinite variety of business, comparable to that of any fifteenth-century noble landowner, and with the queen, helped determine policy, which her officials then implemented. Elizabeth also had a team of lawyers upon whose expertise she and her council could draw when necessary, for the council served as a court of law to determine disputes between the queen's tenants. Her surviving letters suggest that she took a close interest in her business affairs, particularly where her rights were threatened. A sharp reprimand, threatening to seek remedy in the courts, was sent to Sir William Stonor, one of the king's knights of the body, when she discovered that he was usurping her rights in the forest of Barnwood: 'to our great marvel and displeasure, we will that you show unto us or our council your said commission [permitting him to hunt], if any such you have, and in the mean season that you spare of hunting within our said forest and chace, as you will answer at your peril'. Nor did she noticeably tone down letters to members of the peerage, as an astringent letter to the earl of Oxford in 1469 on behalf of one of her gentlemen demonstrates.[9] Although written by officials, letters of this nature, signed by the queen herself, would have expressed her wishes rather than general policy.

One of a queen's chief roles was to grace her husband's court, where she was a leader of domestic society. Elizabeth may not have been of royal birth, but she had been a lady-in-waiting at Margaret's court, and had, so to speak, served her apprenticeship. She knew what was expected of her, and there is no doubt that her reputed beauty helped set the tone of her court. Mancini, in writing of her marriage, says 'the king first fell in love with her beauty of person and charm of manner'.[10] There are several representations of the queen of a type common in the fifteenth century, in miniatures, where portraiture was not intended and in stained glass, where it probably was, but Elizabeth was the first English queen for whom a portrait exists. There are a number of versions in existence, all probably later copies of the one in the Royal Collection, but even that was probably not done from life. Nevertheless there is a strong resemblance between them and her stained glass portrait at Canterbury Cathedral, each showing a shaven forehead, long neck, large eyes and heart-shaped face. Her attire appears rich and elegant in all the representations of her. A new young queen was always good for business in the luxury trades as wardrobes and jewel caskets were stocked and palace rooms refurbished, and thereafter her interests and tastes set the tone of the court every bit as much as those of her husband. The stylish and elegant Elizabeth was a perfect partner for a king who believed that appearing regal was as important as acting regally.

Englishmen also demanded piety and good works from their queen. Here again, Elizabeth did not let them down. Margaret of Anjou seems not to have been particularly pious and her charity was educational rather than religious, but the new queen founded the chapel of St Erasmus in Westminster Abbey and received papal permission to enter Carthusian houses which were royal foundations, and to which women were not customarily admitted, provided she obtained the priors' consent. Papal letters confirm her devotion to the feast of the Visitation of the Blessed Virgin and her particular support of the Austin friars at Huntingdon. Elizabeth also had Margaret's interest in learning, perhaps developed when she was serving the former queen. Henry VI's foundations of Eton and King's College, Cambridge, were nearly extinguished by Edward, though he later eased his persecution of Eton and restored a few of its lands, but the school owed several favours to the queen, who may have helped to temper his attitude. Margaret's foundation of Queens' College, Cambridge, which was intended to complement her husband's foundation of King's, was not adequately endowed, and might well have foundered without the interest of Margaret's successor, which was displayed only a few months after she was acknowledged as queen. In March 1465 Andrew Docket and the college fellows were granted a licence to acquire lands worth £200 p.a., which they had not hitherto succeeded in obtaining, and the college is described as being under the patronage of Elizabeth. In 1475 the college received from her a set of statutes as its true foundress.

In many ways Elizabeth's behaviour as queen can be described as exemplary. She even went some way towards repairing the damage to her family's reputation caused by the Thomas Cook affair* by interceding with the king on behalf of the London Mercers and Merchant Adventurers' Company and securing the substantial rebate of 1000 marks from the sum of £2000 which he claimed in 1479 they had withheld from his customs. The merchants lobbied various members of the court, but even Hastings advised them to apply to the queen and in the end it was 'at the instance of the queen's good grace' that Edward agreed to forego part of his demand. Intercession was one of the traditional roles of the queen and much approved of by her husband's subjects. Other aspects of the queen's behaviour were not viewed so favourably. It was noted that on a number of the

---

* see Chapter 6

occasions when Edward bent the laws of inheritance, it was for the benefit of her family, both royal and unroyal, and contemporaries believed that it was she who influenced the king to behave in such a dubious manner. The first occasion was the manipulation of the Scales inheritance to the advantage of her brother, Anthony, at the expense of the Scales co-heirs. The second and more important was the marriage of their second son, Richard, duke of York. Here the initiative was clearly the king's. The queen would probably not have been blamed if it had not been for the Scales precedent.

The establishment of a landed appanage for a younger royal son by marriage to an heiress was a familiar and accepted method of providing for him, so when the last Mowbray duke of Norfolk died early in 1476, leaving a single infant daughter, Anne, as his heir, and without close male relatives, it came as no surprise that she was immediately earmarked for Prince Richard; she was just three years old and Richard a few months younger. It was rather more surprising that, instead of a mere betrothal, the couple were formally married in January 1478 in the presence of many of those lords assembled in London for the parliament which was to try the bridegroom's uncle, Clarence. At the time of the marriage, a large part of the Mowbray inheritance was in the hands of two dowagers, in particular, Anne's great-grandmother, Catherine Nevill, widow of the second duke. Anne's mother, Elizabeth Talbot, was then persuaded to forego much of her dower and jointure to the benefit of her daughter. Even before the marriage took place, Richard of York had been granted the Mowbray earldoms of Nottingham and Warenne and the dukedom of Norfolk, which had been in abeyance since the previous duke's death in 1476, and which the king had the right to bestow as he chose. The young duchess seems to have been taken into the queen's household, and it was at the royal manor of Greenwich that she died in 1481, just before her tenth birthday. This was unfortunate for the crown, but Edward had already taken steps to mitigate its effects.

Under the strict English laws of inheritance, since she died without children, Anne's lands should then have reverted to the Mowbray heirs-at-law, who were John, Lord Howard, and William, Lord Berkeley, both descended from daughters of the first duke. Edward and Elizabeth, however, had not been prepared to risk the loss of their son's appanage in the event of the death of a small girl. Immediately after the marriage, the 1478 Parliament set aside the law of inheritance in this instance and enacted that, if Anne died without heirs of her body, her inheritance was to remain the property of Richard and his heirs. After her death, a second act confirmed the first, and claimed for Richard any lands which Anne would have inherited had she lived, chiefly the dower held by her great-grandmother. Such legal chicanery had never been practised before on the marriage of a royal son to an English heiress and struck at the heart of the landowning structure of society. From the poorest yeoman to the richest peer, people wanted their family to benefit from their inheritance and not to have it diverted to the benefit of those more powerful than themselves. By age-old custom, the king was not blamed directly; but in the place of 'evil councillors', it was the queen and her family who were held responsible, particularly since the Mowbray lands in East Anglia marched alongside the queen's duchy holdings there and were thereafter administered in tandem with them. Together with her brother's Scales property in the area, this meant that the Woodvilles were by far the most significant force in the region. Thus while in many ways the English widow had proved a good and effective queen, she was not popular in the manner of her predecessor, Joan of Kent, and while the men of her family were efficient administrators, they were seen as using their closeness to the king to feather their own nests. Englishmen probably felt that the rule that forbade foreign queens from bringing male relatives to England with them had much to recommend it.

6

Nevills and Woodvilles

In writing of any royal dynasty, it is unwise to ignore the families closest in ties of blood and marriage. This is particularly true of the Yorkists because of the English nature of the dynasty. Unlike any medieval king since the Norman Conquest, Edward had parents and grandparents who were all English, and only one foreigner (Isabella of Castile, who had married Edmund of Langley) among his great-grandparents. He was therefore related to most of the nobles in England, and his siblings, with one exception, married fellow countrymen or women. In addition, unlike any of his predecessors, he had an Englishwoman as his queen, thus further extending his links to the nobility. It is hardly surprising, therefore, that the king's relatives played a major role in politics. In the first half of the reign it was his cousins on his mother's side, the Nevills, who were dominant, while in the period after 1471, his wife's family, the Woodvilles, played a significant role. The years from 1461 to 1467 have been described as 'the rule of the Nevills'. This is not strictly true and it can be argued that the period of Warwick's greatest success was between the earl's landing in June 1460 and Edward's accession nine months later, during which time he directed Yorkist policy. What is not at issue, however, is the high level of influence that Warwick wielded during those six years. The Nevill family was so closely linked to the Yorkist dynasty that knowledge of it is essential to the understanding of English political affairs from 1452 to 1471.

The senior branch of the Nevill family, descended from Ralph, earl of Westmorland by his first wife, Margaret Stafford, do not play a part in this story. In 1396 the widowed Ralph took as his second wife, Joan Beaufort, daughter of John of Gaunt and Katherine Swynford, and a year later he was elevated to the earldom. He had nine children already by Margaret and went on to have fourteen more by Joan. Such was Joan's influence, however, that much of the Nevill patrimony was diverted to the benefit of her sons at the expense of her husband's children by his first marriage, and subsequently the senior line, the earls of Westmorland, were poorer than they had been as Lords Nevill before Ralph's elevation. From being local peers who concerned themselves only with northern affairs, the Beaufort marriage propelled the Nevills into the major political league, particularly after the accession of Joan's half-brother, Henry IV, to the throne.

The exquisite paintings of Ralph, Joan and their children at prayer emphasizes their sense of the importance of dynasty. The earl and countess promoted the interests of their children ruthlessly – it was, after all, no easy task to provide for them all – and they did so with astonishing success. Their eldest son, Richard, was married to the heiress, Alice Montagu, who brought him the estates and title of the earldom of Salisbury. Three of his brothers were married to the heiresses of the baronial families of Fauconberg, Latimer and Abergavenny (the last lady a lunatic), while a fourth became bishop of Durham, and their sisters were matched to the heirs of the dukes of Buckingham, Norfolk and York and the earl of Northumberland. In the next generation, Salisbury's heir, also Richard, and his sister Cecily were married in 1434 to the two children, Henry and Anne, of Richard Beauchamp, earl of Warwick, the wealthiest of the English earls. Henry, later raised to the dukedom of Warwick, died in 1446 and his infant daughter survived him by only three years. Thus, in 1449, his sister Anne became the Beauchamp heiress (and co-heiress of her mother's Despenser inheritance), and she and her husband, the younger Richard Nevill, were created earl and countess of Warwick in her right. The luck of the Nevills had proved astonishingly good. All medieval baronial families saw their chief aim as the preservation and advancement of their family, but the Nevills excelled at it and never allowed themselves to be diverted from the main chance by any scruple. They outbid their rivals in the marriage stakes; all Westmorland's children by Joan Beaufort married heirs or heiresses, and so did Salisbury's son and heir. It was the most spectacularly successful exploitation of the marriage market in late medieval England.

The Nevills, having benefited so greatly from their connection with the Lancastrian kings, remained loyal to them until the mid 1450s. Their change of heart had nothing to do with Henry VI and his incapacity but was a result of deteriorating relations with their cousins, the Percies. The Percy earls of Northumberland had long dominated northern life, and indeed were to continue to do so for a century to come, but the inexorable rise of the Nevills, and the family takeover of so many northern baronies, had led them into areas, particularly in Yorkshire, which were traditionally Percy domains. Rivalry escalated into private warfare, which neither Somerset nor York, acting for Henry VI, had the power to quash, and each was seen, justifiably or not, as partisan, York favouring the Nevill relatives of his wife, Somerset the Percies. The Nevill change of heart was compounded by a dispute between Somerset and Richard Nevill, earl of Warwick, over the lordship of Glamorgan, which the king had placed in Somerset's custody but which Warwick claimed as part of his wife's inheritance. Warwick was as acquisitive and as ruthless as any Nevill, disputing as bitterly with his uncle and cousin of Abergavenny over their share of the Despenser inheritance as with a family enemy. The Nevill family entity was too large to act as a single unit, and its members were as frequently at odds with each other as they were with outsiders. Edmund Beaufort, duke of Somerset, who was Warwick's territorial rival and was to become a political opponent, was both Warwick's first cousin and his brother-in-law (he was married to Eleanor Beauchamp, half-sister of Warwick's wife, Anne). The ruling elite in England was a small enough class for everyone to be related in some way to everyone else, but blood ties rarely determined action to the exclusion of self-interest.

Warwick remained loyal to the crown until the ending of York's protectorate in 1455, but by that time he was engaged in his own personal battle with Somerset and this dictated his change of allegiance. His success at the first battle of St Albans in 1455, where both his rivals, Somerset and Northumberland, were killed, earned him a military reputation; he had arrived at the centre of the stage of English politics. There is no doubt that Warwick had energy and courage. He also made skilful use of propaganda and recognized the importance of sea power. The first enabled him to harness the views and grievances of the common people to his cause. The second was based on his appointment by York, when Protector, as captain of Calais in 1455, an office he retained through the rest of the decade, often in defiance of royal authority.

It would be easy to overlook the significance of Calais's role in the political troubles of the mid fifteenth century, but in fact it held the only permanent military force of the crown, the payment of whose wages was a continuing struggle for an impoverished crown. Anyone who could provide the Calais garrison with wages and victuals earned their loyalty. The merchants of the Staple, who were based in the town, had little in the way of political allegiance; all they wanted was the peace and stability needed to trade. Most captains functioned through a deputy, but Warwick took up residence there. Although Calais was primarily England's greatest military fortress, and his sojourn there introduced Warwick to both continental military practices and diplomacy, it was for piracy that he earned his reputation. Piracy was nothing new to Calais, but the earl raised it to a new pitch, seemingly not caring whether his victims were from friendly powers or not. Diplomatically his regime was a disaster, financially it was successful and it earned him popularity at home, since those attacked were all foreigners anyway. Over the years he built up his own fleet of ships which was self-financing through a combination of trade and piracy. This gave him an independent fighting force and enabled him to control the shipping in the Channel. Calais was thus able to provide the Yorkists with both a safe bolt-hole in time of need and a springboard for their return. In the last years of the lives of his father, Salisbury, and uncle, York, Warwick had been increasingly influential in determining Yorkist policy and his role in ensuring the accession of his cousin Edward cannot be underestimated.

After 1461, Warwick reaped tangible rewards for his support. The offices

Edward IV granted him were legion, admiral of England, captain of Calais, constable of Dover and warden of the Cinque Ports being only among the more significant. Yorkist success also enabled him to resolve the problems of his wife's Beauchamp and Despenser inheritance entirely in her favour. The death of his mother in 1462 added her Montagu and Holand inheritance to his holdings and made him technically earl of Salisbury as well, though he rarely used the additional title, remaining Warwick to all. It has been calculated that his income from lands was thereafter in the region of £7000 p.a., which together with his offices brought in a total of about £12,000 p.a. This was about twice the income formerly enjoyed by either of the dukes of York and Buckingham, who both, in addition, had financial difficulties, and it enabled Warwick to cut a figure on the European stage from his Calais base in a way that was denied his poorer compatriots. His spending was lavish and his hospitality legendary and available to the poor as well as the rich, which was one reason for his popularity. The Great Chronicle of London observed that he 'was ever had in great favour of the commons of this land, by reason of the exceeding household which he daily kept in all counties wherever he sojourned or lay'.[1] The Burgundian chronicler, Jean de Waurin, summed him up shrewdly after visiting him in Calais when he wrote that 'he had in great measure the voice of the people because he knew how to persuade them with beautiful soft speeches; he was conversable and talked familiarly with them – subtle, as it were, in order to gain his ends'.[2]

Despite his two earldoms and his immense riches, Warwick was never created a duke, a rank to which he almost certainly aspired and which his maternal uncle Henry had achieved. At his coronation, King Edward had created both his young brothers dukes, but this was a rank he seems to have decided to retain solely for use in the royal family. Warwick's desire for elevation was probably lessened by his lack of a male heir. His wife had borne him two daughters, Isabel and Anne, but, in a long marriage, no son. He faced the prospect of much of his great inheritance being divided between the two girls, so his choice of their future husbands became a critical issue. This is the explanation behind his determination to match Isabel to George, duke of Clarence. Once Buckingham had been married off to the queen's sister, Clarence was the only duke single and of the right age, quite apart from the fact that he was the king's heir presumptive. Warwick's daughters were heiresses of the Montagu, Beauchamp and Despenser possessions held by their father in the female line, but many of the entailed Nevill estates would descend in the male line to his brother John's son and heir, George. In the meantime Warwick matched Margaret, his last unmarried sister, to John de Vere, and was probably instrumental in helping him regain the earldom of Oxford, forfeited by the rebellion of his father and older brother in 1462. Warwick's widowed sister, Katherine, Lady Bonville, secured an important alliance when she married William, Lord Hastings, the king's friend and chamberlain.

It was Edward's refusal to countenance Isabel's marriage to George, thwarting Warwick's dynastic plans, as much as his emerging foreign policy threatened the earl's political influence, that proved the catalyst for Warwick's defection. In George of Clarence he had found a son-in-law of suitable birth and malleable ambition with whom to threaten Edward. When he replaced Clarence as an alternative king with the Lancastrian prince of Wales, whose marriage to his younger daughter Anne he made the price of his support, he was probably hoping to repeat his role as the *eminence grise* of a young, untrained king. If he had been successful in placing Prince Edward on the throne, he would, of course, have had to reckon with Margaret of Anjou. It is difficult to find any real mitigating circumstances for Warwick's betrayal of Edward IV. If his political influence was waning in the later 1460s, it was still considerable, and he was the richest, most powerful man in the realm after the king, and at that time he still had the king's affection. In many ways he was similar to Richard, duke of York, in his inability to accept the authority of a king he believed to be wrong, or that his behaviour constituted treason. It is hardly surprising that Edward simply could not believe that his cousin and mentor could betray him in such a way.

By acting as he did Warwick also ensured the downfall of his own male line. Although it is probable that John Nevill's young son, George, duke of Bedford, would not ultimately have married the king's eldest daughter because of the importance of her match in terms of foreign policy, he might well have been given one of her younger sisters instead. As it was, his uncle's treason, which ultimately dragged down Bedford's father, Marquess Montagu as well, sealed Bedford's own fate. Although not involved in the Re-adeption, the attainder passed on his father and uncle and the forfeiture of their estates meant that Bedford could not support his ducal title. Edward might have granted him some of them, but in this instance the king's customary magnanimity deserted him and in 1477 Parliament passed an act degrading Bedford from his dukedom. In March 1480 the right of his marriage was granted to Richard of Gloucester, but he was still single when he died three years later aged about twenty-six.

Three of the men closest in blood to Edward IV, Warwick, Montagu and Clarence, committed treason against him and ultimately paid for it with their lives. In contrast, three of the queen's closest male relatives died for the king because of their relationship to him. Just as contemporaries saw the first reign of Edward IV as dominated by the Nevill family, so they saw the second reign as being the era of the Woodvilles. This was in fact a misconception, since the queen's family did not determine policy as Warwick had done, but they did wield a considerable amount of influence, not all of it in Edward's best interests. One of Edward's most serious flaws was his inability to look ahead and anticipate the consequences of his actions. The position of the new queen's family was probably not one the king had given any thought to while he pursued Elizabeth, but in a number of ways they were to play a significant part in the downfall of his dynasty.

The last time that male relatives of a queen of England had become a political issue was in the thirteenth century, when the Savoyard uncles of Queen Eleanor of Provence enjoyed considerable wealth and advancement from Henry III and were consequently unpopular. Since that time, the numbers of her compatriots a new queen might bring to England had been severely limited and male relatives virtually banned, but this was not a restriction that could be placed on an English queen. It was unfortunate for Edward that Elizabeth was the eldest of a large family and one that was comparatively poor. In the early years of the queen's childhood, the major part of the family income stemmed from Duchess Jacquetta's dower, which would revert to the crown on her death. Despite later charges that they were upstarts, the Woodvilles were a perfectly respectable gentry family which had already contracted marriages for some of its members with members of the lesser peerage. They were certainly the equals of men like Hastings and Herbert who became close friends of Edward's and were raised by him to the peerage. Once Edward had become king, he initiated a reconciliation policy with Lancastrians and the Woodvilles were among many soon pardoned.

There is no record of Lord Rivers's feelings when he learned that Edward had allied himself to his 'inferior' family, and there is no evidence that he, unlike his wife, knew of the marriage in advance or sought to promote it. Six months after his daughter's coronation he was advanced to the post of treasurer, always a source of enrichment for its holder, and was almost immediately created an earl, but he was given very little in the way of land. In 1467 he was made constable of England, the office being granted to him for life, with remainder to his son, Anthony. The latter had been married young to Elizabeth, heiress to the Scales barony, which title he took in her right after the death of her father in 1460, but in 1464 he was the only one of the queen's brothers already provided for. There were four younger brothers and seven sisters. One brother, Lionel, entered the church and advanced up its ranks until he became bishop of Salisbury in 1482 at the age of 29. The third brother, John, was given a post in his sister's household, but the two youngest Woodville sons, Richard and Edward, received virtually nothing from the king, who may have felt that, by the time they needed settling in the world, their father would be able to endow them. Thus far, then, King Edward had managed to provide for his wife's senior male relations without granting much from the crown and had done very little that would offend his nobles. What the Woodvilles received was nothing in comparison to the grants lavished on the Nevills and the king's friends, Hastings and Herbert, both before and after 1464, nor were they given lands which might have set them up as rivals for local influence in a particular part of the country. Rivers was given offices to support his new earldom, not lands, and in return, his son-in-law received loyal service.

Advancing the queen's sisters was more straightforward than providing for her male relatives. Only one of them, Jacquetta, was already married, to John, Lord Strange of Knockin. Marriages were always used to forge links between families and by those arranged for his wife's sisters, Edward benefited from a network of kinship links with senior noble families at little expense to the crown. This would bring him supporters to complement the Nevill network of his own family. It has long been held that it was the queen and her father who were the driving force here and not the king, but the benefits to Edward were considerable and there is no reason to suppose that he did not fully support them and there is certainly evidence that he provided cash for dowries. The series of advantageous marriages arranged for the Woodville girls cornered the higher reaches of the aristocratic marriage market from the time of the king's marriage to his deposition in 1469.

Most of the established nobility were only too pleased to take the opportunity to ally themselves to the royal family. Offspring of such unions might well be able to call the next king 'cousin'. Within a little over two years after Elizabeth became queen, her sister Margaret was betrothed to Thomas Fitzalan, son and heir of the earl of Arundel and a nephew of Warwick; Anne to William Bourchier, son and heir of the earl of Essex; Eleanor to Anthony Grey, son and heir of the earl of Kent; and Mary to the son and heir of William, Lord Herbert. Catherine Woodville made the grandest match, to Henry Stafford, grandson and heir of the duke of Buckingham, and a ward of the queen. Such marriages into the family of a guardian were common, and it would have surprised contemporaries if the queen had not taken advantage of the situation. After he became duke of Buckingham, Stafford is supposed to have resented the marriage, but this may well have been as a result of later political developments.

Having settled her sisters, the queen then paid 4000 marks to Edward's sister, Anne, duchess of Exeter, for the marriage of her elder son, Thomas Grey, to the duchess's daughter and heiress, Anne Holand. This was despite the fact that Anne was already betrothed to Warwick's nephew, the infant George, son of John Nevill, at that point earl of Northumberland, and Thomas was technically contracted under the earlier agreement made by his mother with Hastings before she became queen. The broken betrothal to Anne Holand freed young George Nevill for a subsequent betrothal to the Princess Elizabeth. In contrast to his brother Thomas, the queen's younger son, Richard, received nothing during the king's reign.

One of the new queen's earliest actions had been to arrange a highly unsuitable match for her brother John with the dowager duchess of Norfolk, Katherine Nevill, aunt of both Warwick and the king. The duchess was extremely wealthy, enjoying dower from three previous husbands, but she was more than forty years older than her twenty-year-old bridegroom, who would be able to enjoy her income only during her lifetime. Such a match was not totally without precedent, but it was described as a *maritagium diabolicum* and does seem to have offended contemporary feelings of what was appropriate.[3] The irony is that the duchess survived her fourth husband as well, and was last seen alive in her eighties at the coronation of Richard III.

At least three of the Woodville marriages may have personally offended Warwick, involving as they did two nephews and an aunt, but the Woodville successes do not compare with the Nevill matrimonial achievements of a generation earlier. They did, however, remove any potential husbands for Warwick's own two daughters. The loss of Buckingham's heir left only the two royal dukes of Clarence and Gloucester of a rank that Warwick felt his heiresses deserved and, undoubtedly, he saw the advancement of the queen's family as a threat to his own political influence. Unlike Warwick, however, the Woodville men were loyal servants of the king, supporting his policies and not attempting to impose their own.

By the time of the queen's coronation, a year after her secret marriage, Elizabeth's family was in an unassailable position, and any mutterings about upstart Lancastrians was done in private. And yet the Woodvilles have attracted a reputation for being greedy and grasping which cannot quite all be explained away by Tudor propaganda or peer group envy, though they made useful scapegoats for the propaganda first of Warwick and later of Richard of Gloucester. One of the main reasons for the unpopularity of the Woodvilles was the perceived influence they had on the king, and the fact that influence was not always used for benign purposes. The marriages of Elizabeth's sisters were a normal part of the noble marriage market, and in terms of scooping up heirs were certainly surpassed by the Nevill family, but there seems no doubt that the match of her brother with the elderly duchess of Norfolk was seen as offending the natural order, flexible as that order was, and it was the queen and her father who bore the odium. Likewise, her father was a well-regarded royal servant of proven capabilities, who was probably worthy of the post of treasurer, but no one holding it was ever popular and the fact that Rivers had been a Lancastrian until recently and was advanced to an earldom as well was bound to lead to a degree of envy among his fellows.

There were, however, other reasons for Rivers's unpopularity. One particular instance was the affair in 1468 of Sir Thomas Cook, a former lord mayor of London and, like Rivers, a former Lancastrian. He was apparently approached by a Lancastrian agent on behalf of Queen Margaret for a loan. While unwilling to advance any money, he did not report the matter to the authorities. When the agent was captured and forced to reveal what he had been doing, he implicated Cook, who was arrested for treason and sent to the Tower. Rivers, in his capacity as constable, Sir John Fogge (a Woodville relative and treasurer of the king's household) and their servants then ransacked Cook's London house looking for evidence against him.

So far, so reasonable, but it was Rivers' misfortune that one of Cook's apprentices was the future chronicler, Robert Fabyan, who later recounted the whole sordid story. Cook's wife and servants were turned out of the house, and both that and his house in the country were 'spoiled and destroyed much, much of his jewels and plate, cloths of silk and cloths of arras [came into] the treasurer's hands, which, to Sir Thomas, was a great enemy.'[4] The reason for that last phrase is that supposedly Rivers and his wife, Jacquetta, had taken a fancy to one of Cook's valuable tapestries and were affronted when he refused to sell it to them. There may be little truth in this latter story, but how much of Cook's purloined goods went into the king's coffers and how much, if any, into those of Rivers and Fogge will never be known. At Cook's trial for treason, the jury found him not guilty of treason but guilty of misprision of treason (that is, being aware of treason but not revealing it). For this he was fined the enormous sum of 8000 marks, a sum set by the king himself and an indication not only of the seriousness of the crime, but also of just how much he needed money.

The queen then entered the picture. Elizabeth claimed an additional ten per cent on top of the fine under her ancient right of 'queen's gold'. Defenders of the queen have argued that she was entitled to her share and that, while Cook paid the fine to the king, he negotiated over the queen's gold and in the end was let off, indicating the queen's benevolence, although in the meantime he had had to make 'many good gifts' to her council. In fact, 'queen's gold' was only leviable on a voluntary fine, such as that paid for a licence or a dispensation, and not on one levied as a judicial penalty. If Elizabeth did indeed claim it, then the fact that she eventually let him off is an indication not of her generosity of spirit but that her claim had no validity in law or custom. In whatever light the Cook affair is viewed, the Woodvilles do not come out of it very well, and in London particularly, the attack on such a prominent citizen, even a guilty one, was not forgotten. When the city's chronicles were written much was made of it, although the accounts were undoubtedly embroidered.

While the intrigues and the dangers of the Tudor court are familiar, a great deal less has been made of what were surely very similar conditions a century earlier. A small group of able, ambitious men, all well known to each other and most of them related by blood or marriage were vying for the king's ear. While service at court was multi-faceted, involving as it might military and diplomatic duties as well as responsibilities in the counties, one of the main goals of a courtier was to attract royal patronage. This proved that he had the king's ear and a degree of influence with him, and it was essential for him to demonstrate in turn to his own retainers and clients that he could support them and use that influence to their advantage. The more supporters and clients he could attract, the greater his influence locally and thus the more useful he was to the king. The sudden arrival on the scene of a new group with their own private access to the king through the queen was seen by more than just Warwick and Clarence as undermining their own influence. The small faction which had made Edward king was necessarily being widened and, as his council became more representative of the country as a whole, it was inevitable that those who had most benefited during the early part of the reign would find their noses were put out of joint. During the period in 1469 when Edward was under Warwick's control, however, the earl was able to do something about it, taking the opportunity to dispose of several men he regarded as threats to his interests, among whom were Rivers and his son John. Those threats were less a result of anything the Woodvilles had actually done but of the influence they were believed to have over the king.

The greatest Woodville influence, of course, was that of the queen, about which even Warwick could do little while Edward was on the throne. He did his best by fomenting anti-Woodville propaganda, almost certainly exaggerating their influence, and such was his popularity with the commons that he seems to have been remarkably successful. The proclamation issued by Warwick and Clarence in July 1469 justified their actions in view of the 'deceitful, covetous rule and guiding of certain seditious persons, that is to say, the Lord Rivers, the duchess of Bedford his wife, William Herbert, earl of Pembroke, Humphrey Stafford, earl of Devonshire, Lords Scales and Audley, Sir John Woodville and his brothers'.[5] It is worth noting that William, Lord Hastings, the king's closest friend and chamberlain, and arguably the most influential person at court after the queen, was not one of those on whom Warwick turned. As the earl's brother-in-law, Hastings had wisely attached himself to Warwick as well as to the king.

By the end of Warwick's period in power, most of the men named in the proclamation were dead, and not content with executing the queen's father, he then turned his attentions to her mother. Duchess Jacquetta seems to have been close to her daughter and spent much time at court with her. One of Warwick's followers accused her of witchcraft. This was a handy tool for threatening women powerful enough to be otherwise untouchable. It had been successfully used by Henry V against his stepmother, Queen Joan of Navarre, to deprive her of her substantial income when he needed it for his French wars, and against Duke Humphrey of Gloucester's wife, Eleanor Cobham. On this occasion it is possible that Warwick was hoping that the charge would discredit the king's marriage, if the duchess had used sorcery to procure it, and thus have the effect of bastardizing his children. Even if the Duchess Jacquetta's life was not at risk, the accusation would probably have succeeded in frightening her and the queen considerably. Jacquetta successfully enlisted the support of the mayor and aldermen of London, which suggests that the story implicating her over Sir Thomas Cook's tapestry was untrue, since the city authorities would otherwise have been unlikely to help her. Eventually she won her fight and was cleared of all the charges.

No single man dominated the second half of Edward's reign in the way that Warwick had done in the period 1461–70, but nobody could doubt the influence of the second earl Rivers, nor his important contribution to the culture of Edward's court. Anthony Woodville, the queen's eldest brother, was a contradictory figure. He was intelligent, deeply involved in humanist scholarship and travelled widely in southern Europe. He was an early patron of Caxton; his own translation of the popular *Dictes and Sayings of the Philosophers* became the first book to be printed in England in 1477. His piety, which took a contemplative turn, seems to have been genuine and he made pilgrimages to Compostella and to Rome, where he was robbed and had to be financially bailed out by the queen. Beneath his fashionable dress, the earl was known to wear a hair shirt; not a feature that would have endeared him to the sybaritic king. At the same time he was one of the best English jousters of his day. In 1467, after issuing a challenge to the European champion jouster, the Bastard of Burgundy, he fought him in a splendid tournament at Smithfield. It was a major public display of Woodville prowess and their standing among the European nobility, so it is hardly surprising that the attire of Woodville and his mounts was magnificent. Questions, however, were raised about his actual behaviour on the tourney field, which was held to be unchivalrous. When he accompanied Edward's sister Margaret on her marriage trip to Burgundy, the tournaments at Bruges carefully avoiding pitting him directly against the Bastard again.

Despite Warwick's jaundiced view, the Woodvilles did not push Edward towards the Burgundian match, they merely supported what they knew to be his wish. Anthony Woodville was with the king when he went into exile and on their return was wounded at Barnet. The wounds cannot have been severe because Edward left him in charge of London while he himself went on to fight at Tewkesbury, and Woodville defeated a Lancastrian attempt to take the city. Soon afterwards he asked for permission to go and fight the Saracens in Portugal. Somewhat irritated because there was so much to do at home, Edward gave him permission to go, but not before he had both appointed him to the council of his baby nephew, the Prince of Wales, and replaced him as captain of Calais by Lord Hastings. Whether he went or not is another matter, because in the spring of 1472, he and his brother Edward took a force of 6,000 archers to Brittany to support its duke against the French. The expedition was not a success, the English force suffering much from sickness. Later, in 1476 the Milanese ambassador to Burgundy, observing his behaviour in the camp of Duke Charles, accused him of behaving in a cowardly manner.[6] Nor was Woodville above the scheming that went on around the king and, after having lost Calais to Hastings, attempted to bring the latter into disfavour and was briefly successful.

Before his sister became queen, and probably either just before or just after Edward became king, Anthony Woodville married Elizabeth, widowed daughter and heiress of Lord Scales, in whose right he held that title from 1460. The Scales estates were largely in East Anglia, where he was able to build up a degree of influence, but the only significant grant he received from the king was the Isle of Wight, with the castle and lordship of Carisbrooke, in 1466. In the same year he persuaded his wife to convey her inheritance to his trustees, thus ensuring that, should she die childless, the lands would remain in his possession rather than reverting to her heirs, one of whom was the earl of Oxford, married to Warwick's sister. This was a perversion of the natural laws of inheritance and came into effect in November 1473 when Lady Scales did indeed die without children. The Scales estates were not particularly extensive and even after the death of his father in 1469, Anthony cannot have been particularly wealthy.

Late in 1473, the new earl Rivers was made governor of the Prince of Wales and was thus put in charge of his education and of his household at Ludlow. This appointment was a mark of the respect that Edward had for his brother-in-law's learning and military skills, and while the queen may well have suggested her brother for the post, the appointment would never have been made if Edward had not desired it. As governor, Rivers had considerable power in Wales and the Marches and was not afraid to use it. In terms of the ruthless politics of the Marches, he was well placed to teach his young charge the realities of political rule. In 1477 Edward proposed Rivers, now an eligible widower, as a husband for the young heiress, Mary of Burgundy, and although this was probably more a piece of diplomatic manœuvring than a serious suggestion, two years later considerable progress had been made in negotiations for a match between Rivers and Margaret, sister of James III of Scotland. Both sets of negotiations indicate that Edward saw his wife's brother as a member of the extended royal family and not just a useful royal servant. The Scottish match, too, came to nothing and in 1480 Rivers married Mary, daughter of Sir Henry Fitzlewis, and granddaughter of Edmund Beaufort, duke of Somerset. Anthony was the only Woodville for whom Mancini had a good word, describing him as 'always considered a kind, serious and just man, though one tested by every vicissitude of life. Whatever his prosperity he had injured nobody, though benefiting many'.[7] This last judgement is inaccurate, since Rivers could be as ruthless in his business dealings, even against churchmen and women, as any of his contemporaries, but may reflect the general esteem in which he was held.

In the second half of Edward's reign, the queen and Anthony, Earl Rivers were the only Woodvilles who could be described as influential at court. Their brother, Lionel, who finally became a bishop in 1482 when he was elevated to the see of Salisbury, played no part in politics, and the two youngest Woodvilles, Sir Edward and Sir Richard, were, for the most part, lightweight figures who seem to have been the king's companions in his more dissolute activities. This would not have endeared them to those who preferred the king to behave with more dignity. There is some evidence that towards the end of the reign, Edward Woodville was developing into a useful soldier.

There was, however, one more member of the Woodville connection who cannot be overlooked. This was the queen's elder son by her first marriage, Thomas Grey. Although he was the heir to the Ferrers barony through his paternal grandmother, Queen Elizabeth wanted much more for him. The high price she paid in 1466 for the marriage with Anne Holand, heiress of the king's sister Anne, duchess of Exeter and her husband, and already betrothed to George Nevill, Warwick's nephew, was one of the first signs that the Woodvilles were willing to be ruthless in pursuit of their family interests. Anne Holand died in 1473 before her father, and without issue, which meant that Grey lost the chance of the Holand inheritance. With the king's help, the queen then pursuaded Lord Hastings in 1474 to agree to a match with his step-daughter, Cecily, heiress of the Bonville and Harrington families, who had extensive estates in the southwest. Since Cecily was only thirteen, it was agreed that if Thomas, who was twenty-three, died before the marriage was consummated, then she was to marry his younger brother Richard instead.

Thomas Grey had been created earl of Huntingdon in 1471, when he was twenty, but he resigned that title when he was made marquess of Dorset in 1475. Marquessates, a continental rank which in England fell between dukedoms and earldoms, were rare, but useful; John Nevill had been compensated with one for the loss of the Percy earldom of Northumberland, and that of Dorset had already been held by John Beaufort, prior to his elevation to the dukedom of Somerset. Edward had a clear policy of reserving the creation of dukedoms for members of the royal family, and Thomas was not of the blood royal. Whether the honour of a marquessate was an indication of Edward's affection for his step-son or the queen's ambition for him is impossible to say. As an adult, Grey fulfilled his role as a peer, sitting on commisssions, raising troops for various military campaigns, and emerging as a serious political contender in the later part of Edward's reign. Unfortunately, part of his politics consisted of a feud with Lord Hastings. Mancini says that it was 'because of the mistresses whom they had abducted or attempted to entice from each other. The suborned informers of each had threatened a capital charge against the other.'[8] This was how it may have manifested itself, but the feud almost certainly dated from the early 1460s, when Hastings had driven a very hard bargain when agreeing to help the widowed Lady Grey by securing Grey's future marriage with a daughter of his own on very good terms. The queen's marriage voided the agreement and she was too shrewd not to get on amicably with her husband's closest friend, but Thomas was perhaps not so forgiving. This did not stop the two families doing business together, but it did not help the atmosphere at court and was surely upsetting for Edward, who, Mancini says, loved both men.

Never before in the middle ages had the relatives of the king and queen among the English nobility, not themselves of royal blood, played such key roles in the political fate of the country as they did under the Yorkists. While it is an exaggeration to say that the earl of Warwick and his brothers 'ruled' England in the early 1460s, for this would discount the strong personality of Edward himself, Warwick's influence was immense, and certainly initially was used for the good of Yorkist rule. Later his frustration with the king when the latter's decisions ran counter to his own views, and his ambition to find a more malleable figurehead, led him into unforgivable treason. Montagu's role in pacifying the north and controlling Lancastrian activity was crucial and it is hard not to sympathize with him in 1470–1, when he was forced to choose between his kingly cousin and his brother. Nevertheless, the Nevills played a crucial part both in placing Edward IV on the throne and in keeping him there in the first few tenuous years of Yorkist rule. The Woodvilles, in contrast, had little in the way of a political role, and their influence, even through the queen, was never paramount. They supported the king's policies, never initiated them, and it says much for Warwick's propaganda skills that they were as unpopular as they were. Both Earl Rivers and his eldest son were intelligent, hard-working and efficient royal servants, whose abilities the king was able to put to good use. More than anything else, it was the way in which the laws of inheritance were manipulated for the benefit of the queen's youngest son and her eldest brother that earned them the disfavour of the landowning classes, and on Edward's death, it was fear of their influence over the new young king which initially at least favoured the promotion of Richard of Gloucester to the role of Protector. If Edward IV was unfortunate in the treasonable actions of members of his mother's family, he was loyally served by his wife's father and brothers, who died for that loyalty. This double-sided picture of faithlessness and loyalty was replicated in the behaviour of the king's brothers.

7

The King's Brothers

'These three brothers, the king and the dukes, possessed such outstanding talent that if they had been able to avoid dissension that triple cord could have been broken only with the utmost difficulty.'[1] This was the view of the Crowland Chronicler, a councillor who knew all three men. It was in the inability of the three brothers to avoid such dissension that the seeds of destruction of the Yorkist dynasty were sown. The second of the brothers was George, duke of Clarence, born in Dublin in 1449. The youngest of the three was Richard, duke of Gloucester, born at Fotheringhay in 1452 and better known to history as Richard III.

The sons of Edward III and Henry IV were able to work together despite family disagreements and present a more or less united front to the world. Those of the duke of York could not. Richard of York and his duchess, Cecily, had seven children who grew up, four sons and three daughters. The eldest two boys, Edward and Edmund, were both born in Rouen barely a year apart in age and were treated almost identically while they were young. Edward was given the name of his great uncle, from whom the dukedom of York had descended; his short-lived elder brother, named Henry for the king, had probably died before Edward himself was born. Edmund and his elder sister, Anne, were named for the Mortimer side of the family because Richard of York was proud of his Mortimer lineage, the senior line of descent from Edward III. It was not Edmund, however, on whom his father persuaded the king to bestow the Mortimer title of earl of March, but his heir, Edward. Edmund was permitted to style himself earl of Rutland, a title first borne by Edward, duke of York, during his father's lifetime. Although there is no formal record of either creation, the boys were known by their titles from about 1454.

Once the two boys had left their infancy and outgrown the care of their Norman nurse, Anne of Caux, they were set up in their own household at Ludlow. This was the administrative centre of the great Mortimer holdings in Wales and the Marches, and it was here they were educated and trained in the appropriate manner for the landed inheritance which was to be their future. York had once seen his baby second son as a possible inheritor of his lands in France, but this grand design for Edmund faded as York's position as governor of Normandy came to an end and the English possessions in France became ever more threatened.

The two boys were first noted on the political scene in the early 1450s; Edmund, for instance, is recorded as attending a meeting in the great council chamber in London in February 1454 when he was only ten years old.

In November 1459, after his defeat at Ludford, York was attainted and both his elder sons were attainted with him, an indication that they were now regarded as adult and responsible for their own actions. They were sixteen and seventeen. York escaped to Ireland, taking Edmund with him. Whether the decision that Edward should go to France with the Nevills was his own independent gesture, or more likely a prudent division of the York family in the face of disaster, will probably remain unknown. From this date, Edmund seems to have been continually in his father's company. A year later, after the triumphant return of the Yorkists, the formal Act of Accord which recognized York's right to succeed Henry VI granted him 10,000 marks a year, of which 3500 were to go to Edward and 1500 to Edmund.

When York and Salisbury set out a few weeks later to face the growing tide of Lancastrian opposition in the north, Edmund of Rutland went with them, but Edward was given his first independent command and went west to raise troops from the York estates in the Marches and counter any military action by the Welsh Lancastrians under Jasper Tudor, earl of Pembroke. This decision almost certainly preserved his life. At the battle of Wakefield, where York was killed, Edmund is believed to have been flying from the field across the bridge at the town when he was captured by Lord Clifford and immediately killed, and it is hard to believe that Edward would have avoided the same fate. Edmund's head, severed from his body, was impaled on the gates of York, with that of his father and uncle, Salisbury. Salisbury, too, had survived the battle, only to be executed shortly afterwards. Years later, when York's body was transferred from Pontefract, where he and Edmund were buried, Edmund's body was disinterred too and brought south to Fotheringhay for reburial in the York family mausoleum.

From the start of Edward IV's reign, attention was transferred to his two much younger brothers, George and Richard. George, six years younger than Edmund, had not joined his elder brothers at Ludlow by the time that their formal education came to end ten years later, but he was there with his mother and brother Richard at the time of the rout of Ludford, close by. The town of Ludlow and its castle were sacked and the duchess and her boys taken prisoner. The next that is heard of George and Richard, they, together with their sister Margaret, were with their mother in London in the autumn of 1460. They seem to have been staying in Sir John Fastolf's mansion opposite the Tower of London, which Duchess Cecily had rented. Almost immediately Cecily received news of the duke's landing she set off north to join him. The children stayed in London, 'and the Lord of March cometh every day to see them'.[2] They were still in London at the time their father and brother were killed at Wakefield, after which Cecily took the no doubt difficult decision to send them overseas to safety. The obvious choice of destination was Burgundy, and they were despatched to the care of the bishop of Utrecht, an illegitimate son of Duke Philip. A few weeks later, after their brother had become king and had defeated his opponents at Towton, the two young boys assumed a much greater importance. Duke Philip sent for them and gave them a princely welcome to Bruges. He was keen to display his friendship to the new regime, which he saw as a potentially stronger ally against France than the Lancastrians.

The suggestion seems to have been made at this period that George should marry his granddaughter Mary, so far the only child of his heir Charles, count of Charolais. Duke Philip may not have been serious about it, seeing it purely as a possible negotiating ploy, but the idea seems to have taken root in the mind of George. The boys, now young princes, were back in England in time to attend Edward's coronation in June 1461. George had become heir presumptive to the throne, a position he retained for nearly ten years until the birth of Edward's son in November 1470. Edward appointed his brother as steward of England for the coronation, but because of his youth Lord Wenlock was assigned to perform the duties of the office. Two days later George was created duke of Clarence. The title, borne by Edward III's second son, Lionel, emphasized the superiority of the Yorkist descent, but it had also been borne by Henry IV's second son, Thomas.

It was no longer appropriate for George and Richard to live with their mother, and Edward set up a permanent residence for the two boys and their unmarried sister, Margaret, at Greenwich. The palace, which had been a favourite residence of Queen Margaret, was convenient for London but much healthier than the city. It was here that the boys continued their education in company with three or four other well-born boys. As they grew older, so did the size and grandeur of their household. George was made Lieutenant of Ireland, the post held by his father. Although his office was performed by his deputy, the earl of Desmond, he had estates in England to administer and other formal business to attend to under the direction of his council and the ultimate authority of the king. His chancellor, John Tapton, dean of St Asaph, was the head of his household and probably supervised his education as well. In 1463, not yet fourteen, he was the guest of honour at the reburial of his uncle, the earl of Salisbury, who had died with his father at Wakefield, and a few weeks later he attended his first Garter ceremony. He acted as steward of England at the queen's coronation in 1465, this time in person. We do not know Clarence's reaction to his brother's marriage. It inevitably reduced the chances of George remaining heir presumptive for much longer. Edward undoubtedly sweetened the pill by taking the opportunity greatly to increase George's endowments, but it is unlikely that George learned to love the queen and her relatives as he, like Warwick, saw his influence with the king which he regarded as rightfully his as heir presumptive, slipping away to the Woodvilles.

Although Clarence seems to have been under the nominal tutelage of Humphrey Stafford, Lord Southwick, he was not in his charge. His younger brother, Richard, who was not heir to the throne, became a member of Warwick's household in 1465, as any other noble boy might have done. George was treated very differently and on 10 July 1466 did homage for his lands and ceased to be treated as a minor. He was still only sixteen and this indicates that not only did Edward need him politically, the king was confident that his brother would behave as a responsible adult, because otherwise his coming of age could have been postponed for another couple of years. As a man, Clarence was described as 'a mighty prince, seemly of person and right witty and well-avisaged'.[3] His portrait as constable of Queenborough Castle (sixteenth century in date, but possibly based on a lost original), shows him in full armour, but his face certainly deserves the epithet 'well-avisaged'; like his brothers, he was dark-haired, but his face, slim and large-eyed, looks more like Richard than Edward. There seems little doubt that the deference shown to him as heir presumptive went to George's head, and a degree of arrogance began to show in his behaviour.

This arrogance was increased in 1466 when Edward resurrected the proposal that Clarence should marry Mary of Burgundy during the negotiations for a match between their sister Margaret and Mary's father, Charles. Philip of Burgundy was not willing to pay such a high price even to win an English alliance against France, and the suggestion was quietly dropped. Louis of France, however, in his negotiations with Warwick aimed at thwarting an Anglo-Burgundian alliance, proposed a division of Burgundy whereby Clarence would get the northern provinces of Holland, Zeeland and Brabant while Louis took the rest. Needless to say, Clarence was in favour of this, but Edward was not to be seduced from his pro-Burgundian policy. There were other signs that relations between the king and his heir were becoming strained. Edward's policy of reconciliation included the re-establishment of the Percy family as earls of Northumberland, and Warwick, his brother, John, and Clarence had been the main beneficiaries of the dispersal of Percy estates, Clarence receiving those in Yorkshire and Lincolnshire. Clarence was unwilling to surrender the estates, not least because he knew the king had little in the way of landed compensation to give him. Like Warwick, he had also watched the rise to influence at court of a number of men like Hastings and Herbert, the latter being created earl of Pembroke, as the Nevill influence declined.

The marriage of George of Clarence was of considerable importance to the Yorkist dynasty as in the late 1460s he was still heir presumptive. The fact that Edward was prepared to bid on his behalf for Mary of Burgundy in 1466 shows that the king wished to use his brother's marriage as a diplomatic tool until such time as he had sons of his own of an age to be considered for marriage. Once the Burgundian initiative failed, however, Edward made no further effort on his brother's behalf, since there were no other suitable openings. The alternative was marriage to an English heiress. The only ones rich enough were Warwick's daughters, but a proposal that George should marry the elder, Isabel, was flatly rejected by the king. On the face of it, this seems unreasonable; it certainly seemed so to Warwick and Clarence. If Clarence married abroad but remained heir, however, this might raise considerable problems in the future. If, as seemed likely, he was replaced by a son of the king, then marriage to an English heiress was a well-established means of providing an appanage for a younger royal son. Edward may simply have wished to keep his options open for a little longer, in the hope of a son, but Warwick and Clarence simply ignored the king's wishes. They began negotiations at the Vatican for the dispensation required for the marriage of cousins, aided by the connections of Archbishop Nevill, and it was finally granted in March 1469. Obviously the prime mover in this was Warwick, since Clarence was only in his late teens and dominated by his charismatic cousin, but this does not absolve the latter from the responsibility of putting his own wishes before the needs of the crown. Marriage to a rich heiress had many attractions, not least because the lands the king had been able to grant him were insufficient to enable him to cut the figure he felt his position deserved, and one from which his rivals at court seemed to be shutting him out. Isabel Nevill was the same age (she was born in 1451) and the fact that she was known to him and not some foreign princess probably added to her appeal.

Warwick arranged for the marriage itself to take place at Calais, where he was in total control, but it was not a secret affair. The licence was obtained from Archbishop Bourchier, though Archbishop Nevill performed the ceremony; the duchess of York paid a visit to the wedding party at Sandwich and there were several knights of the Garter in attendance. It seems that there was a general degree of sympathy for Warwick and Clarence and by most observers it was deemed a suitable match. If their disobedience had stopped there Edward would almost certainly have forgiven them and there would have been no serious breach. Warwick, however, had much more ambitious plans. The question is, how much did Clarence know of them in advance and how far was he something more than a tool?

For the previous century and a half, no English king's brother had been anything other than a loyal supporter, and it is hardly surprising that Edward was slow to grasp the degree of treachery involved. While they were in Calais, Warwick's plans for rebellion took shape and there is no doubt that the grievances against the king and his trusted supporters such as Rivers and Herbert were felt across a spectrum of the peers. The claim of Warwick and Clarence that the king was excluding those of his blood from his councils had a strong echo of York's complaints a decade or so earlier. From the time of the marriage until Edward fell into his hands, everything went Warwick's way. He would surely have known, however, that Edward was not going to surrender tamely to being controlled, and the rumours, first current on the Continent and then at home, that the king was a bastard, were a clear threat of deposition if he did not comply with Warwick's wishes. For Clarence, the prospect of supplanting his brother had to be balanced against the disgrace of branding his mother a whore. The first rumours appeared on the Continent after Clarence's marriage and there is no reason to believe they were current when he had last seen his mother at Sandwich.

During Warwick's period in power, Clarence was prominent in the council, taking a particular interest in attempting to end a feud between the duke of Norfolk and John Paston, over the ownership of Caister Castle, which threatened the peace of East Anglia. When Edward gained the upper hand, he had to pay the price. With a number of senior members of the court party recently dead, and with Warwick and Clarence still in control of large numbers of men, the king saw the need for a degree of superficial amity, but he never forgave Warwick for his treachery and for the deaths of his wife's father and brother. He also found it very difficult accept his brother back into the family fold and demonstrated this by his actions. Edward made his younger brother, Richard of Gloucester, now seventeen, heir to Herbert's control of Wales, at least until the latter's son came of age. Then, in compensating John Nevill for the loss of the earldom of Northumberland by, among other things, elevating his son to the dukedom of Bedford and betrothing him to his eldest daughter, he indicated that, with the consent of his council, in the event of his failure to have a son, the crown might pass to his eldest daughter and not to the collateral male line. The Yorkist title had come through a woman and it could continue through the female line. This was a sop to Nevill pride, a warning to Clarence that he would not automatically become king if Edward failed to have a male heir, and possibly an attempt by the king to sow dissension among his opponents. As far as Warwick was concerned, far from controlling policy, he found his aim at being the controlling power in South Wales thwarted, his hegemony in the north threatened by the reinstatement of the Percies, and his pocket affected by the loss of the Percy estates he had held. The slight possibility of his nephew and male heir becoming king in the right of his wife was hardly adequate compensation. Clarence lost his Percy estates worth about £450 p.a. and got nothing in return. In addition, his valuable grant of honour of Richmond looked badly threatened by moves to restore the young Henry Tudor to his father's earldom of Richmond as part of the king's move to bolster suppport from the powerful Bourchier and Stafford connection. Edward was punishing his brother's treachery harshly and few would have blamed him, but he pushed Clarence into a position where he had nothing to lose from further rebellion and the possibility of a crown if he was successful. In 1470 it may have been Clarence and not Warwick who took the lead.

The Lincolnshire rebellion in early 1470 had its origins in a local feud, but there was very little doubt that Clarence was deeply implicated from the start. A similar rising planned for the north by Warwick failed to get under way only because Edward crushed the Lincolnshire rebels decisively. This left Warwick and Clarence with little option but to flee, taking their wives and Warwick's younger daughter with them. When they were refused entry to Calais, the duchess of Clarence was forced to give birth at sea; the baby, a boy, was still-born. Once in France, Warwick regained the initiative from his son-in-law; after all, it was on the Continent that he had felt most valued and in control. After he and Margaret of Anjou had managed to overcome their mutual antipathy in the face of political necessity, Warwick did very well out of the pact and was more than happy to agree with Louis's plans for an offensive against Burgundy. With his daughter Anne to marry the Lancastrian heir to the throne, his security and political influence were assured. He seems to have had no qualms in abandoning Clarence's claim to the throne, while the latter was forced to recognize that there was no support in England for him to replace Edward as a Yorkist king. The settlement negotiated in France accorded him the duchy of York and a place in the succession if the Lancastrian line failed, together with compensation in return for the loss of those lands which he held from Lancastrian forfeitures. He had thus been offered a place close to the throne and seat of power, but it was unclear whether it was enough, since his position would be little different to that he had held as the king's brother.

Once the Re-adeption of Henry VI was under way, the new government found it impossible to compensate Clarence for the lands he had to give up to the queen and Prince Edward, while a large part of the duchy of York was held by his mother in jointure. Although he managed to hang on to the honour of Richmond, he was effectively worse off financially than before. Two of his men became king's secretary and treasurer of the royal household, but Clarence could hardly expect not to be deeply unpopular with both long-standing Lancastrians and the Yorkists he had betrayed. In family terms – not something for which he had shown many scruples in the past – he had two brothers in exile in Burgundy, where his sister was duchess, which was now about to be threatened by an alliance of England with France. Clarence may have given up on his family out of greed and selfishness, but his family had not given up on him. While his mother and sisters Anne and Elizabeth worked on him in England, Duchess Margaret, with whom he had grown up and the sibling to whom he seems to have been closest, put him in touch with Edward.

What Edward promised Clarence at this point is not known, but by the time the king landed on his return from exile 'a perfect accord was appointed, accorded, concluded and assured betwixt them'.[4] The balance of motives, family loyalty, dislike of the Lancastrians and political opportunism which motivated Clarence at this point are impossible to determine, but his actions are clear. As a leading member of the Lancastrian government, Clarence was commissioned to raise troops in the west country, which he duly did, leading nearly 4000 men north apparently to join Warwick at Coventry to confront Edward's growing army of supporters as he moved south. He defected to Edward instead, and his meeting with Edward and Richard of Gloucester marked a formal reconciliation. It is a tribute to Clarence's nerve that he managed to carry out his plan without being suspected.

After his sweeping victories of Barnet and Tewkesbury had destroyed both the Nevills and the Lancastrian line, Edward was safe on his throne. He was unlikely ever to forget Clarence's treacherous behaviour. Yet he seems to have been determined to forgive it, recognizing that his brother's change of heart was a considerable factor in his own victory. This time his treatment of Clarence appears magnanimous in the extreme, but it was almost certainly part of the bargain Clarence drove in returning to the fold. Edward had even allowed his brother to try and negotiate a settlement between himself and Warwick before Barnet, though the terms offered, probably deliberately, were not ones that the latter could bring himself to accept. Once Edward was firmly back in command, Clarence was permitted to keep both his lands and offices (the latter were even augmented by the great chamberlainship which Edward had first given to Gloucester but transferred at Clarence's request) and be seen to protect most of his own and Warwick's supporters from attainder. Although the birth of Prince Edward meant that he was no longer heir presumptive, he was now the wealthiest of the magnates and the king seems to have refused him nothing. The lack of new attainders in 1471 (most of the Lancastrians had already forfeited their lands, which had been regranted to Yorkists) meant that the king had little in the way of lands beyond those forfeited by Warwick and Montagu to redistribute to his loyal supporters, so his generosity to his brother understandably led to a degree of resentment. It also placed Edward in difficulties when he wanted to endow the two youngest males of the House of York, the new Prince of Wales and his own younger brother, Gloucester.

Richard of Gloucester was only nine when Edward became king, but even allowing for the fact that Clarence was his brother's heir, the endowment that Richard received was far less generous. He was created duke of Gloucester in November 1461 and Edward had initially given him the wealthy honour of Richmond, forfeited by the Percies, only for the thirteen-year-old Clarence to demand it for himself in a fit of jealousy. The king gave in, not for the last time, to his brother's greed, and transferred Richmond to him. While Clarence got the endowment of a great noble, Gloucester got the equivalent of a barony.

In 1469, then, if one of the brothers had a grievance it was Richard and not George, since he was now sixteen and eligible to be declared of age and begin to administer his own affairs. He had spent some of the intervening years living in the household of the earl of Warwick at Middleham castle, Yorkshire, so it is surprising that Richard seems never to have wavered in his loyalty and devotion to Edward. That devotion was rewarded in the brief period during 1469 when Edward temporarily gained the upper hand. Gloucester was made constable of England, an office formerly held by Earl Rivers and granted some duchy of Lancaster lands, but chiefly he was advanced to become the chief representative of royal power in Wales, a position Warwick had long coveted himself and never wholly achieved. When Edward went into exile, Richard went with him, and on his return, young as he was, was made a senior commander at both the battles of Barnet and Tewkesbury, and as constable, condemned the surviving Lancastrian leaders to death after Tewkesbury. There is not a shred of evidence that he was involved in the death of the Lancastrian Prince of Wales as he fled from the battlefield, and while he may have been at the Tower of London when Henry VI met his end, if that were so, then he was simply acting on the orders of the king. The complete contrast between the behaviour of Edward's younger brothers in the ten years of his first reign can only partly be explained by their ages. The inescapable conclusion is that Clarence allowed his greed and arrogance to overwhelm his undoubted intelligence. That was not a charge that could be levelled at Gloucester. If Clarence was not to be made to suffer materially for his treachery, how much greater then could Gloucester expect his reward to be?

The trouble was that Edward did not have much in the way of forfeited estates to bestow on his loyal brother. While Warwick had been the richest man in England, much of his wealth was derived from his wife's Beauchamp-Despenser inheritance, which would descend to her daughters. The king did what he could, granting Gloucester Warwick's offices as chief steward of the duchy of Lancaster and warden of the west march among other, lesser, ones together with all the lands which had descended to Warwick from his father. The king was effectively making Gloucester Warwick's heir in the north, though in doing so he replaced him in the Welsh offices. Finally he granted him the substantial estates of the Lancastrian earl of Oxford, who had survived the debacle of the end of the Re-adeption and was living in exile in France. In the course of the 1470s, more grants and offices followed and Richard had little to complain of now in the generosity of the king. He did, however, have cause for bitter resentment over the behaviour of Clarence. Warwick's plans for his daughters had been that they should marry the king's brothers; the first part of his plan had come to fruition when Isabel married Clarence, but Anne had been sacrificed to her father's ambition in France and married off to the Lancastrian Prince Edward. The fact that she was now a widow meant that she was free to marry Richard, if that is what he wanted – and it was. It was most definitely not what Clarence wanted. He would have preferred his wife's sister in a convent, so that the whole inheritance would descend to him and his wife. Anne seems to have been in Clarence's custody and the Crowland Chronicler, usually a well-informed and reliable source, says that 'he had the girl hidden away so that his brother would not know where she was, since he feared a division of the inheritance. The duke of Gloucester, however, was much the more astute, that having discovered the girl dressed as a kitchen maid in London had her moved to sanctuary in St Martin's'.[5] The one prospective husband strong enough to champion Anne's rights against Clarence's disgraceful behaviour was his own brother, Richard. The brothers' quarrel over the Warwick inheritance was to have unforeseen consequences for their house and reflected badly not only on them but on the king as well.

Since Warwick's death his estates had been seized by the crown, and the king had then regranted them, giving his younger brother all those estates that were the dead man's Nevill inheritance, while Clarence received all those to which his widow had a hereditary claim. In this one person had been ignored – the widowed countess of Warwick. It was accepted practice in the fifteenth century for the wife of a traitor still alive to be put in the custody of a lady whose loyalty was unquestioned, to prevent her aiding her husband. All the traitor's lands were confiscated by the crown, which usually then granted the wife an annuity to support herself. This is what happened to the duchess of York after Richard of York fled into exile, and to Warwick's sister Margaret, the unfortunate countess of Oxford, though the latter had to wait a long time for her annuity. If the traitor was dead, however, the procedure was very different. The widow was legally protected and had the right to retain any lands she held in jointure, though she forfeited additional dower rights, and in the course of the fifteenth century it had become customary for her to be allowed to keep any lands which were her own inheritance. In this way, a certain amount of the family inheritance was protected for the heir, allowing for the family's eventual rehabilitation.

After Warwick's death, therefore, the only lands which the Crown might have been expected to confiscate were the earl's Nevill possessions, which should, by inheritance, have gone to his male heir, George, duke of Bedford, less anything held by the countess in jointure; the countess's own lands should have been hers to hold for her lifetime. Clarence did not regard this as acceptable. Royal grants were the least secure form of land holding, because they could be reversed in an act of resumption. What Clarence wanted was land by inheritance, and he persuaded the king to allow him to receive his wife's inheritance in advance of her mother's death. If Gloucester married Anne Nevill, then he would be forced to share that inheritance. Gloucester had to face not only his brother's implacable hostility to the match but other difficulties, such as the matter of a papal dispensation, which had been hard enough to obtain for such close cousins as Clarence and Isabel, whose marriage had then increased the degrees of relationship which had to be set aside for their siblings to marry. The dispensation was granted in April 1472, but whether he and Anne were married that spring, or later, is not known.

Clarence and Gloucester argued their cases in the dispute over the division of Warwick's lands before the royal council in the autumn of 1471 and did it so well that the Crowland Chronicler was moved to the judgement quoted at the beginning of this chapter. In the end, Edward forced a settlement on his brothers. In return for giving up some of the Warwick inheritance, Clarence was given full security in the rest, together with all the Courtenay lands he held. He was granted the titles of Warwick and Salisbury, some Nevill manors in Essex and the earl's town house. Gloucester even gave up to him the office of royal chamberlain. The widowed countess of Warwick, who tried desperately to protect her rights, was ignored in the act of settlement as if she 'were now naturally dead' and despatched up north to Middleham, her former home and now Gloucester's chief seat. The rights of the young duke of Bedford, male heir to both his father and uncle, were also set aside, so that the two royal dukes could be regarded as heirs by law of Warwick's Nevill inheritance.

Edward's imposition of a settlement stifled but did not eliminate the bad feeling between his brothers. Clarence felt aggrieved at the loss of Warwick lands which he had been required to hand over; Gloucester had demonstrated a remarkable degree of forbearance, but he, too, was a willing partner in the treatment of his wife's mother. He had also ensured that in the acts of settlement a clause was inserted guaranteeing his title to Anne's estates if the marriage was eventually declared invalid because of a lack of dispensation, an eventuality which resolved itself in the spring of 1472. In November 1473 an act of Resumption, from which Gloucester was exempted, deprived Clarence of a number of valuable estates, including the honour of Tutbury, which he held by royal grant. It was a warning shot across Clarence's bows that the king would not forever give way to his demands.

It was not, however, to be his greed that caused Clarence's eventual downfall, but Edward's suspicion that his brother was still willing to intrigue with remnants of the Lancastrian party. In April 1472 Archbishop George Nevill was arrested and imprisoned at Hammes, near Calais. His household was broken up and his large personal fortune seized. The king gave no reason for his action, but it was almost certainly because he believed him to be communicating with his brother-in-law, Oxford, who was raiding the Calais Marches with the support of Louis XI. Despite rumours, there is no evidence to indicate that Clarence was involved, but any plotting to remove Edward would almost certainly have focused on him as a replacement. A year later, Oxford attempted a landing in his home territory of East Anglia with French backing. When that proved unsuccessful, he took his ships round to Cornwall, where he seized St Michael's Mount, holding it for some time before lack of supplies and the haemorrhaging of his men led to his surrender. He had received no English support from anyone outside his own small circle, but evidence suggests that Clarence, if not involved, at least had some connection with Oxford at this period. Once taken prisoner, the earl was sent to Hammes, where he remained for ten years before making his escape. When Oxford arrived there, Archbishop Nevill was released, but died a few months later, a broken man.

Over the next few years, while the power of Gloucester in the north and of the Woodvilles in the Marches grew, Clarence was not given a similar area of authority. Indeed, that which he had held, Ireland, was withdrawn from his control. Although he retained the title of lieutenant, the day-to-day governance was delegated directly by the king to Sir Gilbert Debenham, who had been appointed chancellor. Clearly Edward did not trust Clarence out of his sight or with military powers, so the duke was left with little to do and with an increasing grudge against the king. This was not assuaged by a few small grants, nor by the creation of his infant son as earl of Warwick at his baptism in February 1475 by order of the king, who stood godfather. In December 1476 Duchess Isabel died, and was buried with great solemnity in Tewkesbury Abbey. Her death was followed almost immediately by that of Charles of Burgundy, leaving his unmarried daughter, Mary, for whom Clarence had more than once been proposed as a husband, as his sole heiress. The widowed Margaret of York, duchess of Burgundy, immediately resurrected the suggestion of a match with her brother George. King Edward would have none of it. Although it would have removed Clarence from England, it would almost certainly have meant a drain on English military and financial resources, and more importantly, it would have jeopardized the alliance with France and his daughter Elizabeth's prospective marriage to the dauphin. Nor did a proposal from Scotland that Clarence should marry James III's sister, Margaret, find favour. Whatever the excuses, it was clear that the king had no intention of allowing his brother to make an advantageous foreign match and provide himself with a potential launching pad for a further attempt on the throne.

In May 1477 three men were indicted of attempting to encompass the king's death by necromancy. All were known personally to Edward, but the most important was a retainer of Clarence's called Sir Thomas Burdet. After what seems to have been a justly conducted, if political, trial they were found guilty and executed, but died protesting their innocence. At no time during the proceedings did Clarence's name arise and despite suspicions, he would not have been implicated in the affair if it were not for the fact that he confronted a meeting of the council with a declaration of the men's innocence and then walked out. Just what he hoped to achieve is unclear, but his actions drew attention to another occasion when he seemed to have shown contempt for the due processes of law.

When the Duchess Isabel died just before Christmas 1476 it was almost certainly as a belated result of the birth of her second son, Richard, in the preceding October. The baby died almost immediately after his mother. In April 1477 one of Isabel's women, Ankarette Twynho, was charged with poisoning her mistress, a yeoman called John Thursby was charged with poisoning the duke's baby son, and Sir Roger Tocotes was charged with aiding and abetting them. The latter seems to have escaped, but Twynho and Thursby were tried at Warwick, condemned and immediately executed, probably in the presence of Clarence. Tocotes and Ankarette's late husband, William, had been long-term, trusted retainers of Clarence, but although the duchess died at Tewkesbury, the trial was held at Warwick, the main Clarence seat, and there is no doubt that the jury was pressured into returning guilty verdicts. The verdict was later anulled on the grounds that the 'jurors for fear gave the verdicts contrary to their conscience, in proof whereof divers of them came to the said Ankarette in remorse and asked her forgiveness'.[6]

When Clarence was summoned by the king to Westminster in June 1477, he seems to have gone unsuspectingly, which suggests that he thought he had nothing to fear. When he was arrested and sent to the Tower, it was not on a treason charge, but because his behaviour was 'in contempt for the law of the land and a great threat to judges and juries of the kingdom'.[7] To the question of why Clarence acted as he did over these two legal cases there is no satisfactory explanation. The Parliament of 1478, however, did try Clarence for treason. In keeping with the seriousness of the charge, every effort had been made to ensure it was a compliant one. Between a third and a half of the commons were either crown servants or connected to members of the court, and the Speaker was a servant of the Woodvilles. The king himself put the case for the prosecution, but while the charges were numerous and illustrate Clarence's discontent, his unease with his position and a harking back to the old claim that he was the true heir of York, many had been formally forgiven by Edward and they do not add up to anything substantive. In effect Edward was saying that, despite all his forbearance with his brother, Clarence had never learned his lesson and his behaviour was becoming a threat to the safety of the kingdom. No one else was charged with him, which indicates that the king did not believe he was actively engaged in a plot. The Crowland Chronicler recoiled from describing the event, 'so sad was the dispute between two brothers of such noble character. No one argued against the duke except the king; no one answered the king except the duke'.[8] Clarence swept aside all the charges with a disclaimer offering to uphold his case by personal combat, but this was rejected.

Although there was no proof of his guilt, parliament found against him and sentence of death was pronounced. Even then, Edward could not quite bring himself to order the sentence to be carried out and had to be chivvied into action by the Speaker several days later. He was right to hesitate, for the show trial had not produced evidence of recent treason and, however deplorable his general behaviour had been, Clarence did not merit death in 1478 and his condemnation was seen by contemporaries as dishonouring the king. The execution took place on 18 February 1478 and was carried out privately in the Tower to spare Clarence the humiliation of a public execution. This was apparently at the prayers and pleadings of their mother; the feelings of Duchess Cecily, inured to tragedy as she was, can only be imagined. The story that Clarence was drowned in a butt of malmsey, though not absolutely contemporary, may well be true.

While it is difficult not to feel that, by his previous behaviour, Clarence was largely deserving of his fate, it is also difficult not to censure Edward for condemning his brother in 1478 for sins which he had forgiven earlier. How far he allowed himself to be persuaded by the Woodvilles is open to question. The queen almost certainly saw her brother-in-law as a threat to her children, since he had been responsible, at least in part, for the rumour of her husband's bastardy, and probably for casting doubts on the validity of her own marriage. Even if the queen played no role in the affair, the wider Woodville circle were now a considerable force in the council, and in the packed parliament a number of the MPs had Woodville connections. This hardly passed unnoticed and was added to the crimes with which the queen's family were later held responsible. Although the Crowland Chronicler does not mention them, he does say that after the death of Clarence 'many people deserted King Edward'. The king must take full responsiblity for his action, but he had long been patient and forgiving with his brother and was privately distressed by what had happened, 'for (as men say) whensoever any sued for saving a man's life, he was wont to cry out in a rage, "O unfortunate brother, for whose life no man in the world would once make request".[9] He ensured his brother's body was honourably interred at Tewkesbury Abbey, in Duchess Isabel's tomb, and paid for a monument with their effigies.

What of the third brother? Edward could not have tried and condemned Clarence without the support of Gloucester, a number of whose retainers sat in the parliament. The condemnation of Clarence was in reality judicial murder and Richard acquiesced in it. Like Edward, Richard presumably grieved for his brother, but like him saw it as necessary in terms of politics. He was certainly not going to fall out with Edward over it and his rewards were tangible. Even before Clarence died, Richard's small son had been created earl of Salisbury, and he himself regained the office of chamberlain which he had earlier been forced to surrender to Clarence.

In the years since 1471 Gloucester had been consolidating his position in the north. He had become Warwick's natural successor, not just in terms of land, but in power and influence. This was with the express approval and assistance of the grateful king. He had ensured that Richard got the Nevill estates in Yorkshire and Cumberland. In addition he appointed him as warden of the west march and chief steward of the duchy of Lancaster in the north. These were all only royal grants, which is why Richard was so determined to marry Anne Nevill and to obtain at least her share of her widowed mother's inheritance. The act of parliament which broke the entail on Warwick's Nevill lands and disinherited his nephew and male heir, George Nevill, to the benefit of Gloucester and Clarence had one unusual clause: the title was to belong to Richard and his wife only as long as there were male heirs of the disgraced John Nevill, Marquess Montagu. Once Montagu's line died out the title to the Nevill lands would revert to the Nevill heirs general. George Nevill was formally degraded from his dukedom on the grounds that he lacked the estates to sustain it; it was therefore unlikely that he would be in a position to reclaim his Nevill inheritance, now firmly in Gloucester's possession. George himself, fourteen at the death of his father and uncle, was in the wardship of Archbishop Bourchier, though Richard gained custody of his person and was granted his marriage in 1480. It was obviously an unsatisfactory state of affairs which would need resolution at some point. In the meanwhile, Gloucester was allowed to exchange certain parts of his wife's inheritance, hitherto inalienable, for more convenient royal properties and to claim other disputed lands.

When Gloucester took over the Nevill estates in the north, he needed to identify strongly with his new wife's family in order to take over Warwick's northern connections. It should be remembered that Richard had spent his boyhood in Warwick's charge at Middleham and knew most of these men personally. After coming to terms with its most influential member, Sir John Conyers of Hornby, he was able to absorb Warwick's affinity. Many were undoubtedly relieved to enter his service, which offered protection from any prosecution for the treason they had committed in Warwick's train. Although Richard's dominant position was resented by others who had hoped to gain from Warwick's fall, such as Northumberland, Lord Stanley and the bishop of Durham, in the end compromises and accommodations were made. By the time of the French expedition, they had learned to accept that the king's brother would be pre-eminent. In 1475, his was the largest private contingent of the forces which went to France, and evidently he disapproved of the diplomatic end to the invasion.

Richard's interests were not exclusively northern. He held lands in a number of southern counties and in south Wales, and his former de Vere holdings in East Anglia were extensive, particularly after the earl of Oxford's widowed mother had been coerced into surrendering to him all her own considerable inheritance there. These, however, were areas where, if the opportunity arose, he was prepared to surrender land in exchange for property which consolidated his holdings in Yorkshire. Richard was not a northerner by birth or initial upbringing and it was

Edward who first gave him lands and offices there, but the long-term creation of his power base there was Richard's own doing. He gradually divested himself of his more southerly possessions and greatly enhanced his position by his marriage. This was all done with Edward's approval, since his brother's increasing power and influence in the region were at his disposal, thus extending royal authority. Conversely, one of the reasons that Richard's influence was so widespread and accepted by the other noble families in the region was their recognition of his influence with the king. In the last years of Edward's reign, Richard of Gloucester spent most of his time in the north. He was now by far the greatest landowner in the region and his responsibilities for the most part kept him there, based at his main seat of Middleham, where he and his wife Anne had grown up, and where their only child, Edward, was born.

It was during these years when Richard felt secure that he established his reputation as a benevolent lord. His expenditure was lavish, his religious benefactions numerous and his political influence unchallenged. Since everyone sought his good lordship, he was able to pacify old feuds and persuade his followers to replace their quarrels with cooperation. Where his own interests were not directly involved, his administration seems to have ensured that justice was impartial. The war with Scotland in the early 1480s added to his northern preoccupation, since he commanded the English army. During the invasion of 1482, in support of the duke of Albany, his forces reached Edinburgh, but when Albany capitulated, the English were left with no alternative but to retire, with only the capture of Berwick as a consolation. The latter was seen as an expensive white elephant from a southern perspective, but it was viewed differently in the north, where Gloucester's success in taking it further enhanced his reputation. In the subsequent parliament of 1482–83 he was granted palatine authority in any lands he could conquer in south west Scotland, and the wardenship of the English West March as a hereditary office, along with considerable land and royal rights in Cumberland. It would, however, be wrong to suggest that Gloucester cut himself off from London and court life. He spent time there and was present at a number of important occasions, not least the trial of Clarence, and it is unlikely that he did not have a very good idea of what was going on. He may not have been entirely happy with the increasing Woodville influence at court, but it had no bearing on his life in the north. There is no evidence that during Edward's lifetime he was in any sense hostile to, or estranged from, members of the queen's family, and in particular he seems to have worked amicably with her brother, Rivers.

The Nevill Family: The Patriarchs (Bibliothèque Nationale de France, MS Latin 1158, ff. 27v, 28v).

2. Edward IV. Panel portrait (Royal Collection).

3. Elizabeth Woodville. Stained glass (Canterbury Cathedral).

4. Margaret of York, Duchess of Burgundy. Panel portrait (Society of Antiquaries).

Edwardus princeps Wallie primus filius Edwardi quarti

Edwardus dei gracia Rex Anglie et Francie et dominus hibernie

The Princes in the Tower, Richard, Duke of York and Edward, Prince of Wales. Stained glass (Canterbury Cathedral).

6. The Daughters of Edward IV. Stained glass (Canterbury Cathedral).

7. Richard III. Panel portrait (Royal Collection).

ELIZABETHA · VXOR
HENRICI · VII ·

8. Elizabeth of York. Panel portrait (National Portrait Gallery).

8

The King's Sisters

Medieval historians have often been inclined to overlook the role of women, but no family consists solely of its male members. There is evidence of the affection some kings felt for their daughters but they also knew their value in terms of making foreign alliances or reconciling old enemies by linking them to the royal family. In the fourteenth and early fifteenth centuries about half of the English princesses of the period married overseas, but their sisters married into English comital families. Taken with the number of royal sons married to English heiresses, it is hardly surprising that so many English noble families carried some trace of royal blood. A marriage to a royal daughter brought with it the prospect of material gain and a position among the small group of men who surrounded the king. If Queen Elizabeth's family seemed to exercise an undue amount of political influence during Edward IV's reign, were the families of the king's sisters also influential? This might well have been the case, but in fact it was not so. It seems reasonable to spend a little time exploring why.

In the 1440s and 1450s, the question of suitable matches for their children was one that exercised Richard and Cecily of York considerably. The couple were of royal descent, very wealthy and held one of the most senior peerages in the realm, so matches for their children should not have been hard to arrange. Yet on Richard's death in 1460 only the two eldest girls were married and none of the others so much as betrothed. This was largely as a result of the political situation. In the early years of York's career, we have seen that a marriage into the French royal family was mooted, if not entirely seriously, for Edward, but after that, there is no evidence of any other plans for the heir. For Edward, York would probably have been looking in the senior ranks of the nobility for a potential bride, preferably one with royal blood somewhere in her ancestry. The only exception which might have tempted him would have been a substantial heiress from somewhat lower in the social scale – the lesser baronage. If any such heiresses appeared, they were destined for other husbands.* Nor was there any move to try and obtain an English heiress for Edmund, which might have provided him with a suitable estate. While his two eldest sons were still young, this was not a problem, but as they grew older, their father became more excluded

---

* For a possible marriage for Edward in this context, see Appendix 2.

from the seat of power and patronage, and therefore alliance to the York family became less attractive.

That situation had not yet developed in 1445 when York arranged a match for his eldest child, his daughter Anne, then aged six, with Henry Holand, son of the duke of Exeter, who was fifteen. The children were married soon afterwards. Anne's dowry, set at 4500 marks, is one of the largest known in late medieval England. York's motives were at least partly political, for he was hoping that Exeter would be an ally in his attempt to return to France, and partly dynastic. Exeter was Henry VI's closest legitimate male relative after his uncle, Humphrey, duke of Gloucester, since he was the son of Elizabeth, daughter of John of Gaunt. The size of the dowry still raises several questions. Was it because Anne was still so young that the real marriage would have to be delayed for a relatively long time, whereas Henry could marry much sooner? Was it because of the closeness of the Holands to the throne that they felt able to demand so much? Although their descent was through the female line, King Henry as yet had no heirs of his body and in the general scheme of things his uncle Humphrey, the heir presumptive, was likely to predecease him. York was always aware of his bloodline and would have been hardly likely to let a Holand succession go unchallenged, but the linking of the two great houses was an obvious move. Henry Holand's grandmother Anne, the daughter and heiress of Thomas of Woodstock, youngest son of Edward III, had married as her second husband, Edmund, earl of Stafford. Their daughter, Anne, was already the widow of Edmund Mortimer, earl of March, when she married Henry's father. In every sense the match between Henry and Anne of York was the union of two English dynasties and nothing could have been more appropriate. In fact, in both personal and political terms it was a disaster.

In July 1447, on his father's death, young Henry passed into the guardianship of his father-in-law. The death of Exeter removed an experienced soldier from the French scene and a potential ally from the duke of York in his attempts to return to France. Henry was granted livery of his father's lands in 1450, and thereupon became admiral of England, Ireland and Acquitaine and constable of the Tower of London. During Cade's rebellion, he was one of the members of the nobility whom the rebels demanded should be brought into the king's council in preference to Suffolk. He was certainly of the belief himself that his closeness of blood to the king entitled him to a role in government. He seems to have been rather a violent young man. Only two years later during a dispute with Lord Cromwell over the Fanhope inheritance in Bedfordshire, he resorted to armed force when he failed at law, even though he had agreed with Cromwell to submit their competing claims to arbitration. His men were said to have carried off £2000 worth of Cromwell's goods from Ampthill. The king ordered his arrest and he was imprisoned in Windsor Castle for a short period. Given Henry's own claim to the throne, and Henry VI's recognition on more than one occasion that Exeter was his closest blood relation, it is perhaps not surprising that York failed to carry his son-in-law with him when he began to advance his own claim to be considered Henry VI's heir presumptive after the death of Humphrey, duke of Gloucester.

In the serious breakdown of local law and order which characterized the early 1450s, Exeter played a prominent role, not just in Bedfordshire but also, more seriously, in Yorkshire. The fierce rivalry between the Percies and the Nevills, though controlled by the two earls, Northumberland and Salisbury, was largely carried out by their younger sons. It led to a number of violent clashes, made possible because each side in their capacity as wardens of the two Marches, had manpower available. The growing closeness of the Nevills and York meant that Northumberland inevitably supported Queen Margaret, but his sons needed another powerful supporter. They got one in Exeter, partly at least because the niece and heiress of his old enemy, Lord Cromwell, had married Sir Thomas Nevill. Both Percies, Nevills and Exeter turned a deaf ear to royal reprimands and ignored commissions set up to try and restore peace. The seemingly uncontrollable violence in Yorkshire was the biggest challenge to York in his protectorate in 1454. Although he owned large estates in the county himself, he is never known to have gone further north than Fotheringhay in Northamptonshire before 1454. His pleas to his son-in-law to disband his men were ignored. Exeter thought he had a claim to lead the government and seems to have deeply resented the fact that York and not he had been made Protector. At twenty-four he lacked any real experience, and seems to have been as unintelligent as he was violent, which meant that he would have received little support, but in his grievance he took no account of this. He planned a major uprising in the north. According to a contemporary newsletter, 'the duke of Exeter in his own person hath been at Tuxforth beside Doncaster, in the north country, and there the Lord Egremont [Thomas Percy] met him and they two been sworn together, and the duke is come home again'.[1] The threat was serious enough to bring York up from London and Exeter seems to have plotted to murder York when he arrived in Yorkshire. The rising was foiled without much difficulty and Exeter fled to London secretly and took sanctuary at Westminster, from where York 'fetched him out'.[2] He was sent north again to prison at Pontefract at the orders of the council, but his freedom was not long coming once York's protectorate ended.

Exeter was now a very bitter enemy of York and the Nevills and thus a committed Lancastrian. In 1460 Henry VI appointed him as commander of all his naval forces for three years, but he failed to intercept Warwick on his way from Ireland to Calais a few months later. He fought for the Lancastrians at the battles of Blore Heath, Northampton, St Albans and Towton, after the latter, fleeing north to Scotland with Henry VI and Queen Margaret. In October 1461 he appeared in Wales, supporting the military activities of Jasper Tudor, earl of Pembroke, against Edward IV, but again managed to escape overseas. For this he was attainted in the parliament of 1461 and all his honours were forfeit. He remained in exile at Queen Margaret's little court in conditions of considerable poverty until the Re-adeption. It was reported that he was reduced to begging for alms until the duke of Burgundy came to his rescue with a modest pension.

Where, in this political struggle between her father and her husband, was the Duchess Anne? Henry Holand seems to have had an unappealing character: an Italian observer reported that he was viewed as 'fierce and cruel' and it seems unlikely that his wife escaped the animosity he felt against her father. This was compounded by the fact that York had defaulted on the later instalments of her dowry, paying only the 1000 marks due at the time of the marriage. Nonetheless, she bore him a child, probably quite early on in the marriage, who was named Anne after her mother. It seems reasonable to suppose that at some point in the early 1450s the couple became estranged; to live separate lives was a customary solution to a marriage breakdown among the wealthy, being easy to arrange when there was a choice of residences. Anne then found a solution to her personal problems. His name was Thomas St Leger, and he came from a family of Kent gentry. When he became the duchess's lover is unknown. That the relationship was already established by the time Anne's brother Edward came to the throne is suggested by the fact that, very early on in his reign, St Leger was made an esquire of the body and received a grant of eight manors in Buckinghamshire and Cambridgeshire ostensibly for the services in battle he had rendered. This was a very considerable grant and was followed by a stream of wardships and minor offices and more lands, including the royal manor of Kennington. This was presumably a result of the king's tacit acceptance of his sister's awkward position. In 1465 this royal favour nearly came to a premature end when St Leger was involved in a fracas at Westminster, wounding another esquire, Stephen Christmas, one of the marshals of the king's hall. A law which stated that if any man strike another within the palace of Westminster, he should lose his right hand was invoked and the case was tried by the steward of the royal household, John, earl of Worcester, who was also constable of England. St Leger was condemned to lose his hand and was only saved by a royal pardon on account of his good services to the king's father and himself. Services to the king's sister went unspecified, but it was probably she who begged her brother for mercy. She may even have been the cause of the quarrel in the first place, if Christmas had passed some slighting remark about her relationship with St Leger.

When Exeter was attainted, his wife was granted all the lands they had held jointly under her marriage settlement, and all his goods, the maximum that was customarily permitted. In addition a large proportion of his forfeited estates were settled on Anne and her heirs by King Edward. In this Anne certainly benefited from being the king's sister; Margaret, countess of Oxford, who was Warwick's sister and in the same position ten years later, was left virtually a beggar. Anne promptly conveyed all her lands to trustees, who included the Archbishop of Canterbury and William, Lord Hastings, for the use of herself and her heirs by the duke. Edward also granted her other forfeited lands, but she was in an anomalous position. She was neither a widow nor a wife, and her affair with St Leger had to be conducted discreetly if she was to avoid censure by both the church and public opinion. The fact that St Leger was an esquire of the body meant that the couple were often at court; Anne was, after all, the third lady in the land after the queen and the king's mother.

At some point early in the reign Duchess Anne reached an agreement with her cousin Warwick and his brother John that her only child, Anne, should marry John Nevill's son, George. There is no evidence of Anne's view of her brother's imprudent marriage, but in October 1466 she was prepared, probably under some pressure from Edward and Elizabeth, to break the Nevill marriage contract for her daughter in order for Anne to marry the queen's elder son, Thomas Grey. Queen Elizabeth was willing to pay 4000 marks to secure the Holand inheritance for Thomas. In August 1467 an arrangement was made which settled the Holand inheritance on young Anne, with remainder to the Duchess Anne 'and the heirs of her body' – at this date the duchess had only one child, Anne herself – with a second remainder to the queen, which was presumably intended to benefit her son in the event of the death of Duchess Anne and her daughter. The difference in wording between the first settlement on the duchess and 'her heirs by the duke' and this second one 'and the heirs of her body' was to prove crucial when Anne Grey died childless in 1473, predeceasing both her parents.

Once the Re-adeption of Henry VI was under way, Henry Holand returned to England, specifically to his London house of Coldharbour, which had been granted to his wife in 1461. If there was a meeting between the couple, no chronicler noted it, and we have no idea of whether they ever met again. At Barnet 'the duke of Exeter fought manly there that day, and was greatly despoiled and wounded, and left naked for dead in the field, and so lay there from 7 of the clock till 4 after noon; which was taken up and brought to a house by a man of his own, and a leach [doctor] brought to him, and so afterwards brought in to sanctuary at Westminster'.[3] Exeter's courage had never been in question, and it seems that he was capable of inspiring loyalty among his own servants. He was removed from sanctuary into the Tower, but he had escaped with his life. He remained there until May 1475 when he was released in order to join the king's French expedition, presumably a step on the road to rehabilitation. On the return journey he drowned in the Channel, but exactly what happened is not recorded.

Soon after her husband was taken into custody in 1471, Duchess Anne obtained a divorce. The source for this is the sixteenth-century annalist, John Stow, but he is surprisingly specific, saying that the divorce was obtained on 12 November 1472. Whether the word divorce is technically accurate is questionable, since in the fifteenth century it is far more likely that what was obtained was an annulment. Whatever the means, Anne was freed from her husband and able to marry her lover. The death of her only child without issue soon afterwards meant that all the Holand inheritance reverted to her, thus depriving the queen's son of his wife's lands. Duchess Anne died in January 1476, almost certainly in childbirth. Her second daughter was also baptized Anne, and her birth ensured that St Leger and his child retained the Holand lands, thanks to the settlement of 1467, which stated that the remainder was to the heirs of the duchess's body. When Anne St Leger married George Manners, Lord Ros, in 1490, she carried the inheritance and her Plantagenet genes with her and lived to see her son raised to the earldom of Rutland in 1525. After Richard III seized the throne, his brother-in-law, Thomas St Leger, for reasons we do not know, joined Buckingham's rebellion. Captured at Exeter, he was condemned to death by the king, despite large sums of money being offered for his pardon. If the Duchess Anne had still been alive, it is unlikely that he would have died. It is possible that the pious Richard disapproved of Anne's relationship with St Leger, or he may simply have been punishing family disloyalty, but for whatever reason, he was not willing to be merciful. Thomas was buried with his wife in the chantry chapel he had founded in St George's Chapel, Windsor, at the time of her death; there is a brass to them there, in the Rutland Chapel. Far from exercising political influence at the Yorkist court, Anne of York's first husband, the duke of Exeter, remained implacably opposed to it. Her second husband, though of too junior a rank to wield much influence, finally also opposed Richard III.

The married life of Elizabeth, the second daughter of Richard of York, followed a very different path to that of her elder sister. Elizabeth was born in April 1444, at Rouen, like her brothers Edward and Edmund. She had a grand christening in the cathedral there, and her godparents included the veteran soldier, John Talbot, newly created earl of Shrewsbury, and Jacquetta, duchess of Bedford, by then married to Richard Woodville. The presence of such important people in Normandy was almost certainly related to the formal betrothal of Henry VI to Margaret of Anjou, which had just taken place at Tours, and for which there were festivities in Rouen. Some time before October 1460, and possibly a year earlier, Elizabeth married John de la Pole, duke of Suffolk, who was nearly two years her senior. Negotiations for the match were under way in 1458 at a time when York was politically marginalized and by the time it took place he was in active opposition to the crown. It is possible that the match was based on council attempts to reconcile the two opposing parties, or that the duke's mother, the formidable Alice Chaucer, was playing a clever political game to ensure that her son was well placed with both the conflicting parties. As a child, Suffolk had been married to Margaret Beaufort, infant daughter and heiress of John, duke of Somerset, but the marriage was dissolved soon after Suffolk's father had been murdered in 1450, certainly by March 1453. Initially John de la Pole was in the wardship of the king, but in May 1453 the wardship was confirmed to his mother, Duchess Alice, and it was she who arranged the York match for her son. It was, by any standard, a suitable marriage and meant that York had captured two of England's dukes for his elder daughters. Unlike her sister Anne, Elizabeth produced a string of sons for her husband: John born in 1462, Edmund in 1471, Humphrey, who became a priest, in 1474, William born about 1478 and Richard, whose birth date is unknown. There were two more possible sons, Edward and Geoffrey, whose identity cannot be confirmed for certain, and daughters, Anne, Katherine, Elizabeth and Dorothy. Elizabeth had clearly inherited her mother's Nevill fecundity, but with the exception of her husband, an only son, the de la Poles had also produced a large number of sons in each generation.

Unlike his brother-in-law Exeter, John, duke of Suffolk, did not come of age until after Edward IV's accession, but by that stage he had already fought for the Yorkists at St Albans and Towton. He was lord high steward at the coronation and received his confirmation as duke of Suffolk and licence to enter all his lands a few months before attaining his majority in 1463. Although his father had not been attainted before his death in 1450, all his royal grants had been resumed and his mother Alice retained substantial parts of the Suffolk estate in dower as well as her own Chaucer inheritance. For a duke, Suffolk was poor. Even after his mother's death he barely held an estate worthy of his title; in addition he had a large family of sons to support. While he might have counted on the generosity of his brother-in-law, his rewards were not lavish. High birth and closeness to the royal family were not attributes that Edward rewarded so much as loyalty and ability. Since Suffolk's loyalty was never in doubt, it was presumably his ability that the king had reservations about; the duke never even attended a royal council meeting. While his rank inevitably gave him a certain prominence, he is rarely mentioned as playing any part in national politics. In East Anglia he seems to have been unable to step into his father's shoes and it may be true, as the Pastons suggest, that he remained under his mother's thumb. The king's lack of confidence in him probably also played a part. The duke played his proper role in ceremonial, bearing St Edward's sceptre at the queen's coronation, and sat on various local commissions, and together with his wife, was granted the constableship of Wallingford Castle, but that was all except for the creation of their heir, John, as earl of Lincoln with an annuity of £20 in March 1467.

In 1469 when the king visited East Anglia and saw the ruins of the manor of Hellesdon which Suffolk had created during his violent feud with the Paston family, the Pastons were not promised redress at the duke's expense; indeed the king told William Paston that 'he would neither treat nor speak for [Sir John Paston], but for to let the law proceed and so he sayeth that they departed'.[4] Since the Pastons had been trying to get legal redress for years without success, this oblique favouring of the king's brother-in-law was cold comfort and perhaps partly explains their willingness to desert Edward the following year. Suffolk remained a notable supporter of Edward throughout the upheavals in the period 1469–1471 and as a reward he was created a knight of the Garter and he and Elizabeth were granted the wardship of Francis, Lord Lovell. He and his contingent were part of the army which went to France in 1475 and, in a slightly surprising move, Edward made him lieutenant of Ireland in 1478. During his reign Edward had in general been content to leave Ireland to be run by Anglo-Irish deputies, firstly the earl of Desmond and then the earl of Kildare. In 1478, when he appointed Suffolk, the king sent over an English deputy, Henry, Lord Grey, who encountered such a level of Anglo-Irish resistance that he was powerless and returned to England the following year. Suffolk, like other lieutenants of Ireland before him, never took up his appointment. Since he certainly used violence against the Pastons, it was clearly not dislike of it that kept him at home, though there is some suggestion that his health was not good. Suffolk's concentration on local affairs at the expense of a national role perhaps indicates that he made a decision to avoid politics. Often dismissed as a nonentity, he may simply have been rather wiser than many of his contemporaries.

On a more personal level, the duke sold a very elaborate jewel to the king in 1478, which was described as an image of Our Lady with Our Lord in her arms and the images of Saint John the Baptist and Saint Katherine on either side of Our Lady. The gold jewel had two other images with seven angels and was garnished with great numbers of precious stones. Edward was prepared to pay £160 for it and may have intended it for his new chapel of St George at Windsor.

Like her husband, Duchess Elizabeth does not appear to have taken a prominent role during her brother's reign and her name tends to occur only when family affairs were the issue. She and the duke, together with her young brother, Clarence, represented the York family in February 1463 when Warwick reinterred his father and brother Thomas in a grand ceremony at Bisham Abbey, Berkshire, following their hasty burial after Wakefield. In 1471 Elizabeth, her sister, Duchess Anne, and their mother, Duchess Cecily, were all named as mediating between Edward and George of Clarence in what turned out to be a successful attempt to get the straying Clarence back into the family fold. In 1478 the family was less forgiving and Suffolk's Irish appointment can perhaps be seen as his payment for not opposing Clarence's trial and death; it had certainly been Clarence's office. At the same time, in an act of parliament exchanging some lands between the king and himself, the duke was permitted to come off rather better than Edward in the deal.

A vivid vignette of Elizabeth in London in 1476 comes from the hands of the Oxfordshire family of Stonor. Duke John's illegitimate half-sister, Jane, was married to Thomas Stonor and two of their daughters served in Duchess Elizabeth's household. The girls' brother, William Stonor, married a wealthy London widow, and on 22 October 1476 Elizabeth Stonor wrote to her husband from London describing two visits she made to the duchess and the meeting between the king and his mother, and adding*

> And sir, my lady of Suffolk is half displeased because my sister Barantyne is no better arrayed, and likewise my sister Elizabeth. And she says without they be otherwise arrayed, she says, she may not keep them.[5]

During much of Elizabeth's married life, the duke's mother held a large portion of the de la Pole lands in jointure, including Ewelme in Oxfordshire, the Chaucer family home, which had long been her main residence. The young couple settled at Wingfield in Suffolk. The dowry Elizabeth brought to her marriage, 2300 marks (£1533), was only a third of the sum York had paid for her sister Anne and was handed over in instalments, some of which were still unpaid in 1472. In 1465 Edward granted the duke 100 marks a year during Duchess Elizabeth's life until he could provide lands of equal value. Suffolk and his wife were the York family's poor relations, but there is no obvious reason why so little came their way. How much time they spent at court is unclear, but given the rate of Elizabeth's child-bearing, it is perhaps reasonable to suppose that much of their time was spent on their estates rather than in London. In 1471 the duke refused to attend parliament because he could not afford to bring a retinue that reflected his status adequately. His relations with the court seem to have been perfectly friendly, but his interests remained local and during the upheavals of the Re-adeption he seems to have been content to acquiesce in the change of dynasty. He stayed at Ewelme while Elizabeth returned to Wingfield, whence it was easier to communicate with her brothers in Burgundy. The fate of his father may have discouraged the duke from playing a role in national affairs, and certainly the minor appointments and offices he received were in East Anglia and Oxfordshire, where his family interests lay.

The duke and duchess were in no sense excluded from court, but when she came to court Elizabeth seems to have had no special privileges and, if the royal household was outside London, suitable accommodation was usually in short supply. Towards the end of Edward's reign, Elizabeth arrived at court, possibly at Windsor, without arrangements having been made in advance for her reception. She was forced to dash off a quick note to John Paston, asking if she might have the use of his rooms for three or four days until another lodging could be found for her. The note is highly unusual because the duchess wrote it herself. Most fifteenth century gentlewomen could write but they almost always used a clerk for

---

* see p. 66

all their correspondence, however intimate, and very, very few holograph letters have survived. 'For God's sake, say me not nay', she wrote, and signed it 'Your friend, Elizabeth'.[6] Despite her husband's attempts to wrest some of the Fastolf manors from the Pastons in the 1460s, the duchess was more favourably inclined towards the family, particularly after the land disputes were settled. As a knight of the Garter, the duke and his duchess received licences in mortmain for gifts to St George's Chapel, Windsor, in 1479 and 1480. Neither was at court, however, when the king died and the duke was not present at his funeral.

Both King Edward's elder sisters were married before his accession and neither played a significant role in the life and politics of his reign. It was the youngest girl in the York family who found herself in the role of princess in 1461. Margaret was born in May 1446, probably at Fotheringhay but possibly at Waltham, and of the six children who followed, four, William, John, Thomas and Ursula, all died as infants, leaving only George and Richard to grow up with her. After Edward's accession the three of them shared a household at Greenwich until Margaret reached the age of eighteen. By a fortunate coincidence, this was at the time of the king's marriage and nothing could have suited the new queen better than to have the king's sister as one of her ladies. Duchess Cecily may have had a diplomatic illness and avoided attendance at Elizabeth's coronation, but her daughter was there, sitting at the queen's left hand.

Margaret had now become a diplomatic asset, and several husbands were suggested for her, including James III of Scotland. The one whom Edward and Warwick most favoured was Don Pedro, pretender to the throne of Aragon, but just as the betrothal was being formalized, the prospective bridegroom died. Even before that another suitor had appeared on the scene, in the person of the newly widowed Charles of Burgundy. In 1446 Charles's mother, Isabella of Portugal (herself the daughter of Philippa of Lancaster, daughter of John of Gaunt) had suggested Anne of York as a possible match, but in 1454 Duke Philip finally decided on his son's cousin, Isabelle of Bourbon. It was a happy marriage, but had produced only a single daughter by the time Isabelle died in 1465. Soon afterwards a Burgundian envoy arrived in London to discuss a possible match between Charles and Margaret, despite her betrothal to Don Pedro. With both Burgundy and France bidding for his support, Edward was willing to turn down a French husband for his sister when King Louis suggested his brother-in-law, Philip of Savoy. Duke Philip of Burgundy died in June 1467, adding to the attraction of his son as a husband, but raising the cost. The marriage treaty was settled in the spring of 1468 and Margaret appeared before the great council to give her formal consent.

Edward had to provide a large dowry for the bride, some 200,000 gold crowns, of which a quarter was due on the wedding day. He raised it with some difficulty by way of loans from Italian bankers, the Calais Staple and London merchants, after the marriage had been delayed for two months because the money was lacking. One guarantor of the loan furnished by London merchants was Sir Thomas Cook. When his arrest looked like causing further delay Margaret apparently intervened personally and appealed to her brother for Cook's liberty, which was granted 'for as long as she was in the land'.[7] Contributions from the clergy provided her with suitable rich apparel and furnishings and her travelling expenses. She finally sailed from Margate to Sluys and on 3 July was married to Duke Charles at Damme amid celebrations of unparalleled splendour. Edward was determined that the English contingent should uphold the honour of his sister and their family name, no matter what the cost, while Duke Charles was equally determined to outshine his father at the first major event since his accession. John Paston, who formed part of Margaret's train, could hardly find words to express the wonder of it all: 'And as for the duke's court, as of lords, ladies, gentlewomen knights, squires and gentlemen, I heard never of none like it, save King Arthur's court. And, by my troth, I have no wit nor remembrance to write you half the worship that is here.'[8]

Margaret referred to herself as 'margarete dangleterre' when she presented a book to the Poor Clares of Ghent, but in Burgundy she was usually called 'marguerite de yorch'. She used the York emblem of a white rose, not only in the crown she wore to her marriage but also in one of her portraits, which shows her wearing a collar bearing the initials of herself and her husband and with alternate white and red roses. Her marriage to Charles was in many ways a union of similar characters. Both were serious, hard-working and deeply pious. The Burgundians described their new duchess as 'reserved and seldom smiling', which means that she was very unlike her brother Edward and may have taken after their father. At her wedding Margaret was described as being tall, like her brother, which suggests that for a woman her height was noticeable, while Duke Charles was below average height, and as having 'an air of intelligence and will'.[9] She is the first English princess for whom portraits survive, and one, painted at about the time of her wedding, shows a young woman not beautiful, but pleasant looking, with large eyes, a straight nose and a well-shaped mouth. There are also numerous representations of her in illuminations, all of them religious in tone. Charles was generous to her, despite the fact that Edward never completed payment of her dowry, settling on her the towns of Malines, Oudenaarde and Dendermonde, with other estates worth an annual income of 16,000 crowns. The duke paid her every formal courtesy but his military interests abroad meant the couple spent much of their time apart. This left the duchess to take a prominent part in the administration of Burgundy. She did not bear him the son he needed, though he seems never to have reproached her for it; she did, however, establish a very good relationship with her stepdaughter, Mary, who was only eleven years her junior.

Margaret's notable piety was almost certainly an inheritance of her mother, Duchess Cecily. This not only determined her reading, which was largely devotional, but also her interest in charities and in the establishment and reform of religious houses. Childless herself, she particularly favoured the care of orphans. While always elegantly and richly dressed, she was not, unlike her royal brother, noted for display, and her major extravagance was her library of beautiful manuscripts, inspired by the collections she saw in her new duchy. Her spoken French was fluent when she left England, because the York nurse, Anne of Caux, had remained in the household she shared with her two younger brothers, and we know that she could read French fluently enough to correct Caxton's translations, but her written French remained flawed. While she learned some Dutch, her Latin was minimal and she preferred to read French translations of Latin authors. Ghent and Bruges were centres of the book trade, and many manuscripts were produced there for the luxury end of the English market. William Caxton, a London mercer, was governor of the English Merchant Adventurers in Bruges and a major figure in commercial relations between England and Burgundy. His business acumen enabled him to recognize the potential of the new trade of printing and his first venture was to translate a French version of the history of Troy, hitherto unavailable in English, which he showed to Margaret. He went on to learn printing and published at least four French and two English texts at Bruges before returning to England in 1477 and setting up in business there. One of the latter texts was his *History of Troy*, which he presented to Margaret in 1473.

It was not unusual for English princesses married to rulers of nearby states to retain a close interest in the affairs of their native country and to return there for visits to their parents. In Margaret's case, the close trading ties between England and Burgundy and the latter's dependence on a political alliance with the former against their common enemy, France, meant that her role as intermediary took on extra significance. Her marriage had been arranged by her brother as part of an anti-French policy and despite the offer of a suitable husband by Louis XI. The thwarted French king retaliated by trying to prevent the issue of a papal dispensation for the Burgundian marriage and then spreading rumours about the bride's lack of virginity. These rumours were completely without substance, but Edward's way of life and her eldest sister's liaison with Thomas St Leger gave some degree of colour to the charge.

Louis' behaviour was almost certainly one of the reasons for Margaret's strongly anti-French bias, but the latter also reflected the reality of Burgundian politics. Prior to the invasion of France in 1475, Edward sent Lord Dacre (who had accompanied her on her wedding trip as her chamberlain) to his sister, asking for her help in recalling Charles to his treaty obligations, but his wife's pleas were ineffectual against the stubborn duke's wish to continue with the siege of Neuss.

His death in January 1477 at another siege created a crisis. His heiress, Mary, was twenty and as yet unmarried, and the threat of an invasion by France was very real. Charles had been negotiating for a match with Maximilian of Austria for his daughter, but while Margaret might have liked an English husband for Mary, the only possible royal candidate was George of Clarence and this was a marriage Edward would not permit.

Faced with a French invasion, Mary wrote three weeks after her father's death that Margaret was 'fully occupied in dealing with the very high and mighty prince, our well beloved lord and cousin the king of England, to persuade him to come to our aid and to uphold the everlasting alliances and treaties which were signed between him and our late lord and father'.[10] England was bound by treaty to come to Burgundy's aid, although after 1475 the alliance was nominal. More importantly, Margaret was appealing to her brother on a familial and chivalric level. Both her younger brothers were in favour of a major military expedition in her support, Clarence because he still had the illusion that a marriage with Mary was possible, Gloucester because he wanted to add to the military reputation he had gained at Barnet and Tewkesbury and of which he had been thwarted by the treaty of Picquigny in 1475. They were supported by Lord Hastings, who as captain of Calais, saw it seriously threatened by a French invasion of the Low Countries.

While Edward sanctioned Hastings to cross with a force for strengthening the Calais garrison, he refused to permit armed intervention. He did not want such a marriage for Clarence and he did not want to lose his French pension and the French marriage for his daughter Elizabeth, let alone find the money to fit out an army. In a contest between pragmatism and chivalry, Edward always came down on the side of the former. The French price for English non-intervention was to be further guarantees over payment of the pension and the marriage. Louis's army invaded Picardy, capturing many Burgundian towns, and then laid siege to Boulogne. Hastings, in Calais, rebuffed Louis's overtures and offered help to the garrison of Boulogne, even attempting to bring English troops into the town in direct opposition to his royal master's wishes, but probably with the knowledge and support of the king's brothers. Boulogne surrendered after six days, but the Burgundians did not forget his attempts to help, though it earned him a severe reprimand from Edward.

In allowing Louis a free hand, the king failed to prevent his sister's dower lands in Flanders being ravaged and deserved the reproach she sent him, describing herself as 'one of the poorest widows, deserted by everyone, especially by you'.[11] Not only had he failed to come to her aid, Edward had continually defaulted on the payment of her dowry, half of which was still owed. This in turn meant that her dower would have been substantially reduced but for the generosity of her stepdaughter, Mary. The young duchess demanded that it be paid in full because

Margaret held 'our person and our lands and lordships in such complete and perfect love and good will that we can never sufficiently repay and recompense her'.[12] Edward had in fact granted Margaret herself several valuable trading licences, which the businesslike duchess put to good use, but these were not included in her dowry.

Once it became clear that an English match for Mary was unrealistic, Margaret put her considerable energies into hastening the marriage with Maximilian of Austria. Within nine months of Charles's death it had taken place and Burgundy had received help from the east. It was a happy though brief marriage and Margaret gave Maximilian her support and loyalty for the rest of her life. In turn he and Mary made her godmother to their two children; their son Philip was largely brought up in Margaret's care after the premature death of his mother and it was at her hands that he was trained to govern his Burgundian inheritance. Margaret's reaction to the trial and death of Clarence is not recorded, but they took place at a time when all her attentions were focused on Burgundian affairs. There is no evidence that she made any attempt to intercede for him, but then the same can be said for both her sister Elizabeth and their mother, Duchess Cecily.

Despite Edward's refusal of help when she needed it most, Margaret continued to work for a strong Burgundian alliance with England against France. To this end she made a state visit to her native land in the summer of 1480. Her brother took the occasion to lay on lavish ceremonies as well as family events, but drove a very hard bargain with the Burgundians, who were in too weak a position to demur. The marriage alliance between England and Burgundy which Margaret wanted was confirmed with the betrothal of Duchess Mary's infant son, Philip, and Edward's daughter, Anne, but the king's determination to gain such a matrimonial coup without paying a penny in dowry meant that Maximilian inevitably broke off the match when it suited him to do so. Once again Edward's parsimony had defeated his sister's superior diplomatic sense.

On a more personal note, Margaret was probably the influence behind Edward's decision to introduce the order of Observant Franciscans to England and offer them a site for a new house adjacent to his palace of Greenwich. She had strong connections with the order and had spent much of her summer visit of 1480 at Greenwich, where she had lived during the early years of Edward's reign. Maximilian's governance of his wife's territories inevitably led to the dowager duchess's gradual retirement from public life. She settled herself in her dower town of Malines, but her influence on English affairs was not yet done. It was to re-surface after the downfall of her family.

9

Edward V

Edward V reigned for only a few weeks, and was never crowned, but he is one of the best known medieval kings, not as Edward V but as one of the Princes in the Tower. It was a sad end to a life that had seemed so full of promise during the reign of his father. In the few months after the prince's inauspicious birth on 2 November 1470 in sanctuary at Westminster Abbey, Edward IV ensured the final destruction of the Lancastrian threat to his throne by his victories of Barnet and Tewkesbury. Nothing, it seemed, could challenge his son's right to succeed him. The baby prince was almost immediately granted the rights and titles of the heir to the throne: prince of Wales, duke of Cornwall and earl of Chester, and oaths of loyalty to him as his father's heir were sworn by members of a great council which included members of the royal family and almost all the senior peers and clerics. His father's earldom of March was added to the prince's holdings rather later, in 1479. Before Prince Edward was a year old, he had his own household and a council to administer his lands. During the visit to England of Louis de Gruthuyse in September 1472 he made two formal appearances in robes of state – possibly the long gown of cloth of gold on damask bought for him at a cost of £1 – and was carried by his chamberlain, Thomas Vaughan. In 1475 at the age of four the prince was knighted, together with his baby brother Richard and his two Grey half-brothers, preparatory to being formally installed as keeper of the realm at Westminster when his father departed with his army to France. By then he and his household were normally resident at Ludlow.

Ludlow was the administrative centre of the earldom of March and of those duchy of York lands which lay in the west and Wales. It was where Edward IV had himself grown up, though it was not sentimentality which dictated the king's choice of Ludlow for his heir; he had decided to use the prince's household to bring a measure of peace and security to the turbulent marcher lordships at the expense of family life. The queen, and probably the king also, escorted their son to Ludlow when he first moved there in 1473, indeed his brother Richard was born at the neighbouring town of Shrewsbury. The little prince was with his parents as frequently as could be managed and must, in fact, have spent a good deal of his young life travelling, since his parents rarely left the tranquillity of their Thames valley residences. Nor could he have known his siblings well, spending time in their company only on special occasions and at major feasts.

The prince had no London residence of his own and is known to have stayed in Thomas Vaughan's house at Westminster on visits to the capital. Vaughan had long served the house of York. He had held posts under both Edward IV and his father, serving on numerous embassies in the first half of Edward's reign and becoming treasurer of King Edward's chamber. His patent of appointment as the prince's chamberlain granted him 'all power and authority belonging to the office' because the prince 'is of so young and tender age that he cannot yet guide or direct himself'.[1] Edward IV planned his son's upbringing carefully and from an early point. Ordinances for the government of his household, regulating every hour of his daily life and how he was to be raised were drawn up under the king's instructions in September 1473, and these were updated ten years later. The prince's upbringing was aimed at combining the education required for any aristocratic English boy with training for the additional responsibilities of kingship. It goes without saying that religion was a major part of this, but Edward also learned Latin and French and needed to be able to read and write in English. By the time he was twelve, the prince had read widely, far more so than most aristocratic boys of his age, and probably more so than his own 'henchmen' or companions, young boys of noble birth who shared his schooling and leisure time.

While a separate household for the prince was customary, establishing it as far away as Ludlow when the prince was only three probably came as a surprise to many. The queen in particular would have found it hard to part with her son while he was still so young, but her influence over his household remained very strong indeed. She had been appointed to his council in 1471 and since nothing, including the appointment of new officers, was done without the council's advice and the queen's express assent, her role was a powerful one; she was also one of the three members of his council who held a key to his treasury. When the prince's household first moved to Ludlow a number of his council who fulfilled other roles at court had to remain in London, so new members were appointed specifically to go with him, and they included the queen's cousin, Sir Richard Haute, and her confessor, Edward Story. Queen Elizabeth remained closely involved in the prince's Welsh administration for a number of years and then seems to have handed over much of her responsiblities to her son, Sir Richard Grey. Her brother, Anthony, Earl Rivers, had been appointed the prince's governor, 'that he may be virtuously, cunningly and knightly brought up'.[2] In many ways it was an obvious appointment. Earl Rivers combined the skills of a noted jouster with some, not entirely successful, military experience and the intellectual interests of a pious and well-educated humanist. In addition, as the prince's uncle, he could be trusted completely to guard him and raise him as the king and queen would wish. Whether it was an entirely wise choice remained to be seen.

In 1479, when the prince was given his father's earldom of March, the scope of his government in Wales and the west was further extended, also taking in duchy of Lancaster holdings in the region. For Rivers, his post meant authority and wealth in Wales far in excess of anything he had from his own modest estates in East Anglia; in the prince's name he became the virtual ruler of Wales. It was, for example, Rivers who raised the contingent of several thousand men from the region who served in the Scottish war of 1482–3. Even his brother-in-law, William Herbert, second earl of Pembroke, was required to exchange his Welsh earldom and his largest estates there for the title earl of Huntingdon and lands in the south west. Rivers also used his position to appoint his own men to minor offices, exercising the prince's electoral influence in the duchy of Cornwall, and Prince Richard's Mowbray interests in East Anglia, on behalf of men for whom he wished to find parliamentary seats, though this was customary noble practice. It should be pointed out, however, that Rivers's power came from office rather than landholding and that offices could be removed overnight, making him more vulnerable than peers whose power was based on their own great estates. Men serving under him were, with some exceptions, royal servants whose loyalty was to the office and not the man. They were certainly not all Woodville clients, but it is hardly surprising that they came to be identified with Woodville interests. Rivers could not be in Ludlow all the time, and indeed went overseas on several occasions during the 1470s. His deputy in Wales seems to have been his nephew, Richard Grey, who was probably the most visible and active of the Woodvilles in the region, and who was granted the lordship of Kidwelly.

The man appointed directly to oversee the prince's education was John Alcock, bishop of Rochester, who was translated to the more convenient see of Worcester in 1476. He was a pious reformer, extremely learned and the author of many good works. He was also a longstanding Yorkist civil servant, a former keeper of the great seal, and well qualified to be president of the prince's council and supervise his day-to-day upbringing. Like Thomas Vaughan, he had no previous connection with the queen's family, but because of his appointment inevitably came to be associated with them and their interests. For instance, when the mayor of Bristol, William Spencer, was accused of treason by a fellow merchant, Thomas Norton, in 1478, the city council sought the help and support of their bishop, Alcock. It later thanked him for obtaining the good lordship of several of the king's council, including Rivers, Dorset, Vaughan and Sir Richard Grey, all of whom were also fellow members of the prince's council. In 1475, when the king went to France, taking Chancellor Rotherham with him, Alcock was made acting Chancellor.

As Edward IV lay dying, he had strength enough to add to his will and to attempt to heal rifts between those closest to him at court. Neither he, nor anyone about him, however, seems to have made any attempt to send for his heir so that the boy might see his father for the last time and receive his blessing.

The omission seems strange, even if it is unlikely that the prince could have reached London before his father's death, and certainly by custom would not have attended his father's funeral. As it was, Ludlow did not receive the news of Edward's death until 14 April, five days after it took place. Even then it was not until 24 April, with his coronation already fixed for Sunday 4 May, that the young king set out for London. In the capital, there had been considerably less dilatoriness. A high proportion of the peers and senior clerics had managed to get there in time for the funeral and to constitute a representative council to make the decisions necessary to the running of the administration. With the death of the king during the minority of his heir, royal authority had devolved on them, as it had done in similar circumstances in 1377 and 1422, though that authority was customarily shared with the deceased king's surviving sons or brothers. Precedents also established that the council was not obliged to follow the wishes of the deceased king, which, rumour said, were that the young king and the realm be placed in the care of his brother, Richard of Gloucester. As with Ludlow, the distance of London from Yorkshire meant that Gloucester and the northern lords had also been absent from Edward's obsequies.

One of Edward IV's greatest achievements, in such contrast to the previous dynasty, was to control his nobles. This he had done by a combination of character, firmness and generosity, but it was a very personal loyalty that they owed him, and his most conspicuous failures were with members of his own extended family. It was Warwick and Clarence who forced him off his throne, and Gloucester, Clarence and the queen who inveigled him into actions of dubious legality to ensure that estates went where they wanted them to go, regardless of the laws of inheritance. The test of the success of any regime is its ability to ensure a smooth succession and, by this test, Edward ultimately failed. It should not have been so. His heir was an intelligent, educated boy, almost into his teens. In about eighteen months he would be fourteen, the period of River's guardianship would have come to an end, and at sixteen, he would have been declared of age, as his royal uncles had been. As king he was already old enough to have some say in the decisions made in his name. England had weathered worse on the death of Henry V when his son was still a baby, and, as in 1422, the late king had a loyal, capable brother to protect the interests of his son and realm. Unlike France, England did not appoint a regent in such situations but a Protector who worked with the royal council as first among equals. Although Richard of Gloucester had of recent years spent most of his time in the north, running his estates, representing royal power in the region and prosecuting the war against the Scots, he had returned to London regularly for every major event at court. Whatever his views on Edward's foreign policies, the death of Clarence or the queen and her family, he had kept them to himself. He was the obvious, indeed the only, choice to be Protector and it may have been Edward IV's own wish. There is no evidence to substantiate this, but it certainly seems possible. Gloucester, however, was not in London to put his case in person.

Instead of appointing Gloucester as Protector, the council followed another precedent. The protectorate under Henry VI came to an end in 1429 at his coronation when he was only seven, after which he was regarded as an adult. Edward V's council decided that if their new king was crowned immediately, he, too, could be declared an adult and would thus have no need of a Protector, for government would then be carried out on his behalf by his council. It was a perfectly reasonable decision, but its consequences were to be calamitous. Even as a crowned king, Edward was still only a boy and was bound to turn informally to those he knew and trusted – his mother, his uncle Rivers and others of his former household. While the Woodville family would not hold formal power, their influence would be even greater than it had been under his father.

The first to foresee the danger was Hastings, sensitive to his own vulnerability. He was no longer in the highly influential post of king's chamberlain, he knew that Rivers coveted his position as captain of Calais, and his feud with the marquess of Dorset, though personal rather than political, meant that he could no longer hope for preferment. He seems to have been responsible for keeping Gloucester informed of events in London, and to have argued strongly, but unsuccessfully, for him to be made Protector. Rivers was in a very strong political position because he had been in Ludlow at the time of Edward's death. This was either fortuitous, or an indication that Edward's health was giving concern before his final illness. Only a few weeks before, on 27 February 1483, Rivers' patent as the prince's governor had been renewed, and whereas his first patent had given him general powers, 'with and in as ample power and authority as unto the same office of Governor appertaineth or belongeth',[3] the new one was much more specific, granting him the right to direct the prince's household, every man of which was to be issued with horse and harness, to receive and pay out the prince's revenues, and remove the prince's person from place to place at his discretion. In March, Rivers had instructed his business agent in London, Andrew Dymmock, to forward his patent to Ludlow, proof that he could raise troops and receive revenue in the prince's name in case any challenged his right to do so. With these powers and their control of the young king's person, the Woodvilles held the political initiative. In London, Rivers had been quietly making arrangements with the constable of the Tower, John, Lord Dudley, to transfer the office of deputy to his nephew, Dorset. A scholar and a courtier Rivers may have been, but he was also a skilful political animal and, when required, a hard-headed and ruthless businessman.

Having confirmed his wife's family control over the person of his heir only weeks before his sudden death, if Edward IV decided as he lay dying to bestow political control of the country on Gloucester, he may well have believed he

was continuing the balance of power which had worked so smoothly during
his lifetime. There is, however, no independent evidence that he did so, and
Gloucester's claim that the Woodvilles were aiming to prevent him holding such
an office may well have been simply propaganda. Edward's own personal form of
government – dispersing regional power to a handful of men he trusted – worked
well when he was there to hold the reins. In a minority there was less chance of
such a system continuing harmoniously. Nevertheless, there is no evidence of
any previous major rivalry between Gloucester and the Woodvilles before the
spring of 1483 and suggestions that Gloucester deeply resented their influence
and retired to the north in dudgeon seem to have been a product of hindsight.
Where their local interests coincided there was apparently no friction, and it
seems that only the circumstances of the prospective minority brought them into
conflict. If Edward IV had been aware of any trouble between his brother and his
brother-in-law, he would probably have made different political dispositions. The
Woodvilles may not have been particularly popular, but they were an established
group on the political scene and the person who was most hostile to them was
not Gloucester, but Hastings.

One of the major problems for the understanding of the reign of Edward V
is the lack of contemporary narrative sources. The only neutral eyewitness, the
Italian visitor, Mancini, wrote after the event and was inevitably influenced, albeit
subconsciously, by hindsight. He was hampered by his lack of understanding
of the English political system, while his main source, the king's doctor, John
Argentine, moved only on the fringes of the court circle. The man who did
understand the system, the second unidentified continuator of the Crowland
Chronicle, who describes himself as a councillor and was personally at the centre
of affairs and thus the most reliable source, also wrote after the event. He describes
the general and entirely reasonable feeling among the councillors that the queen's
family should not be allowed to retain unfettered control of the king's person
and the arguments at the council over the size of the entourage the young king
should bring to London. Young Edward's delay in leaving Ludlow was probably
caused by Rivers' desire to raise a large contingent of men to accompany him. It
was Hastings, feeling personally threatened, who argued most strongly for its size
to be limited. However, wrote the Crowland Chronicler, 'the benevolent queen,
desirous of extinguishing every spark of murmuring and unrest, wrote to her son
that he should not have more than 2000 men when he came to London'.[4] Hastings
was perfectly content with this, since he was certain that Gloucester would bring as
many. Queen Elizabeth may have hoped for some role during her son's minority,
though it was not customary for a queen dowager to play a political part, but her
behaviour toward the council seems to have been exemplary. The council had
acted sensibly up to this point and in accordance with precedent. By appointing
an early date for the coronation, it had deprived Gloucester of the possibility of

EDWARD V

becoming Protector, leaving him only an influential member of their own body. The council had also prevented the Woodville faction from bringing a large armed force to the capital. It appeared to be doing its best to remain even-handed and to continue Edward IV's own policy, and almost certainly his own wishes, of balancing the power between the influential wings of his family. The one thing all the council members keenly desired was that 'this prince should succeed his father in all his glory'.[5] If, as Mancini reports, some of the concillors were uneasy about such major decisions being taken without the presence of either Rivers or Gloucester, they were overruled. As the queen's son, Dorset, was able to claim, 'We are so important, that even without the king's uncle we can make and enforce these decisions'.[6] While it is possible that he was referring to his family, it is more likely that Dorset meant the council in general.

Rivers and the young king, with their large entourage, left Ludlow on 24 April. On 29 April they arrived at Stony Stratford, Northamptonshire. Here they learned Gloucester was in nearby Northampton, also on his way to London from the north. Was this by arrangement, to enter London with a united front, as Mancini suggests? The Crowland Chronicler says that when they heard that Gloucester was in Northampton, Edward sent Rivers to Gloucester to pay his respects. Whatever the circumstances, Rivers seems to have had no suspicion he was walking into a trap. This suggests that he had no reason to believe that he and Gloucester could not work amicably together. The two parties spent a convivial evening and then dispersed to their various lodgings. At dawn, Rivers and his party were arrested and Gloucester went to Stony Stratford to take possession of the king's person. In a single stroke he had deprived the Woodville party of the initiative.

In the coup, Gloucester had been supported by Henry Stafford, duke of Buckingham, who seems to have sprung from nowhere onto the centre of the political stage. He had inherited the title from his grandfather, who had died at the battle of Northampton in 1460. While under age he had been married to the queen's sister, Catherine, something which he is reputed to have resented deeply as a disparagement to his birth and rank. He had fulfilled the role of steward of England at the trial of Clarence, was present at such major royal functions as the marriage of Richard of York and Anne Mowbray and had received a few minor favours; but otherwise he seems to have been ignored by Edward IV. He was allowed no part in the exercise of authority in Wales, despite holding major Marcher lordships, and although he contracted to join the French expedition in 1475, he seems not to have gone. He was certainly not given any of the appointments or offices a man of his rank might have expected. Edward IV, a good judge of men, undoubtedly had his reasons for ignoring him, but for Richard of Gloucester he was an unexpected ally, of royal descent, untainted by the court and eager to take his place in the political world which had ignored him for so long. The sources are silent on exactly when and how the two joined forces.

According to Mancini, Gloucester told his nephew at Stony Stratford that Rivers and his supporters had attempted to deprive him of the protectorate that Edward IV had intended, and were even conspiring his death. The young king put up a spirited defence of the men his father had chosen to serve him and said he placed every confidence in the peers and the queen to govern the kingdom, but in the end he had to give way to *force majeure*. The demands of the two dukes, both of them his uncles and thus presumably well known to him, were put politely but they were demands nonetheless. The scene was reported by Mancini and is the only time that Edward comes alive as a person. It shows him as intelligent, brave and loyal, even when deprived of those closest to him, but it can hardly have calmed Gloucester's fears of Woodville power and influence once his nephew was crowned. The night of 29–30 April was a brilliant coup, ruthless, bloodless and a complete surprise to its victims. Rivers, Vaughan, the new king's chamberlain, Sir Richard Grey, his half-brother, and Sir Richard Haute, the queen's cousin and comptroller of his household, were dispatched north under arrest.

The news of the coup reached London the same evening and caused consternation. Two armed parties formed, one at Westminster in the queen's name, the other in London under Lord Hastings. Queen Elizabeth had no confidence in Gloucester's good faith and fled with her daughters and younger son into sanctuary in Westminster. Gloucester wrote both to the council and the mayor of London justifying his actions. In this he was supported by Hastings, who was presumably pleased at the outcome of the coup, since he asserted that 'nothing had so far been done except to transfer the government of the kingdom from two blood-relatives of the queen to two nobles of the blood royal' and 'that this had been accomplished with only so much bloodshed in the affair as might have come from a cut finger'.[7] The Woodvilles were unable to attract enough support for their cause to fight for it and Dorset joined his mother in sanctuary, while Sir Edward Woodville, having previously received authorization from the council, rapidly put to sea with a fleet, and part of the late king's store of ready cash, to take action against the French.

It was not until 4 May, the day originally fixed for his coronation, that Edward V entered his capital, accompanied by Buckingham, Gloucester and only five hundred men, but with four cartloads of weapons bearing Woodville devices which Gloucester claimed were clear proof that his enemies were plotting against him and intended to slay him. This was purely for propaganda purposes: if Rivers had indeed been involved in a plot against Gloucester, he would never have walked so trustingly into his hands. King Edward was met outside London by a gaily clad delegation of the mayor, aldermen and citizens, as was customary, and thence escorted into the city, where he was lodged in the bishop of London's palace at St Paul's. Gloucester summoned the lords spiritual and temporal and the mayor and aldermen to swear fealty to his nephew and a new date, 24 June, later altered to 22 June, was fixed for the coronation. This meant that in the discussions over the arrangements to be made for government after Edward was declared of age Gloucester would be able to play a leading role.

The effect of Gloucester's coup had been to raise suspicions over his intentions. He did his best to allay these fears, but was never totally successful. The council, while arranging for Edward's coronation and formally appointing Gloucester as Protector until the coronation, refused to condemn Rivers and his friends as traitors on the grounds that, when they were arrested, Gloucester held no formal authority. The council remained strictly non-partisan; it acknowledged the natural justice of Gloucester's claim to be Protector, and while respectful to the queen, its members had refused to support Woodville dominance over the young king. It was determined to press ahead with the coronation and to recognize the king's majority on that day. This was deeply worrying for Gloucester, since the king would then be able to summon back to his service the Woodville members of his former household. It was why he pressed so hard for their execution as traitors, and why his plan seemed to be to retain some sort of control of the government after the coronation. He was at least able to keep them imprisoned, but this added to the sense of unease in the capital, as did the fact that the new Protector 'did not show sufficient consideration for the dignity and peace of mind of the queen'.[8]

It is impossible to tell from the available sources what negotiations had gone on behind the scenes between council members as Woodville control of the king, and hence of the kingdom, was replaced by that of Gloucester and Buckingham. The feeling of insecurity was heightened by the queen's refusal to come out of sanctuary, which also had the effect of ruling out the palace of Westminster as an appropriate place for her son to stay. The young king's lodgings at St Paul's were too small for his retinue, for when the most senior members of his household were imprisoned, his previous personal attendants were dismissed and he passed into the care of his late father's household servants. While alternative places for him to lodge were being canvassed, Buckingham suggested the royal apartments in the Tower, always used by kings immediately prior to their coronations, and the suggestion was generally accepted as appropriate by members of the council.

A further problem for the council was that the new regime was acutely short of money. The funeral of Edward IV had been expensive, the naval campaign against the French had absorbed cash, so did the newly acquired fortress of Berwick, yet everyday administration had to continue and there was a coronation to organize. Inevitably there were changes to administrative personnel. At the top, the long-standing chancellor, Archbishop Rotherham, identified as being too supportive of the queen, was replaced by another well-qualified churchman, Bishop Russell of Lincoln, while the treasurership, vacant by the recent death of the earl of Essex, was filled by his deputy, Sir John Wood. Hastings retained his captaincy of

Calais, while Buckingham got his reward by being given the governance of Wales and the Marches, completely replacing the prince's council, as well as control of all the royal lands in Somerset, Dorset and Wiltshire. The size and scope of this delegation of royal authority was without precedent and was never to be repeated, but it indicates just how much Gloucester both valued and needed the support given to him by Henry Stafford at the time of the usurpation. Rivers was treated as though attainted and his and other key Woodville posts were reallocated to Gloucester's supporters or men regarded as neutral.

Gloucester seems to have been anxious to maintain the status quo as far as possible, and his actions in general seem to have done little to antagonize the wider circle of royal servants, who on the whole were willing to acquiesce in the curtailment of Woodville influence. The strong desire of the political community for continuity and the fulfilment of Edward IV's wishes was undoubtedly a major reason for the success of Gloucester's claim to be Protector. It looked as though, after the coup at Stony Stratford, things had settled down sufficiently for a somewhat uneasy calm to reign. Most contemporaries felt able to accept the new situation; the exception, of course, was the now powerless Woodville family. The queen refused to leave sanctuary with her other children. Dorset managed to escape from sanctuary and fled abroad. Although Gloucester was able to obtain the surrender of most of the royal fleet under Sir Edward Woodville, the latter, with two ships, was also able to make his escape.

Late May and the first half of June saw the government functioning normally. Parliament was summoned to sit immediately after the coronation, as it did at the beginning of every reign, so that the new king might be granted the customs revenues. The chancellor, Bishop Russell, even drafted his opening speech, though this seems to have contained suggestions that Gloucester's powers be prolonged after the coronation. Suddenly, in the middle of June, a crisis emerged, or was manufactured. Gloucester wrote to two of his supporters, and presumably to many others though the evidence has not survived, commanding them to London with as many troops as they could speedily raise because of a plot by the queen and her adherents to murder him and Buckingham. This was clearly only a means to an end, as the queen was in sanctuary, Rivers was in prison, Dorset was in exile and Sir Edward was away at sea. Even if the resentful Woodvilles had been plotting, they were hardly a threat to a Protector who currently had all the powers of a king. Gloucester was using the Woodvilles as a screen for his own actions, and the family was just unpopular enough for him to be able to get away with it. There is no contemporary evidence of such a plot, and it can only be presumed that those in London were unaware of one, or of the content of Gloucester's letters. If Hastings knew, he certainly did not anticipate that, on 13 June, Gloucester would have him arrested in the middle of a council meeting, charged with treason for participating in the queen's plot and executed immediately without trial. Hastings may have supported Gloucester in his claims for the Protectorate against the Woodvilles, but his ultimate loyalty was to the son of his lord and friend, Edward IV. Moreover, he was the natural leader of the moderate loyalists in the council, who had already refused to agree to the execution of Rivers on the grounds of treason and would certainly resist any attempt by Gloucester to take the throne.

The pre-emptive strike against Hastings, following the coup at Stony Stratford and the lack of evidence of any serious Woodville plotting except that produced by Gloucester himself, suggests strongly that he had no intention of relinquishing power. All his actions, from the death of his brother to his own coronation, show a consistency and strength of purpose which negates any suggestion that he was acting solely in response to events. After the elimination of the Woodvilles, Hastings was his greatest obstacle, so Hastings had to go and he was 'killed not by those enemies he had always feared, but by a friend he had always trusted'.[9] There is also the suspicion that Buckingham may have had a hand in Hastings' downfall; the latter's powerbase in the midlands had to some considerable extent been built up at Stafford expense. At the same time, three other councillors, Lord Stanley, Archbishop Rotherham and Bishop Morton of Ely, were also arrested and imprisoned. In one fell swoop the strongest supporters of the young king were disposed of in a coup as sudden and as ruthless as that at Stony Stratford. If Gloucester was by this time aiming at the throne, he judged that it was not yet the time to make his plans public; ostensibly he was still planning his nephew's coronation. If members of the council were growing suspicious, they were clearly reluctant to challenge the duke.

Three days later, on 16 June, the aged archbishop of Canterbury, Cardinal Bourchier, entered the sanctuary at Westminster (he was 'compelled' to do so according to Crowland) in order to persuade the queen to allow her younger son, Prince Richard, to join his brother prior to the coronation. Bourchier's arguments were reinforced by the armed men the Protector saw fit to station around the sanctuary and whatever misgivings the queen may have had, she was realistic enough to know she could not retain the child with her any longer, and entrusted his safety to the archbishop. As soon as Prince Richard had joined the king at the Tower, Gloucester issued writs cancelling the parliament called for the end of June and postponing the coronation until November. News that armed men summoned from the north and from Wales by the Protector were approaching London spread through the city, causing alarm. The northern forces had been gathered ostensibly to support Richard as Protector, and it was the background threat of the arrival of an army from the north that underpinned his seizure of the throne.

A few days after that, on Sunday 22 June, Dr Ralph Shaa preached a sermon at St Paul's Cross, declaring the young king and his brother illegitimate because of their father's previous precontract of marriage, though at this stage there seems to have been some doubt about the identity of the lady in question. According to a London chronicle, the sermon was very ill received by its hearers and Shaa never recovered from the ignominy of having preached it. Only Commynes identifies Gloucester's informant as Robert Stillington, bishop of Bath and Wells: 'the bishop said that he had married them when only he and they were present'.[10] This seems intrinsically unlikely. No claim was made in England that Edward had actually married Eleanor Butler, only that he had contracted to do so; if he had indeed gone through some form of marriage ceremony that he planned later to reject, he would hardly have chosen the keeper of his privy seal, in preference to an obscure chaplain, to perform it. The old rumours of Edward IV's own bastardy, first put out by Warwick in 1469, were already circulating, but there was one other factor for the Protector to take into account. His other nephew, the eight-year-old Edward, earl of Warwick, who after Edward's children was next in line to the throne, was brought to London and placed in the care of his maternal aunt, the duchess of Gloucester. It was declared that the attainder of his father, Clarence, barred him from the throne, a technicality which had not prevented Gloucester's father, Richard of York, from claiming the throne and which was now conveniently overlooked.

On Wednesday 25 June, the duke of Buckingham addressed a gathering of lords and prominent men who had assembled in London for the coronation with the suggestion that Richard should be offered the throne. Mancini says that overawed by the two dukes and their armed supporters, and having themselves been told not to bring large retinues into the city, and lacking any obvious leader, the gathering rather feebly acquiesced. Many of them may well have been in a state of shock at the speed and ruthlessness with which Gloucester had acted, unable to comprehend how the late king's loyal brother could have metamorphosed into an uncle of such treachery. The following day, joined by the mayor and aldermen of London, they progressed to Baynard's Castle, where Gloucester was staying with his mother, and duly petitioned him to take the throne. The next day, Richard of Gloucester acceded to the throne as Richard III. In this process the council, the governing body of the kingdom, had played no part, according to Crowland. Mancini suggests that the lords of the realm, gathered in London, as they thought for Edward V's coronation, were intimidated by both the numbers of armed men at the disposal of Richard and Buckingham, and the fate of Hastings, into asking Richard to take the throne. In their desire for continuity, the political community had supported Gloucester's coup against the Woodvilles, and on the whole approved of his protectorship, but his second coup had to be backed by armed force because most of that community did not approve of the usurpation of the boy they regarded as the rightful king.

There had been usurpations in the previous two centuries, but these had been in protest against the rule – or in Henry VI's case, non-rule – of the king. That against Edward V was unprecedented. It was not against the king himself, who had done nothing, but was either in anticipation of the power and influence his accession might bring to his maternal relations or a result of pure ambition on the part of Gloucester, or more probably a combination of the two. The excuse was the young king's bastardy, something over which he had no control, and which was suddenly and conveniently divulged. His father's licentious behaviour, both before and after his secret marriage to the queen, had come back to haunt his dynasty. *Titulus Regius*, the act of the 1484 parliament which formally endorsed Richard III's title, gives three reasons for setting the young king aside on the grounds of bastardy. The first, which was that his parents' marriage was clandestine, is irrelevant, since this did not invalidate it and such marriages were recognized by the church. It might certainly be argued that a truly clandestine marriage was one where the couple concerned took their vows in private, without witnesses and then consummated their union. The king's marriage, though private and unsuitable for a king, was, as far as the evidence goes, conducted by a priest and before witnesses.

The second ground, that it was procured by the sorcery of the queen and her mother, the Duchess Jacquetta, was rather more serious. It had arisen before, in 1469, and Jacquetta had been tried and acquitted of the charge, but, while suspicions may still have been circulating, there would certainly not have been enough evidence so many years later for her to be tried again. The claim that Edward's marriage was invalid because of a previous precontract to Lady Eleanor Butler was much the strongest charge, largely because of his own behaviour. But, however plausible, even this could not be proved either way because the lady was conveniently dead. The suspicion remains that she was sufficiently well connected to have protested against the Woodville marriage in 1464 if she had any reason to believe she was indeed contracted to the king herself. It had never been raised during Edward's lifetime, not even by Warwick and Clarence, who had not hesitated to use every other weapon at their disposal. Nor after Eleanor's death in 1468, as far as is known, did the king and queen go through any form of remarriage to ensure the legitimacy of their own union and of any offspring, including both princes, born thereafter.

Even if a precontract had existed, and there is no evidence that it did, the marriage of Edward and Elizabeth had been recognized as legal by church and state for nearly twenty years. If it had been found to be technically invalid, this would not necessarily have bastardized children born of it. By English law children who were regarded as legitimate during their father's lifetime might continue to be so regarded by the law, even if they were later found to have been illegitimate. Canon law as practised in England, however, had specific views on the legitimacy of bigamist marriages subsequent to the death of the first spouse, which were complicated by the clandestine nature of the royal marriage. The arguments were technical and, if they had been tested in law, it is unclear as to whether the decision would finally have been in favour of Edward V's legitimacy or not. In 1483, if the princes were to be declared bastards, this could only legally be done by submitting the issue to a church court, which would have examined all the circumstances of their parents' marriage. If the marriage was found by the court to be invalid, this would have had to be confirmed by the civil courts, in this case, parliament. None of this due process of law took place. In terms of practical politics such a slow process, with such an uncertain outcome, would have been quite impossible. The fact remained that Edward V had been regarded as his father's heir from the moment of his birth, he had received the fealty of all the peers more than once and he had been declared king on his father's death. Bastardy, even if technically proved, did not necessarily bar him from the throne, since it had not prevented William the Conqueror and a number of more recent European rulers, including Henry of Trastamara, king of Castile, from becoming kings. It was power that counted, not legitimacy, and in reality the grounds for Edward's deposition were irrelevant. Gloucester's usurpation was a *fait accompli*.

When he succeeded to the throne, all the titles Edward V had previously held, prince of Wales, duke of Cornwall, earl of Chester, were automatically subsumed to the crown, to be held in abeyance until he had a son. When declared a bastard and dethroned, Edward was left without any title or status. The same, however, was not true of Prince Richard. His titles of duke of York and duke of Norfolk had both been conferred by act of parliament. Bastardy was no bar to the awarding of titles, as many a king's illegitimate son could bear witness, and there was no legal reason why he should not have continued to hold the titles and the lands that went with them. This was not what happened. On 28 June, two days after Richard III assumed the throne, and well before anyone has seriously suggested that the princes were dead, since the last sightings of the boys were apparently in July, he granted the titles and estates of the Mowbray inheritance to the two co-heirs, John, Lord Howard, and William, Lord Berkeley. No act of parliament deprived the prince of his Mowbray holdings, and Richard III's grant was therefore illegal. In the politics of early summer 1483, this, like the charges of Edward V's alleged bastardy, was irrelevant. In deposing the king, Gloucester was hardly likely to allow his heir presumptive to retain his position as a premier peer. He had not even waited until he was king to order the execution of Rivers, Grey and Vaughan; they died without trial on 25 June.

How much the young king Edward knew of what was going on or the fate of his uncle Rivers, his half-brother, Richard, and the chamberlain he had had since a baby, Thomas Vaughan, in faraway Yorkshire, or that of Hastings nearby, is unknown. He was too intelligent and too well educated not to be aware of the fate of dethroned kings and his state of mind is painful to imagine as all his attendants were withdrawn, he and his brother were removed from the royal apartments to inner rooms and allowed less and less freedom within the Tower, until finally they were fully prisoners. His doctor, John Argentine, a fellow Italian and Mancini's main source, was one of the last independent witnesses to see him alive and reported that the young king, 'like a victim prepared for sacrifice, sought remission for his sins by daily confession and penance, because he believed death was facing him'.[11]

In all the millions of words expended on the mystery of exactly how and when the boys were killed and on whose orders, it is important to stick to one basic fact: within a few weeks of Richard III's accession they had disappeared from view and were never seen alive again. There is some evidence that there was a failed plot, whose leaders were caught and executed, at the end of July to release them from the Tower, and that it was after this that Richard made the decision that the boys should die. It will never be possible to be sure when they were killed, how, by whom and on whose orders. In many ways it is unimportant. Within a few months of his deposition, rumours of the death of Edward V and his brother were in circulation, both in London and on the Continent. Whether or not those rumours were justified is immaterial. Mid-fifteenth-century England was a place of ruthless politics and during the civil war a considerable number of men had been put to death after they had fallen into the hands of their enemies. In the final analysis, the deaths of Rivers, Hastings and the others can be seen in this context, even though England was no longer at war. But, however hardened their sensibilities were, English men and women drew the line at the deaths of innocent children. The political reality for the new king was that as long as the boys were alive he would be plagued by fear of rebellion aimed at restoring Edward to his throne and if they were dead then he had to bear the odium of being believed to be a child-murderer. We will never know for certain whether Richard of Gloucester left Yorkshire determined to take the throne or whether he merely aimed at gaining the political initiative so that he could dominate the politics of the minority and then found that each step took him inexorably nearer to a usurpation. What is not in doubt is that from the beginning he seized the initiative and, with a mixture of charm and force, never released it. The brother whom Edward IV had most trusted to protect his son had betrayed him in the most heinous fashion and in doing so had destroyed all those in a position to defend the young Edward V.

10

Richard III

Richard III is one of the most controversial kings ever to have occupied the English throne. For centuries the popular image of him derived from Shakespeare's arresting portrait of the monstrous hunchback. More recently opinions have changed and a society has dedicated its efforts to rehabilitating his character from the view of him disseminated by Tudor propaganda.

It is clear that Richard was a highly complex man. He was intelligent and pious, qualities reflected in his extensive collection of books. He almost certainly had considerable personal charm, he was a good soldier and capable of establishing a just and benevolent regime in his area of influence. Where his own interests were concerned, however, he was also ambitious, aggressive and ruthless. All in all, it may be said that he was a true man of his times. By the time of his brother Edward's death he was all-powerful in the north, save for Stanley-dominated Lancashire and Cheshire, and Edward had crowned his success by granting him palatinate powers in the west march and any lands in south west Scotland that he could conquer. Yet all was not quite as well as it seemed. His pre-eminent position in the north had been established partly through his wife's inheritance, partly through his own abilities, and partly through royal favour with its grants of lands and offices. It suited Edward to have his loyal brother in charge of that perennially turbulent region, but Richard was still dependent on the maintenance of that royal favour for his palatine powers, and his title to the Nevill inheritance (though not to his wife's share of her maternal inheritance) was insecure. George Nevill, the former duke of Bedford and the Nevill heir male, had never married. Since he died in May 1483, he may already have been ill before Edward's death. His death meant that, according to the settlement made in 1472, the Nevill lands would revert from Gloucester to the Nevill co-heirs unless Gloucester could persuade the king to push through another act of parliament in his favour. Edward's death was in many ways a catastrophe for him, since he and his brother had worked together for many years to their mutual advantage. Now he would become dependent on the favour of his successor.

Richard of Gloucester's motives for usurping his nephew's throne were undoubtedly mixed. In the last years of his brother's reign he was without question the second most powerful and influential man in the kingdom, and both the coups which brought him to the throne came from a position of strength, not weakness. Whether he thought that this power was likely to be threatened during the reign of his nephew by the closeness of the Woodville family to the new king, whether he succumbed to temptation and seized power because he could, or whether he genuinely believed that his own rule was a better prospect for the country than the factionalism possible during a minority, we will never know. It was probably a combination of all these. Richard III had the attributes necessary to be a successful king by medieval standards. If he had come to the throne in natural succession he would have had the opportunity to put them to good effect, but he did not. The whole of his short reign was to be overshadowed by the means he took to gain the throne.

Richard III and Queen Anne were crowned on 6 July 1483 in a ceremony of much splendour attended by most of the lords and gentry who had originally come to London for quite a different coronation. Most of his own supporters from the north had also had time to reach the capital. The level of attendance disguised the air of unease and it was the new king's first task to calm and reassure people and attempt to win their real support. He may even have believed that, because he had been able to seize the throne with such little overt opposition, he had indeed carried most of the Yorkist establishment with him. Thus his ends were best served by changing as little as possible and presenting his rule as a natural continuance of that of his brother, so there were one or two changes of senior personnel but no major redistribution of patronage. Richard had few doubts about the loyalty of the northern gentry, but in the southern half of his new kingdom he was little known and it was the servants of Edward IV there that he had to win firmly to his cause.

His first move was a wise one – he set out on a progress. Travelling along the Thames valley, across to Gloucester and then slowly up through the midlands to York, the journey was a public relations triumph. The new king brought a magnificent train with him, pageants and ceremonies were staged all along the route, and when the cities of London, Gloucester and Worcester offered him money, he declined, saying he would rather have their love than their money. He also took the time to hear the petitions of ordinary men and administer due justice on their behalf. The king was joined by his young son and heir, Edward, from Middleham for a ceremonial entry into the city of York, which surpassed itself to welcome home the king it regarded as a Yorkshireman, its celebrations marred only by the refusal of its archbishop, Thomas Rotherham, to have anything to do with them. Richard stayed there for three weeks in late August, during which time his young son, Edward, aged seven, was invested as Prince of Wales. The progress had been largely through areas where the king or his more committed supporters had influence, but he would have done better to have turned his attention further south and west, for it was here that the trouble began.

Richard was too intelligent not to have anticipated that there would be plots against him and to have taken measures to ensure he was kept informed of what was going on. Plotting aimed at releasing the princes from the Tower and their sisters from sanctuary began almost as soon as he left London; indeed the plot may have been the trigger for the princes' murder. The plan was for the daughters of Edward IV to be sent abroad so that, in the words of the Crowland Chronicler, 'if any mishap should befall the male children, nevertheless through the saving of the persons of the daughters the kingdom might some day return to the rightful heirs. When this became known the sacred church of the monks of Westminster and the whole neighbourhood took on the appearence of a castle and a fortress'.[1] Crowland was sure that the king knew about the conspiracy through his spies and the chronicler also named correctly the many southern and western counties from which the disaffected came.

By autumn the rebellion had spread right across southern England among the leaders of the gentry society, the very men who had sustained Yorkist rule for Edward IV, many of them members of his household. Despite for the most part continuing them in office, Richard had completely failed to win them over and their loyalty remained vested in Edward's son. These royal servants were the very men who would normally have been the leaders of the forces used to suppress rebellion. The rebels had August and September in which to organize, and at some point during this period the rumours concerning the fate of the princes became widespread, and their plans perforce changed. Until then it was not a rebellion led by peers, though some became involved later, and towards the end of August, two crucially important women became involved in the conspiracy. Queen Elizabeth and Margaret Beaufort, countess of Richmond, together planned to secure a marriage between the queen's eldest daughter, Elizabeth, now the heir to her father, and Margaret Beaufort's exiled son, Henry, earl of Richmond. The latter, who had a remote Lancastrian claim to the throne only if the parliamentary act barring the Beauforts from the succession was set aside, was to lead an invasion from Brittany. It is inconceivable that the queen dowager would have helped to promote such a match unless she was convinced that her sons were dead. By far the most extraordinary and inexplicable event in the late summer of 1483, however, was the defection of the duke of Buckingham from the king he had been instrumental in assisting to the throne. He had left the king when the royal progress reached Gloucester to continue into his new Welsh domain, and then made public proclamation that he repented what he had done and would lead the rebellion. That Richard was personally shaken by this defection is clear from the postcript he added in his own hand to a more formal letter written to his chancellor, Bishop Russell, 'Here ... all is well and truly determined, and for to resist the malice of him that had best cause to be true, the duke of Buckingham, the most untrue creature living; whom with God's grace we shall not be long till we be in those parts and subdue his malice. We assure you never was false traitor better provided for …'.[2] Who knows whether Buckingham aspired to the throne himself, for he had a distant claim, whether he jumped on a bandwagon he thought would be successful, or whether he foresaw that his rule of south Wales would be threatened with the establishment of a new council under Edward, Prince of Wales, and resented it. Whatever his motives, he failed to raise any support for the rebellion in Wales. His lack of judgement underlines Edward IV's wisdom in excluding him from any form of political responsibility.

Richard III had little difficulty in suppressing the rebellion. The fact that it was so widespread was the cause of its downfall, since it proved impossible for its leaders to coordinate and concentrate their forces. The north and midlands held firm, John Howard, the Mowbray co-heir and new duke of Norfolk, easily fended off the Kent rebels' attempt to take London and Richard, sweeping down from Yorkshire, contained Buckingham's forces, which were trapped by floods west of the Severn. The duke himself was captured and brought to Salisbury to the king, who had no compunction about summarily executing him, before moving on to confront the last stand of the rebels at Exeter. One of these was the king's brother-in-law, Sir Thomas St Leger, who was executed there.

Many of the conspirators simply melted away or submitted, though some, including Dorset and his uncle, Edward Woodville, Edward Courtenay, earl of Devon and his brother, the bishop of Exeter, managed to leave the country. Henry Tudor, arriving off Plymouth too late to have any effect, simply hoisted his sails and put to sea again. Within three weeks it was all over, but its effects were to last for the rest of the reign. Even if Richard had anticipated something of the sort, and although his military skills enabled him to contain the uprising, its widespread nature was a severe blow to the new regime. He had been unable to take over his brother's network of loyal supporters in the south and a new contender for the throne had risen from obscurity. He had now to find a way to fill the large gaps in the royal household and in central and local administration created by the rebellion, and ensure that his authority could never again be challenged by southern England.

The king's first action was to appoint trusted supporters to posts as sheriff in the disaffected counties and to ensure that they were also constables of strategically important castles, and this remained the case for the rest of the reign. Although many of the rebels submitted to the king's mercy, almost a hundred were indicted for treason in the parliament that sat in January 1484. Most of those attainted early in Edward IV's reign had come from the highest echelons of society and were permitted to gradually work their way back into the king's favour. In contrast, most of those who lost their lands and offices in 1484 were from lower ranks and the general view seems to have been that they would never be permitted to regain their places. There was no doubt about the outcome of the trials and even before they took place, the estates of the rebels were confiscated and granted to men the king could trust. The problem was, that with one or two exceptions like the Howards, Richard could not really trust anybody in the south. Whereas in the past, members of the county gentry might differ as to which side to support in times of civil unrest, enough of them would always be available to support whichever regime was in power and local administration could remain in the hands of local men. In January 1484 this did not hold true, since almost all the ruling strata of county society was disaffected. The confiscated estates and offices were therefore largely granted to members of Richard's northern household and affinity. Men from loyal areas, such as Sir Richard Radcliffe, Sir Marmaduke Constable and Sir Robert Percy, all from Yorkshire and northern peers such as Ralph, Lord Nevill and Richard, Lord Fitzhugh also benefited. These men, who may never have set foot south of the Thames before, now controlled the government of southern England. They held the offices and sat on the commissions and while numerically they may have been in a minority, it was they who had the real rule and influence. It was not the quality of their administration which was in question, and there is no reason to suppose they were particularly tyrannical, but the Crowland Chronicler speaks of the 'shame of all southern people' and of how they 'murmured ceaselessly and longed more each day for the return of their old lords'.[3] This is probably an exaggeration, particularly as time went on and more local men were absorbed into the new regime, but by then the idea of the 'northern plantation' and its tyranny had taken hold in London and the south.

By the time Richard III's only parliament sat in January 1484 the king had subdued rebellion, but he had not been able to assuage the doubts about the legitimacy of his title to the throne. The first act of the parliament was therefore to set out this title in the *Titulus Regius*, after which it could be widely publicized. It was a major piece of propaganda, quoting the petition of the three estates which had asked Richard to take the throne and condemning the evils and immoralities of Edward's reign, which were set out in detail and were then contrasted with Richard's own virtues. The charge of corruption levelled at Edward's regime was also an implicit attack on the royal servants who had rebelled. While parliament was sitting and almost all the lords spiritual and temporal were still gathered in London, they subscribed to a new oath of allegiance to the king's heir, Prince Edward. Most of those so swearing must have been aware of the irony – that they had all sworn a similar oath a good deal more freely to Edward V as prince. Despite these efforts, hostility to the king continued to bubble away under the surface. In the summer of 1484 the south western counties were already stirring again, since a commission was appointed to investigate 'great treasons' there.

Like Edward IV, Richard relied on a handful of magnates to control various areas of the country. With the exception of the handful who had fled into exile and joined Henry Tudor, the peerage, ever pragmatic, accepted his rule. Even Lord Stanley, with a history of conflict with Gloucester in the north during Edward's reign and imprisoned during the usurpation, had ultimately come down on the king's side during the rebellion, though if, as Buckingham may have hoped, he had joined the rebellion, its outcome might have been different. As Tudor's stepfather, Richard had to keep Stanley onside. While he could never trust him, he needed him in the north west and in north Wales. East Anglia was another matter. Here the power and authority had been granted to John Howard and his son Thomas. Since they owed their dukedom of Norfolk and earldom of Surrey to Richard, they served him as loyally as they had his brother. Even the Howards, however, had failed to control the region completely during the rebellion, in which several members of the former Mowbray connection were implicated, and Richard was forced to augment the local commissions of the peace with men from the north.

In the midlands, Hastings' role was replicated by the new king's chamberlain, Francis, Viscount Lovell, who had been a personal friend of Richard's since they had been boys together in Warwick's household. The king also relied on his own new son-in-law, William Herbert, earl of Huntingdon, who took over from Buckingham in south Wales. Herbert had been badly treated by Edward IV, who forced him to surrender his father's great earldom of Pembroke to the prince of Wales in return for the much poorer earldom of Huntingdon. His first wife, the queen's sister, Mary Woodville, had died, leaving him with an only daughter as his heir, and Richard offered him his bastard daughter Katherine, sweetened with a very generous dowry worth 1000 marks a year. In the north, although the earls of Northumberland and Westmorland benefited from lands and annuities, Richard showed that he intended to retain the power he had amassed as duke in royal hands, initially through the household of his son, the Prince of Wales, based at Middleham and Sheriff Hutton. In the case of Northumberland at least, this was not well received. Members of the nobility were not the only high-profile supporters of the new king. In the summer of 1484 seditious ballads and rhymes appeared in London, the best known attributed to William Collyngbourne: The Cat, the Rat and Lovell our Dog Rule all England under a Hog.[4] Collyngbourne paid the ultimate penalty, not for his witty lampoon but for his support of Henry Tudor during and after the 1483 rebellion. Apart from Francis, Lord Lovell, the two men to whom he referred were William Catesby and Sir Richard Ratcliffe. The latter has already been noted as one of the northerners given lands and power in the south. He was a long-time member of Richard's council as duke and one of his most trusted men, his rewards being probably greater than those to any other member of the gentry. Catesby, by contrast, was a midland lawyer and was already a confidential servant of Richard's, when, according to Thomas More, he was given the task of sounding out Hastings's attitude to Richard taking the throne; the negative response he took back to his master in effect signed Hastings' death warrant. Catesby was a fixer for Richard before he was selected as speaker for the king's only parliament and he was well rewarded. Others who had formed part of Richard's circle of most trusted servants for years, though not named by Collyngbourne, were Sir Marmaduke Constable, Sir Robert Brackenbury, who was entrusted with the security of the Tower of London, and Sir James Tyrell, an East Anglian who had been in the wardship of Cecily of York. Despite the undoubted loyalty shown to Richard by those who had been in his connection as duke, support was seeping away elsewhere, even among those of Edward's former household who had initially remained loyal. One of the reasons was the existence of an increasingly credible alternative in Henry Tudor.

When Richard became king, England was at war with Scotland and he had been the chief military commander. Relations with France were verging on war and Richard did nothing to ease either situation, though his activity was limited to naval activity against both countries, and in the winter of 1483/4 he was certainly contemplating another invasion of Scotland. In the previous autumn's rebellion, Duke Francis of Brittany had supported Henry Tudor's invasion and continued to give him and other exiles refuge, so Brittany was included as a target in the naval campaigns. In the spring of 1484 it looked as though the king was using the age-old technique of distracting attention from domestic problems by focusing on foreign enemies and, in addition, playing to his own military strengths. The projected expedition against Scotland was cancelled when reports that Henry Tudor was planning another invasion reached London, but the naval campaign was successful and Richard prudently set to work to settle matters with Scotland, agreeing a three-year truce with James III's envoys at Nottingham and arranging that the latter's son should marry his niece, Anne de la Pole. He then turned his attention to Brittany, attempting to negotiate the surrender of Henry Tudor to him, but before matters could be settled, Henry learned of the plans and escaped to France. Vergil says that it was John Morton, bishop of Ely, exiled in Flanders, who 'being certified of that practice from his friends out of England, gave intelligence to Henry forthwith of the plot that was laid and advised the earl that he should get himself and the other noble men as soon as he might out of Brittany into France'.[5]

The failure to capture Henry was a serious blow to Richard and made a military showdown almost inevitable. Henry was far more dangerous in France than in Brittany, since it was unlikely that France would give up such a valuable pawn and might well give serious backing to an invasion. Richard's plan had turned into disaster and all he could do was attempt to make political capital at home by denouncing Henry's refuge with the country's long-term enemy. It was hardly effective, as more and more men made their way discreetly overseas to join him. They were virtually all gentry rather than peers, but one of the

most significant exceptions was John, earl of Oxford, freed from his prison at
Hammes by its commander, James Blount, who also went with him to France.
Calais was of vital importance with the prospect of invasion from France. While
its resident lieutenant, Lord Dinham, was loyal, early in 1485 Richard replaced
its captain, Lord Mountjoy, brother of James Blount, with a member of his own
family, his bastard son John. That he should have done so indicates the lack of
men in whom he could place real trust. John was probably born about 1470,
before the king's marriage, and was old enough to be knighted in 1483 at his
half-brother's investiture at York, but he was still under-age at his father's death.
He was imprisoned after Bosworth and his subsequent fate is unknown, but one
source says that he was put to death by Henry Tudor at the same time as Perkin
Warbeck and Edward of Warwick.

The appointment of Richard's bastard son to such an office also highlights
the critical state that the Yorkist dynasty had by then reached. In early April
1484, on or about the first anniversary of Edward IV's death, the king and the
realm had been shaken by another death. Edward, Prince of Wales, died at
Middleham after a short illness. His parents were at Nottingham and even the
hostile Crowland Chronicler describes them as 'almost out of their minds for a
long time when faced with sudden grief'.[6] He was unlikely to be the only one who
saw it as retribution for the death of Edward IV's sons. The date of the prince's
birth is uncertain, though the place is recorded as Middleham. It is usually given
as 1474, but the Tewkesbury chronicle refers to a birth of a son to the duchess
at Middleham in 1476. While this may refer to a second, short-lived, son, it
may equally well refer to the prince himself. Following the death of his uncle
Clarence, the small boy received the earldom of Salisbury, and soon after his
father's coronation was made titular lieutenant of Ireland. He did not travel to
London for his parents' coronation but remained in Yorkshire, joining them on
their progress just before they arrived at York. On 24 August 1483 he was created
prince of Wales and Richard seems to have made the sudden decision to hold
his investiture there in York, because it was a week later that he sent to London
for the appropriate robes and regalia, and Edward was invested on 8 September
in the archbishop's palace. Whether Archbishop Rotherham was there is open
to question, but the solemn mass in the Minster which preceded the ceremony
was performed by the bishop of Durham. The little prince remained in Yorkshire
when his parents returned south and it seems unlikely that he joined them for
Christmas, so the chances are that they never saw each other again. There is no
record of where he was buried, though Middleham seems likely.

His son's death posed a terrible dilemma for the king. He and his wife, Anne
Nevill, had been married for nearly twelve years and she had probably borne him
just the one child after three years of marriage, so there seemed little chance of
another one now, despite the couple's comparative youth – the queen was not yet

thirty. The king's nearest male relative was his nephew, Edward, earl of Warwick, just a little older than the dead prince. Edward of Warwick had been knighted at the prince's investiture and formed part of his household, but Richard's own claim to the throne was based on the barring of Edward by his father's attainder. His nearest adult male heir was another nephew, John, earl of Lincoln, eldest son of his sister Elizabeth and her husband, the duke of Suffolk. Lincoln, who had been born very soon after Edward became king, had already taken his place as the king's eldest nephew during Edward's lifetime, playing a prominent role at family occasions such as the reburial of Richard, duke of York and the marriage of Prince Richard and Anne Mowbray. He was then chief mourner at Edward's funeral. The title granted him, the earldom of Lincoln, was a former duchy of Lancaster one, and was the only one ever to be reused. Following Prince Edward's death in 1484, the king spent some weeks in the north, establishing a council to represent his authority in the region. He placed it in the charge not of one of the dominant northern magnates, but of Lincoln. The duke of Suffolk was a political nonentity, but his son was beginning to be a figure of some political importance. The earl, however, was never formerly appointed president of the new Council of the North, which was based at Sandal, Wakefield, rather than at Middleham.

Among other duties, Lincoln was responsible for presiding over the household of royal children at Sheriff Hutton; these included Warwick and his sister Margaret, Elizabeth of York and possibly some of her sisters, and probably Richard's own bastard son, John, all of them Lincoln's own first cousins. Somewhat later in 1484 he was appointed Lieutenant of Ireland. As with the Council of the North, this new post reflected his close blood links to the king, but despite what has been claimed, there is no contemporary evidence that Lincoln was ever publicly recognized as heir-presumptive. The king found it easier to shelve the problem for the moment.

Just before the death of Prince Edward, a combination of inducements and threats had finally brought Queen Elizabeth and her daughters out of sanctuary. She was no longer queen dowager, since her marriage had been declared invalid and her dower removed by parliament, but as Dame Elizabeth Grey she was granted an annual pension of 700 marks for the support of herself and her daughters and the king promised to find suitable husbands, 'gentlemen born', for the five girls, giving each a dowry worth 200 marks a year. Whatever her feelings, Elizabeth knew she had little choice but to accept, for they could not stay in sanctuary at Westminster indefinitely, and while she believed Richard to have murdered her royal sons, and knew him to have killed her brother and the younger son of her first marriage, her agreement with the king obtained the best deal she could get for her daughters as long as his reign lasted. There is no record of where they lived when they left sanctuary. The king may have lodged some of his nieces with trusted supporters or they may all have been at Sheriff

Hutton, but during his brief reign only one of his nieces was found a husband. Cecily, the second surviving daughter of Edward IV and thus her sister's heir, was married off to Ralph Scrope, brother of the king's ally, John, Lord Scrope of Bolton. The Princess Elizabeth, who was the greatest threat to Richard's security, was sent away from the disaffected south, to live at Sheriff Hutton, though she was not in any sense treated as a prisoner. One of Henry Tudor's main attractions to potential rebels was his promise to marry Elizabeth of York, and it was to this that Richard turned his attention. He had persuaded Elizabeth Woodville to bring her daughters out of sanctuary in March 1484, but increasing fear of Henry led to a more serious rehabilitation and by the Christmas of 1484 they were re-established at court. In the following months Richard set about a more serious rapprochement with the Woodville faction, pardoning a number of them, including Richard Woodville, the dowager queen's brother, and receiving their allegiance, though they and their sureties had to pay a substantial cash price for it. Elizabeth Woodville was even persuaded to write to her exiled son, Dorset, urging him to abandon Henry Tudor and return home to the king's grace.

The problem of what to do about Princess Elizabeth remained. The obvious solution was to marry her to someone else, but any other candidate for her hand would become as dangerous as Henry Tudor. The Crowland Chronicler believed that as early as Christmas 1484 Richard was considering marrying her himself. Apart from

> many other things besides, which are not written in this book and of which it is grievous to speak, nevertheless it should not be left unsaid that during this Christmas feast too much attention was paid to singing and dancing and to vain exchanges of clothes between Queen Anne and Lady Elizabeth ... who were alike in complexion and figure. The people spoke against this and the magnates and prelates were greatly astonished; and it was said by many that the king was applying his mind in every way to contracting a marriage with Elizabeth either after the death of the queen, or by means of a divorce for which he believed he had sufficient grounds [there had been no papal dispensation for the marriage of cousins]. He saw no other way of confirming his crown and dispelling the hopes of his rival.[7]

It is not easy to deconstruct this crucial passage, even setting aside the element of hindsight. It certainly suggests that the Chronicler was at court that Christmas, or at the least he talked to many who were. His clerical disapproval of the singing and dancing seems unreasonable, since Edward IV's court festivals were as merry, but perhaps he was protesting at Richard's apparent hypocrisy in condemning the loucheness of his brother's court and then emulating it when it suited him. It was not uncommon for leading court ladies to wear similar gowns, and for the queen to lend a pretty but impoverished niece suitable attire can be read as nothing more than a kind gesture. The political dimension was a clear message that the bastard daughters of Edward IV had been fully restored to their place at court and therefore in the royal family, but it certainly need not be read as an indication that Richard was seriously considering marriage to Elizabeth, even if that was what people thought. The unknowable quantity is the health of Queen Anne.

Anne Nevill is the least known of all medieval queens and even more than most seems to be defined purely by the men in her life: daughter and co-heiress of Warwick; child bride of Edward, the Lancastrian Prince of Wales; and then married to Edward IV's brother. The chronicler Rous, who knew her, described her, 'In presence she was seemly amiable and beauteous and in conditions full commendable and right virtuous and according to the interpretation of her name Anne, full gracious'.[8] Rous may have been accurate, but equally he may have been providing the sort of description desirable for any noble lady. Anne's sister Isabel, duchess of Clarence, had died young, almost certainly of complications following the birth of her third child within seven years, but Anne probably bore only one child. While she had doubtless visited Edward's court with her husband, most of her married life had been spent quietly in Yorkshire, chiefly at Middleham, her childhood home. It was the connections of her Nevill inheritance which were a key factor in winning Richard the service and loyalty of northerners, and it was in the north that she was well known. As a considerable heiress, her jointure settlement was presumably substantial when she married Richard, but once he became king there is little evidence that he attempted to settle on his wife the customary queen's dower based on lands worth approximately £4500 p.a. However, certain duchy of Lancaster lands, which had formed part of Queen Elizabeth's dower, were assigned to pay the expenses of the king's household shortly after Anne's death, and she may have been assigned them earlier, though there is no record of it. It usually took several years to settle a queen's dower satisfactorily, and there may well not have been time before Anne's death to accomplish it. In the interim, she may have supported her household as queen with the income from her own inheritance, though even this was managed by the king's officers rather than her own. It was certainly from her inheritance that she made generous endowments to Queens' College, Cambridge, following in the footsteps of her sister-in-law, Queen Elizabeth; Richard had also granted the college a manor in the late 1470s.

In the brief time she was queen, shorter than any previous queen consort, Anne seems to have spent most of her time in her husband's company except when he was on military campaign. She was crowned with him at Westminster, accompanied him on his progress to York and was at Nottingham with him to receive the Scottish embassy when the dreadful news of their son's death reached them. This suggests that her health was not a cause for alarm in the first eighteen months of the reign. For many kings, their wife was the only person they could trust completely, whose interests were more or less identical with their own. For Richard this was doubly true. He and Anne were cousins, they had grown up together and had been married for a decade before they came to the throne; it is likely that they were closer than many royal couples in a dynastic foreign match. Crowland says that the queen fell sick shortly after Christmas 1484 and her condition worsened as the weeks went by 'because the king himself was completely spurning his consort's bed'.[9] This is an illuminating comment, not so much because it shows Richard rejecting his wife as has often been suggested, but first because it suggests that her illness was infectious (modern suggestions that it may have been tuberculosis, though not based on any real evidence, are not completely implausible). Secondly it implies that the couple had previously spent their nights together and that this was a matter of note at court, where it was customary for the queen to have a separate suite of chambers where the king might visit her privately as frequently or infrequently as he chose. Queen Anne died on 16 March during an eclipse of the sun and was buried at Westminster with all the ceremony befitting the funeral of a queen.

A widowed king without an heir of his body was not in a position to grieve quietly for any length of time. Names of possible foreign brides were soon put forward, and emissaries left England for Portugal only six days after the queen's death to negotiate for the hand of Joanna, the sister of John II of Portugal. Not only that, but they were to negotiate for a second marriage, between the king's niece, Elizabeth of York, and the duke of Beja, a cousin of the Portuguese king. This was an almost perfect solution to Richard's dilemma over Elizabeth: a suitable foreign match away from the main diplomatic axis of northern Europe. Richard might have seen such a match as the solution to a number of his problems but it would certainly have created others. It is against this background that a letter written by Elizabeth to her uncle's supporter, John Howard, the new duke of Norfolk, asking for his aid in furthering her marriage, must be interpreted. The letter was seen by the seventeenth century historian George Buck in the Howard collection, but no longer survives and is known only from Buck's version. Buck understood it to mean that the princess was eager to marry her uncle, but an equally valid interpretation is that she was seeking the aid of Norfolk, a highly experienced diplomat, to further the Portuguese match.

The idea of a Portuguese marriage was swept away amid rumours that the king was planning to marry Elizabeth himself. While a union between uncle and niece was not strictly forbidden by the church, provided dispensation was obtained (and it was later not unknown in European royal circles), the idea caused revulsion among his councillors. Richard was warned by Ratcliffe and Catesby, the men he trusted most, that, unless he abandoned the idea and publicly denied any such intention, his northern supporters would rise against him for causing the death of Warwick's daughter in order to enter into an incestuous marriage to his niece. There is no reason to believe the charge that Richard murdered his wife, but the fact that people, even his loyal northerners, believed it possible indicates the air of unease and suspicion surrounding him. The threat of their revolt was enough to bring the king to the humiliating position of making the public denial demanded of him. It was not moral revulsion driving his inner circle, but the self-interested fear that a marriage to Elizabeth would bring about a Woodville revival, with revenge for the deaths of her uncle and half-brother, and the rehabilitation of many of Edward IV's household men at the expense of those who had supported Richard both as duke and king.

As the spring of 1485 wore on, questions of the king's remarriage and a safe husband for Elizabeth were set on one side as it became clear that Henry Tudor, with French backing, was intending a summer invasion. Richard was probably relieved to be able to turn his attention to something as straightforward as military preparations to defend the country from the threat that had been hanging over it almost since the defeat of the 1483 rebellion. The king mustered his army at Nottingham, but sent Lord Lovell to Southampton to guard the south coast. Henry Tudor, with his band of exiles stiffened by about three thousand seasoned French troops, headed south west, as he had done before, but this time to his homeland of Wales, landing at Milford Haven in Pembrokeshire and then moving east, gathering men as he went.

Crowland reported that the king sent letters to every county ordering that every man of property should join his army under threat that, if they failed to do so, the victorious king would deprive them of possessions and life. Despite the threats, a great many of the gentry stayed at home. Richard should have been confident of victory; unlike Henry, he had military experience and he had all the resources of the country at his back, but if Crowland's report is correct, what he really feared was lack of a loyal turnout from ordinary gentlemen. In the event, a great many dragged their feet and failed to reach the rendezvous at Leicester on time, or like Thomas, lord Stanley, fell 'sick'. As Tudor's stepfather, Stanley had everything to gain from a Tudor victory, but he had in the end remained loyal to Richard during the 1483 rebellion and had been well rewarded, though Richard had retained in his own hands offices he had held before becoming king and did not distribute them as the Stanleys might have hoped. This time, when Stanley left court to return to the north west to raise men, he was forced to leave his son and heir, George, Lord Strange, behind as a hostage, hence his plea of illness. Strange tried to escape and when captured confessed that the Stanleys were this time indeed planning to support Henry, but swore he would write and urge his father to come to the king's aid. In the event his uncle, William Stanley, led the family contingent to join the king. In contrast to the lower ranks of county society, virtually every peer, or, if old or infirm, his heir, brought a force of men to the king's army.

Very little is known for certain about the course of the battle which came to be known as Bosworth; even its exact location is disputed. It seems probable that for much of the battle only the vanguard on each side was engaged. Richard's, led by the veteran duke of Norfolk, battled it out against Henry's under the command of the long-time exiled earl of Oxford. The death of Norfolk turned the tide and William Stanley, sensing it, finally threw his forces behind Henry, while the earl of Northumberland declined to bring his northern strength up in support of the king. While it was understandable that the Stanleys saw their future with Henry, Northumberland's motive is more obscure. The earl was probably calculating that a new king, ignorant of the north, would give him the free hand in the region which he regarded as his right, but it was a double blow to the king, because Northumberland had brought not only his own forces, but had overall charge of other northern contingents who would have fought for the king if they had been given the chance. Richard, with his numerical superiority now lost, finally staked everything on a desperate personal charge against Henry Tudor. He had almost reached his target before he was hacked down, many of his household knights and closest adherents dying with him. He was the first king of England since Harold in 1066 to die on the battlefield. In the end, the future of England had turned on the treachery of one northerner, William Stanley, and the treacherous inactivity of another, Northumberland.

Richard's body was discovered among the dead. Even the hostile Crowland, who by the time he wrote was certainly not immune to Tudor propaganda, condemned the lack of decency with which it was treated: 'many other insults were offered and after the body had been carried to Leicester with insufficient humanity (a rope being placed round the neck) the new king, adorned with the crown he had so remarkably won, went on to Leicester'.[10] Northumberland and Norfolk's heir, Thomas, earl of Surrey, were among those taken prisoner. William Catesby, 'who was pre-eminent among all the counsellors of the late king was also captured; as a final reward for excellent service his head was cut off at Leicester'.[11] The defilement of Richard's body and the decision to execute Catesby were deliberate acts of propaganda by the new Tudor king and designed for maximum effect. Later, he was perfectly willing to give his rival an honourable burial in Grey Friars at Leicester and to allow the Catesby family back into favour. At the Dissolution of the Monasteries by Henry's son, Richard's tomb was destroyed and his bones were probably gathered with those from other graves and reburied locally en masse. He is the only English monarch since the Conquest to have now no known grave.

The character of the last of the Yorkist kings was a contradictory one. The man who was responsible for the deaths of his nephews was also pious. The exact nature of that piety is harder to discover. Whether it was essentially conventional or something more personal and contemplative is the subject of some debate, and is unlikely to be resolved five hundred years later. The debate is largely based on

Richard's own book of hours, the popular means of personal devotion, but this was not new when he obtained it, though the selection of psalms and prayers must have appealed to him; not even the prayer he caused to be added to at the end, with its appeal to Christ to deliver the supplicant from all manner of sin, grief and danger, is unique to him. Like many of his peers, Richard's main form of religious benefaction, before and after he became king, was the establishment of chantries or secular colleges of priests, whose main purpose was the saying of prayers for his parents, himself and his family; he seems to have chosen not to include any of his ancestors, which was uncommon in an age where a sense of dynasty was highly developed. He endowed ten in total, not all of them large, but in 1478 he obtained a royal licence to found two on a much more lavish scale, one at Barnard Castle in County Durham, the other at Middleham. He intended Middleham's college to have a dean, six chaplains, five clerks and six choristers, while that at Barnard Castle was to be even grander. The preamble to statutes for the constitution and organization of the Middleham college may well have been composed under Richard's own direction and emphasized the trials and tribulations faced by man, speaking of how God in his infinite goodness had chosen 'not only to endow me with great possessions and of gifts of his divine grace, but also to preserve, keep and deliver me of many jeopardies, perils and hurts'.[12] Even foundations on this scale were eclipsed by the king's later plan for a college of no fewer than one hundred priests at York, a plan which lapsed with his death. It is noteworthy that all three of these foundations were in the north, having no connection with earlier Yorkist foundations at Fotheringhay or Windsor. It would appear that Richard was planning for his own burial to be at Middleham. In the Middleham statutes, of the six saints named other than the Virgin, two, Cuthbert and Ninian, were particularly significant in the north. Another was St George, the warrior saint.

Richard chose to present a martial self-image, and was fascinated by the concept of crusading and feats of arms, yet his military experience was really not very great – a divisional command at Barnet and Tewkesbury and the leadership of one expedition to Scotland, which was only moderately successful. It was Edward who was in reality the soldier king, with a string of successful battles to his name. It was Edward who led a court where jousts and tournaments were an essential part of the chivalric image the king wished to display and who rebuilt St George's Chapel, Windsor, as the chapel of the Order of the Garter. Yet in the end, it was only an image that Edward was projecting. Richard seems to have believed in the ideals themselves, which was presumably why he was so devastated by his brother's behaviour in France in 1475. Honouring those who had died for the cause of York is implicit in his own foundation of a chantry chapel at Towton and in the lavish endowment of Queens' College, Cambridge, where prayers were to be said, not just for his father and brother Edmund who died at Wakefield, but for humble soldiers under his own command who had died at Barnet and Tewkesbury. If he had reigned for longer, there is every possibility that he would have tried to unify his fractured realm by an overseas campaign against the old enemy, France, where his father had been militarily successful. When the ultimate test came, however, he lost a battle he should have won.

In many ways the entire reign of Richard III was a propaganda battlefield, as vicious and as negative as anything modern times can show. Public opinion had generally supported Richard's claim to the protectorship, but in order to justify his claim to the throne he was willing to blacken his brother's character and rule, and in particular to denigrate the Woodvilles and their influence on Edward. Once king, the *Titulus Regius* was a major propaganda tool, circulated widely throughout the country to disseminate his justification for usurping his nephew's throne. When the revolt of southern England was under way, Woodville supporters took the opportunity to begin the rehabilitation of their leaders' image, particularly that of Rivers. The spinning continued throughout the reign, and while it was Tudor propaganda which won the day and has affected how Richard has been seen ever since, it was not only posthumous. There was plenty of briefing against Richard during his lifetime. Rumours that he had murdered his wife, and that he had been responsible for the death of Henry VI were widespread during his reign and, more importantly, believed. The type of lampoon for which Collyngbourne was responsible was equally effective, and while it was all aimed at preparing England for an invasion by Henry Tudor, it was not necessarily coming directly from France. We simply do not know who was responsible and how it was disseminated, but there were plenty of disaffected sources at home. To justify his usurpation, Richard had not hesitated to discredit Edward and his queen; to justify a Tudor invasion, Richard had, in his turn, to be blackened, but, with the death of his nephews, he had handed his enemies a huge propaganda coup. In short, he lost the propaganda war before he was defeated on the battlefield. It was from the disaffected south that most of Henry Tudor's supporters were drawn, and from their perspective that the subsequent chronicles and histories were written which gave birth to the Tudor tradition of Richard as a monster and a tyrant. Again, Richard had brought this on himself by bringing major changes to the way the south was governed. In the north, his regime was judged very differently, both before and after he became king. There he was seen as a firm, just and pious ruler, with the military prowess to take on the Scots, and his loss was deeply felt. If Richard had succeeded naturally to the throne with the support of most of his subjects, he would almost certainly have been able to rule in the same manner over the whole country and his reputation would be very different. If he had defeated Tudor at Bosworth, he might still have achieved it over time. As it is, he was the man who destroyed the Yorkist dynasty by usurping his nephew's throne.

11

Elizabeth of York and the Pretenders

The defeat of Richard III by Henry Tudor in 1485 was long seen as a watershed in the history of England, with the battle of Bosworth signifying the death of the middle ages and the birth of the early modern state of the Tudors. Only comparatively recently have historians explored the continuity between the reigns of Henry VII and Edward IV. Contemporaries, of course, did not see a watershed. The Yorkist dynasty was not extinct; rather it was embodied in Edward IV's daughters, his nephew, Edward, earl of Warwick, and the sons of his sister Elizabeth, duchess of Suffolk. Henry VII's hold on the throne in the first few years of his reign was shaky: his dynastic claim to be the Lancastrian heir was dubious and he ascended the throne only by right of military success and the death of his predecessor. He had no experience of running a major estate let alone a kingdom of which he knew little, having spent most of his twenty-eight years in exile. He did, however, have some advantages over Richard III. First, he did not have the crime of child murder laid at his door; secondly, he did not have a universally agreed pretender on whom all the Yorkist hopes could be centred, and thirdly, his supporters included those key royal servants from the south of England who had deserted Richard. Henry's greatest weapon in his struggle to keep the throne he had so surprisingly won was his own political adroitness. This is not the place for study of the person and reign of Henry VII, but perhaps some light can be thrown on his relations with his wife, Elizabeth of York, and other members of her family still alive at his coronation.

Henry's position as the recognized Lancastrian claimant in the year or so before Bosworth owed much to the conspiracy of two women: his mother, Margaret Beaufort, countess of Richmond and the former queen, Elizabeth Woodville. The latter's involvement implies that by the autumn of 1483 she believed her sons to be dead and that the only hope for her family's survival lay in a marriage between her eldest daughter, Elizabeth, and Henry Tudor. Whether she altered her views as she and her daughters were re-established at Richard's court in 1484 is unrecorded, but by then the die was cast. On Christmas Day 1483, in Rennes Cathedral, Henry vowed to marry Elizabeth as soon as he became king, and this was one of the chief reasons for his acceptance as the figurehead of the Yorkist revolt against Richard. Once he had gained the throne, however, the question of his marriage presented Henry with a problem. If he married

Elizabeth immediately he would be seen as owing his throne purely to her title, while her death, with or without children, would in theory lead to his removal. On the other hand, her claim to the throne was so strong that he could not afford to let her marry anyone else. Henry temporarily shelved the problem by ensuring that he was crowned before he married her, thus emphasizing that he owed the crown purely to his own claim and efforts. The new king's coronation took place two months after Bosworth, just enough time for the preparations to make it a sumptuous and impressive occasion. Although Henry was always careful of his expenditure, he was well aware of the necessity of avoiding anything that looked cheap. Being crowned alone gave him the breathing space he needed to repeal Richard's *Titulus Regius*, ending the question of Elizabeth's legitimacy, and also to try and find out what had happened to her brothers and if possible, confirm their deaths. It can only be presumed that he could find no evidence of what had happened to them, and was forced to proceed with the marriage in the knowledge that by repealing the act, he had restored legitimacy not only to his bride, but to her brothers, if by any malign act of fate they were still alive. In a letter to the pope, Henry explained that while he could have made a useful foreign alliance, the lords of England had requested him to marry Elizabeth solely on account of her beauty and virtue; no mention was made of her superior claim to the throne. Henry might pretend that her blood was of no significance, but nobody else in England thought so. In the meantime, Elizabeth had been brought out of the Tower, where Richard III had installed her for safekeeping prior to Henry's invasion, and restored to the care of her mother. One effect of the repeal of the act was that Elizabeth Woodville had regained her position and property as queen dowager.

In terms of establishing his position on the throne, Henry was undoubtedly right to delay his marriage until after his own coronation, but there was strong pressure on him thereafter to make good his vow to Elizabeth as soon as possible. The marriage took place on 18 January 1486, though the formal papal dispensation, since the two were distant cousins, did not arrive until March. Little is known about the ceremony itself, but the aged Archbishop Thomas Bourchier, who had crowned Henry, was said to have performed it. The coronation of the queen should have followed hard on her marriage. Even the fact that she became pregnant almost immediately should not have delayed it if preparations had already been set in train. As it was, Elizabeth had to wait for an unprecedented two years before she was crowned; it is hard to see this as anything other than a deliberate policy by Henry to minimize the status of his wife. The coronation, when it took place in November 1487, generally followed custom, though the queen made her state entry into London not by land but by barge from Greenwich, and the civic pageantry which greeted her also took place on the river. She was greeted by Henry at the Tower, as if she were a foreign princess making her first entry into the city. She was not, however, dowered as befitted a foreign princess. Technically she was an English heiress, for she and her sisters should have inherited the estates which had been held by their father before he became king, chiefly those of the dukedom of York and the earldom of March. There was little likelihood that the king would allow his wife to hold either of these as her dower, since they were too valuable for his own purposes, though when he granted away Irish lands belonging to the earldom to James Ormond in 1494, the grant did acknowledge that he held them in her right: 'all which possessions are parcel of the lands and tenements of the earldom of March, now in the king's hands in right of Elizabeth the queen consort'.[1] Elizabeth was unfortunate that she had no royal father or brother to arrange the details of her dower before her marriage, and there is no evidence that the customary formal sum that was to be its value was ever set. In the first two years of her marriage the expenses of her household and her personal needs were paid for by the king. Henry did not have much in the way of confiscated land with which to be generous to his new wife. The queen-dowager, restored to her former position, had to have her dower rights restored also, though she certainly received less than her formal due. After his wedding to her daughter, Henry granted her nearly thirty manors, including a number of traditional dower lands she had formerly held, and a cash income from the city of Bristol and a number of other sources. Henry's own mother, Margaret Beaufort, countess of Richmond and Derby, deserved grants befitting her new status, the queen's sisters had somehow to be provided for, and her grandmother, Cecily, generously dowered from the dukedom of York, lived longer than might have been expected, finally dying in 1495.

Any new queen had initially to receive grants of fee farms, wardships, and other interim solutions before royal lands worth the sum agreed for her dower could be settled on her, particularly if there was a queen dowager alive. Henry had no desire to commit himself to a specific amount. It was not until the queen's coronation that he made a formal landed settlement on her. He was only able to do this because her mother moved into Bermondsey Abbey, surrendering her lands in return for an annuity of 400 marks. Henry may not have intended Elizabeth Woodville to retain her dower lands for long because he made an attempt to secure her future in a totally different way, negotiating with the Scots for a posssible marriage with the widowed James III, but the argument that the queen dowager was stripped of her lands and sent to Bermondsey as a punishment for complicity in the rebellion of the earl of Lincoln seems inherently implausible. Why should she plot against her own daughter and grandson? As early as the summer of 1486 she had taken the lease of the abbot's house at Westminster, so clearly she did not intend to live at court, and the negotiations with the Scots continued after she surrendered her lands. Her position as the queen's mother was unprecedented and the role of queen dowager had been taken, naturally enough, by the king's own mother. Elizabeth Woodville was in her late forties and her health was apparently not good; it was cited as the reason for her retirement. There is no reason to disbelieve it because she died only five years later. If she had been younger, and had not had to bear the violent death of so many male members of her family, she might have been willing to carve out a role at court for herself, as she almost certainly would have done if Edward V had lived. As it was, it is hardly surprising that she followed another precedent for royal dowagers: retirement. The most recent example was the king's grandmother, Catherine of Valois, who had also spent the last months of her life at Bermondsey. The abbey had been founded by the Clare family. As the widow of the heir of that family, Elizabeth had certain privileges there. After 1485 Cecily of York, though she did not enter a convent, led a life that was monastic in all but name. By giving up her lands, Elizabeth was in effect giving them to her daughter and in return, the king showed his gratitude by increasing her pension to £400 p.a., an increase of a third. She occasionally came to court and received the odd additional gift of money from Henry. In December 1488, for instance, more than a year after the collapse of Lincoln's rebellion, Henry made a grant of one hundred marks to 'our right entirely and right well-beloved queen Elizabeth, mother unto our dearest wife the Queen'.[2]

The surrender of the queen dowager's lands was formally handled by the council and the new queen initially received only the income from them, but later the estates themselves were made over to her. Elizabeth Woodville, who had received a considerably smaller dower than Margaret of Anjou, managed her affairs prudently and remained solvent. Elizabeth of York received only part of the dower her mother had held as queen and therefore enjoyed less than half her mother's income, leaving her heavily dependent on the king's cash generosity in the early years of her marriage. It is hardly surprising that she accumulated substantial debts and Henry had to give her £2000 from his chamber expenses to pay them off. In 1492 she was granted the reversion of some of the duchy of York dower lands of her grandmother, worth £1400 p.a. and when Duchess Cecily died in May 1495, she was confirmed in their possession. Only then did her income begin to approach the annual sum of £4500 that her mother had enjoyed as queen, but even then, in the last years of her life, Elizabeth's income was only just over £3500.

While Henry was not ungenerous to his wife, since gifts of clothing for herself and her servants were provided from his own resources, he seems to have had no intention of allowing her the financial freedom and the independence of a large landed estate of the type generations of previous queens had held. Neither did he scruple to leave her to support her two younger sisters out of her inadequate income. The delay in her coronation and the frugality of her endowment suggest that Henry was deliberately slighting his queen. If so, he had his reasons, but they did not include animosity towards his wife in person. By all accounts, the marriage was a success and Henry and Elizabeth enjoyed a deep and loving relationship. The king had endured a lonely and unhappy childhood, much of it in exile, and was permanently scarred by it, but Elizabeth provided him with a warm and happy family circle. By the time she was crowned, she was already the mother of a son, born on 22 September 1486, almost exactly nine months after her wedding. He was christened Arthur in attempt to link the new dynasty with one of the great mythical figures of the British past (Edward IV had given a bastard son the same name). Henry also ensured that Prince Arthur was born in Winchester, a city with Arthurian connections.

It is often argued that Elizabeth's marriage was overshadowed by her husband's relationship with his mother. Margaret, countess of Richmond and Derby, had been separated from her son for most of his life, their contact maintained only by letter, but despite this the pair remained devoted to each other. She had been instrumental in his gaining of the throne and, once he sat there, she became immensely influential, much as Cecily Nevill had been in the early days of Edward IV's reign, but her role did not diminish with the king's marriage. She was certainly seen more about the court than was usual with a king's mother and frequently accompanied the royal couple on progresses. She was probably pleased to see the retirement of the dowager queen to Bermondsey, since Elizabeth would always outrank her. Those seeking a powerful intermediary with Henry recognized that there were two queenly candidates for this office rather than one, even if the elder did not bear the title of queen. It says much for Elizabeth of York's skill, her confidence in the strength of her relationship with the king and her own quiet influence with him, that there was never any outward show of a struggle between the two women. Indeed, they probably settled into an affectionate co-operation and a number of senior household members seem to have served them both. They jointly presented a book to their lady in waiting, Mary Roos, and at Margaret's palace of Collyweston a suite of rooms was permanently reserved for the queen. When Princess Margaret's wedding to the adult James IV of Scotland was being planned, both women were adamant that she should not be sent north as young as nine, because 'they feared the king of Scots would not wait but injure her and endanger her health'.[3] Margaret Beaufort, bearing Henry at twelve, and never to have another child, was speaking from the heart and from personal experience. In the event, the princess was not married until she was fourteen. Both Elizabeth and her mother-in-law also wrote to the Spanish court, requesting that Arthur's future bride, Katherine of Aragon, be taught French so that they would be able to converse with her when she arrived; presumably on the grounds that there would be nobody at the Spanish court who could teach her English.

One example of Elizabeth's strong influence in the family sphere was displayed at her eldest son's christening. Not only was her mother asked to stand as sponsor for the king's heir, a considerable honour, but her sister Anne carried the chrisom cloth, while her sister Cecily carried the baby prince and her sister-in-law, the marchioness of Dorset, the prince's train. Her half-brother Dorset, her cousin, Lincoln, and several Woodville relations also took part in the ceremony. The principal representative on the king's side, the earl of Oxford, who was the prince's godfather, arrived too late to perform his role. The king's stepfather, now earl of Derby, was present, but Margaret Beaufort was absent. The ceremony was obviously intended to make clear Arthur's position as the true heir of the Yorkist dynasty, but there was little reason for Dorset and the Woodvilles to be there unless at the queen's wish. When Henry later set up the prince's household, it was John Alcock, bishop of Worcester, formerly tutor to the queen's brother, Edward V, who was appointed president of his council. Another member of Edward's household who joined Arthur's was the doctor, John Argentine. It is very likely that the queen had a role in these appointments; she certainly did when Elizabeth, Lady Darcy, who had been mistress of the nursery to Elizabeth Woodville's children, was given the same role for the queen's own children.

It was highly unusual for a queen to have sisters about her at court, let alone bear responsibility for them. Elizabeth's second sister, Cecily, who had been married off to Ralph Scrope by Richard III, found that marriage rapidly annulled under Henry, who disposed of her safely soon after the queen's coronation by bestowing her on John, Lord Welles, younger half-brother of Margaret Beaufort. What financial arrangements the king made is unknown, but the king's mother had no difficulty in ensuring that her brother was in royal favour. The marriage produced two daughters, who died before their father. When Welles died in 1499 he managed to ensure that all his lands went to his widow for life, to the detriment of his heirs, but Cecily jeopardized this by marrying a mere esquire, Thomas Kyme, in 1502. The king was furious at the disparagement and took the entire Welles estate into his own hands. The couple might have fared even worse but for the unexpected support of Margaret Beaufort. She seems to have been very fond of Cecily, offering the couple sanctuary at Collyweston and managing to negotiate a compromise over the lands which left Cecily in possession of at least some of them. Cecily died in 1508, without heirs.

Queen Elizabeth's younger sisters, Anne, Catherine and Bridget, were all under ten in 1485 and their marriages consequently a less urgent matter. It was nearly ten years later that Elizabeth felt herself in a financial position to arrange a match for Anne, then nearly twenty, with Thomas, Lord Howard, son and heir of Thomas Howard, earl of Surrey. The Howards had been loyal supporters of the Yorkist regime. The earl's father, John, duke of Norfolk, had died at Bosworth and the earl, who survived the battle, had been imprisoned in the Tower and attainted. When Henry gave him the opportunity to rehabilitate himself, Surrey served Tudor as loyally as he had York; a royal match for his son in the spring of 1495 was a suitable reward. It was not, however, a marriage which benefited the Howards financially. It was four scattered Howard manors which initially provided a jointure for the couple, together with the reversion of lands held by Elizabeth, the widow of the last Mowbray duke upon her death, but the trustees of the jointure were headed by Queen Elizabeth's small son, Henry, and her half-brother, Dorset. Henry VII was certainly not going to give his sister-in-law a landed endowment, though he was willing for some manors in Norfolk and Suffolk to go to them on the death of the queen dowager. The queen had no lands at her disposal, but in the marriage contract she agreed to pay an annuity of £120 to Surrey for the support of Anne's household, consisting of two gentlewomen, a girl, two gentlemen, a yeoman and three grooms, and to provide all Anne's clothes until the young couple came into possession of their lands. In fact she was still buying them just before her death: in May 1503 she paid for 'seven yards of green satin of Bruges for a kirtle for my lady Anne', as well as £6. 13s. 4d. 'given her by the queen's grace for her purse'.[4] Although Anne bore four children, only one lived long enough to be baptized and, when she died in 1511, her line died with her.

Having successfully settled Anne, the queen moved on to establish her next sister, Catherine. The husband chosen was William Courtenay, son of Thomas, earl of Devon, and four years older than his sixteen-year-old bride; the family had been Lancastrian and, while they had been reconciled under Edward IV, the earl had been attainted by Richard III and had joined Henry in exile and fought for him at Bosworth. He was immediately restored to the earldom when Henry became king, and continued to serve him loyally, so his son was therefore politically acceptable to the king as a brother-in-law. This marriage contract does not survive, but the trustees were the same and presumably the queen made similar financial arrangements. The Courtenays were not as wealthy as the Howards, but Catherine was a good deal more successful in bearing living children than Anne and the queen ended up paying for their support. When William Courtenay died in 1511, Catherine took a vow of chastity which lasted until her death in 1527. Their only surviving son, Edward, eventually fell foul of his cousin, Henry VIII, and was executed by him. Queen Elizabeth's youngest sister, Bridget, made rather fewer demands on her purse, since she entered the nunnery at Dartford, but the queen still sent her regular payments.

It is clear, therefore, that Henry VII had little problem with his queen's female relatives, allowing her to settle their futures with little cost to himself. He was unlikely to find dealing with the surviving male members of the Yorkist family as straightforward. In the first instance he had tried and failed to discover the fates of her brothers, a defeat which surely irked him considerably at the time and was to have serious repercussions in later years. In 1485 the only surviving male member of the direct Yorkist line was Edward, earl of Warwick, who had been living at Sheriff Hutton with his cousin, Prince Edward, and continued there after the prince's death. Henry VII sent a trusted servant to remove him immediately after Bosworth before he himself had even reached London. He placed Warwick initially in the custody of his mother, Margaret Beaufort, but it was not long before the unfortunate fourteen-year-old was sent to take up residence in the Tower, where he remained for the rest of his life. His sizable inheritance, particularly after the death of his grandmother, Anne, countess of Warwick, in 1492, remained firmly in the king's hands.

If Edward did not present Henry with any problems, the same could not be said of the senior adult male representative of the Yorkist dynasty, John, earl of Lincoln, nephew of Edward IV and Richard III, and heir to the duke of Suffolk. Whether or not Lincoln was at Bosworth is unclear; only one source puts him there but since he was with his uncle the king shortly beforehand, it seems very likely. Whether he was or not, he quickly made his peace with the new king, probably through his father's agency, and was not attainted. Suffolk had immediately come to terms with Henry and retained his offices but, not unnaturally, Lincoln lost the major ones he held. Both he and his father played prominent parts in the coronation procession and he was made a member of the council, but Henry played safe by keeping Lincoln close to him. He accompanied the king on the great progress Henry made through his new kingdom in the spring of 1486, and was with him when the news arrived that Francis, Lord Lovell had escaped from sanctuary, where he had been since Bosworth, and had made his way safely to Flanders. Several rebellious disturbances followed, but far from being involved, Lincoln was appointed to several commissions to enquire into the treasons and conspiracies. He was still with the royal family for the baptism of Prince Arthur, where he played a prominent role, and he was not finally permitted to leave court until Christmas of that year. In terms of bloodlines, the baby prince had now replaced him as the senior male representative of the Yorkist dynasty. This made Lincoln slightly less dangerous to the new regime and he could now look forward to a future as one of the only two dukes in the country (the other was Bedford, Henry's uncle Jasper Tudor), and a career close to the centre of court life.

Late in 1486 or early 1487 disturbing rumours reached London from Ireland of the arrival there of young Edward, earl of Warwick, who had been helped to escape from the Tower. Ireland had been Yorkist in inclination ever since the benevolent governorship of Richard, duke of York, and it welcomed and made much of the boy who claimed to be his grandson. Henry dealt with that by bringing the real Warwick out of the Tower and parading him through the streets of London under the escort of the earl of Derby to a service at St Paul's. There he could be seen by the assembled clerics, including Cardinal Morton, and the mayor and aldermen of London. His imprisonment was subsequently relaxed for a short time and he stayed at Sheen, where, according to Polydore Vergil, 'Lincoln daily spoke with him'.[5] Thereafter, having served his purpose, Edward was escorted back to imprisonment, but there can be no question that Lincoln knew whether the boy in Ireland was an imposter or not. The remote possibility that it was the London Edward who was the imposter and not the Dublin one cannot be entirely discounted, and if so, Lincoln would have known it. The news from Ireland made Henry jumpy, but there is no indication at all that Lincoln was under suspicion, which makes his action in slipping away from Sheen to Flanders almost inexplicable, except in terms of personal ambition. There he joined Francis, Lord Lovell, with whom he had almost certainly been in communication; the pair knew each other well because Lovell had grown up in the de la Pole household as Suffolk's ward after the death of his first guardian, Warwick. Financial help from Lincoln's aunt, Margaret, duchess of Burgundy, enabled the pair to hire a force of German mercenaries and they sailed to Ireland to take part in the coronation in Dublin of 'Edward VI'. The event was marred by the refusal of the archbishop of Armagh to take part, making Lincoln so angry that he could barely be restrained from doing him physical harm.[6] Even if Armagh was sceptical, most of the Irish elite seem to have accepted the genuineness of 'Edward'.

The Irish contingent of the small army which landed with their 'king' in remote Lancashire was led by Thomas Fitzgerald, chancellor of Ireland and brother of Henry's deputy, the earl of Kildare. They were reinforced by Martin Schwartz's German mercenaries, but apart from a few freebooters Lincoln and Lovell found that few if any Englishmen were willing to join their cause. They made their way south to Nottinghamshire, where, at Stoke in June 1487, they were heavily defeated by the army Henry had raised against them. Lincoln, Fitzgerald and Schwartz were killed and Lovell, who seems to have escaped, was never seen again and his fate is unknown. The boy pretender, known to history as Lambert Simnel but whose real identity can only be guessed at, was captured and Henry, appreciating the power of mockery, spared his life and put him to work in his kitchens. Unless Lincoln had already been in treasonable correspondence with Lovell or persons in Ireland and feared discovery by Henry, his motive was presumably to use Simnel as a mask until success enabled him to make his own claim to the throne. It was a foolish gamble and Lincoln paid for it. Even his father, Suffolk, refused to get involved and managed to retain Henry's trust. After his son's death and attainder, the duke was permitted to save those family lands held by his son, though for his own lifetime only. When Suffolk died in 1492, the de la Pole inheritance, much of it held by Duchess Elizabeth in dower, became a shadow of its former self. Lincoln, married to Margaret Fitzalan, daughter of Thomas, earl of Arundel and Margaret Woodville, had no children and on his father's death the Suffolk heir was his brother, Edmund.

The failure of the Yorkist attempt to dethrone Henry VII is hardly surprising. Henry had played his cards carefully from the start, admitting almost all of Richard's supporters back into royal grace. Englishmen were also tired of dynastic upheavals. The birth of a son to the queen, a grandson of Edward IV, had directed Yorkist loyalties to him and away from Lincoln; still less were men prepared to gamble on a supposed son of Clarence. Stoke was the last time Henry would have to defend his throne on the battlefield, but it was not the last time that members of the de la Pole family caused him concern. Lincoln's rebellion had determined the actions and fate of his brothers.

Henry was allowed four or five years' breathing space before the next Yorkist pretender appeared in 1492. Again he surfaced in Dublin, this time purporting to be Richard, duke of York, the younger of Edward IV's sons. According to his later confession, Perkin Warbeck was a native of Tournai in France. He seems to have been apprenticed to the cloth trade, spending time in Flanders before he moved to Portugal in the household of Lady Margaret Beaumont, wife of the Anglo-Portuguese Jewish convert, Sir Edward Brampton. There he transferred to the service of a royal councillor, Pero Vaz de Cunha, before moving on yet again to that of a Breton merchant, with whom he sailed to Cork. In Ireland he was pursuaded by Yorkists, undeterred by the Lambert Simnel debacle, to impersonate the duke of York. What was it about this much travelled youth that made them choose him, a native of France, speaking some Flemish, perhaps some Portuguese and probably a little English which was so important in the cloth trade? He must presumably have looked the part, and his brief sojourn at the Portuguese court may have added a little polish, but it seems unlikely that he had many of the attributes of the gently born. The conspirators managed to gain the backing of the earl of Desmond, but found that in general the Irish were not going to be taken in a second time. Their greatest success was in securing the support of Charles VIII of France, not because he believed in the genuineness of the pretender but because he needed a weapon to deter Henry from supporting Breton opposition to the French annexation of their duchy.

Warbeck and his supporters were brought to France, where presumably his coaching continued. France's support declined six months later, after Charles made peace with Henry, but Perkin moved swiftly on to Burgundy and the court of the dowager duchess, Margaret of York. The conspiracy had taken on an international dimension which that of Lambert Simnel lacked. Margaret, who had paid a long visit to England in the summer of 1480, was perhaps in a position to know if the young man before her was an imposter or not. Whether she convinced herself that he was indeed her nephew, or whether she merely had the intention of using him to embarrass Henry, will never be known, but she never withdrew her support, and she was certainly able to supply high level coaching. Whatever the pretender's background, his personal style was convincing and he became very friendly with Archduke Philip, the heir to Burgundy.

Margaret of York's role in the conspiracies against Henry VII is an important one, and she was on the receiving end of the full force of Tudor propaganda. Polydore Vergil said that she 'pursued Henry with insatiable hatred and with fiery wrath never desisted from employing every scheme which might harm him'.[7] She did, however, have reasons for her behaviour, some personal and some diplomatic. Immediately after he came to the throne, Henry was as generous to the surviving representatives of the house of York as he could afford to be, but he overlooked Margaret. Edward IV, who had never paid the full amount of his sister's dowry, had nevertheless granted her lucrative trading licences. Renewed under her brother Richard, these lapsed under Henry. This would have made a significant difference to the business-like Margaret's income. In 1494, 'Richard, duke of York' promised to restore them. Nor did Henry, aided to his throne by France, make any attempt to renew Anglo-Burgundian commercial treaties or make any friendly overtures to Archduke Maximilian. Margaret and Maximilian always worked closely together on Burgundian affairs and, whatever her personal feelings, all her political actions were sanctioned by Maximilian, who used her as a cover for his own diplomatic policies.

Neither Maximilian and his son Philip, nor Henry himself, could fail to be aware that Philip had a more direct and legitimate descent from John of Gaunt (via Gaunt's daughter, Philippa, who married into the Portugese royal family), and thus a greater hereditary right to the English throne than any Tudor. Maximilian had no designs on the English throne but, in his war with France, it made sense for him to encourage conspiracies against Henry to prevent him forming an Anglo-French alliance, and English exiles always received a warm welcome at the dowager's court. A rapprochement with Henry meant that there was no Burgundian involvement in any of the conspiracies against him in the years between 1488 and 1492 and Maximilian was far too busy with his war against France, which was deeply unpopular in the Low Countries. The Perkin Warbeck affair began in France and there can be no serious suggestion that Margaret created the pretender. When French support ceased, it was only then that Warbeck moved to Burgundy. Margaret had last seen her nephew in 1480 when he was seven. Did she truly believe that 'Perkin' was 'Richard' or did she merely put up a convincing act to further Maximilian's policies? Vergil certainly thought she did believe Perkin to be her nephew, welcoming him 'as tho' he had been revived from the dead so great was her happiness that pleasure seemed to have disturbed the balance of her mind'.[8]

In England, old Yorkist loyalties began to make themselves felt early in 1493. If the young man calling himself Richard, duke of York, was indeed the son of Edward IV, then many would consider backing him, even if they had shown no interest in supporting Edward of Warwick and Lincoln. Significant men began to be drawn into the conspiracy, men like John, Lord Fitzwalter, Sir Robert Clifford, William Worsley, dean of St Paul's, and even Sir William Stanley, chamberlain of the king's household. At this period, Henry was becoming increasingly unpopular and suffered a number of defections by men who had previously been loyal; in the next four years 150 people were tried for treason. Henry's spies and informers kept him abreast of the plots and he fought back. Ireland was brought to heel and some of the plotters captured.

Pressure was brought to bear on Burgundy by a threatened trade embargo, which caused considerable trouble for Philip, but he refused to give up Perkin, sending him off to his father, Maximilian, in Vienna. Here, too, Maximilian was won over. As an experienced diplomatist he was well aware of Perkin's nuisance value, and had every intention of exploiting it, but that does not quite explain his decision to take the young man with him, as a favoured companion, to the funeral of his father, the emperor. Perkin was equally honoured on his return to the Low Countries with Maximilian for the ceremonies installing the now adult Philip as their ruler. What had seemed an extraordinarily successful debut on the European stage was dealt a serious blow at the end of 1494 when Sir Robert Clifford defected to Henry, taking with him evidence of the treachery of Stanley, Fitzwalter and others, which led inevitably to their trials and death. Clifford may have been acting for Henry all along; he was certainly pardoned and rewarded. A number of those involved had connections with Cecily, duchess of York, who died in May 1495, soon after the plot had been exposed. Despite the setback, Margaret and Maximilian provided their pretender with ships and men to attempt a landing in England, timed to coincide with a renewed uprising in Ireland. A landing at Deal in Kent was a disaster, with the advance force overwhelmed while Warbeck and most of his men were still on board ship. He turned tail and fled to Ireland, from there making his way to the court of James IV in Scotland.

Once again the Pretender was received as York. James demonstrated his commitment by giving him a distant relative, Lady Katherine Gordon, daughter of the earl of Huntly, as a wife. This suggests that perhaps, at least initially, he believed the new arrival to be who he said he was. He also paid for the support of the fifteen hundred or so men Warbeck had brought with him. James raised an army to invade England in 1496, something he was planning to do anyway, but York's cause was a useful excuse to break the truce. Warbeck's second military outing was as disastrous as his first. Daunted by the failure of any Englishmen to offer their support, and the military depredations he witnessed, he abandoned James's army and withdrew back to Scotland. No-one had expected 'York', lacking military training as he did, to emulate Edward IV's success in battle, but serious doubts were cast upon his courage, and by association, his pretence of royal birth.

As his usefulness as a diplomatic lever waned, James's support rapidly cooled, but once again Warbeck's luck held. A serious rebellion against Henry's heavy taxation broke out in Cornwall, and the rebel army was able to advance all the way to London without resistance. It was easily dealt with by the king at Blackheath, using forces he had raised to deal with the Scots and diverted swiftly south, but those who escaped made their way back to Cornwall. There the suggestion that York should come and lead them found favour. He had deemed it prudent to leave Scotland with his wife, but a short stop in Ireland had not been encouraging. He landed near Land's End in September 1497, but although a few thousand locals initially joined him, forces from Exeter under the earl of Devon drove them off and the news of an advancing royal army caused the rebels to melt away. Some of the more important rebels fled to France, but Warbeck sought sanctuary in Beaulieu Abbey with a few companions. There he was recognized and surrendered. He was brought before Henry at Taunton, where he made a complete confession as to his origin, and was treated remarkably leniently. It might have proved difficult to charge him with treason, since he was not an English citizen, so he accompanied the court on its return to London; although he was carefully watched, he was not put under any form of restraint. His greatest punishment was that he was separated from his wife. Lady Katherine was placed in the queen's household but the couple were not permitted to live together – Henry wanted no offspring to continue the myth. Henry and Elizabeth treated Katherine generously, granting her lands to support herself, and she remained in England, remarrying three times before she died in 1537.

Emperor Maximilian made strenuous efforts on behalf of his protégé, including the offer of a reward of 10,000 florins to anyone who could obtain the release of 'monsieur d'York' and made the promise on York's behalf that he would renounce all claim to the throne, but to no effect. Warbeck seems to have settled into the life of a minor courtier for the next few months. Then in June 1498 he inexplicably slipped away from his quarters at the palace of Sheen and went on the run. By doing so he sealed his fate, for he was soon captured, forced to repeat his confession and imprisoned in the Tower for life. What happened next is a matter for debate; either he was framed or he became involved in a plot by a few Londoners to release the earl of Warwick. The plot in 1499 certainly existed and probably Henry and his agents allowed it to run until all involved had been implicated. The king then took the opportunity to have Warbeck hanged. More importantly, the unfortunate Warwick, the last Yorkist in the male line, was executed for treason. For nearly six years Warbeck had threatened Henry VII and had been recognized by the kings of Scotland and Denmark and princes of the Empire as the 'duke of York'. While these rulers were more interested in 'York' as providing a hold over Henry than in assisting him to the throne, it was Duchess Margaret's recognition that made the rest possible. Yet the pretender could find no significant support in England, and only the wild Irish and the rebellious Cornishmen turned out for him. Whoever he was, and it is worth remembering that Henry controlled his confession, he had the style and presence to convince Maximilian, Margaret and James IV that, even if he was not Richard of York, he could certainly act the part. They, and he, may in the end have even come to believe he was who he claimed to be.

Even with the death of Warwick and Warbeck, Henry was still not free of Yorkist challenges to his throne. When John, earl of Lincoln, died at Stoke, he left a number of younger brothers. The duke of Suffolk and his wife, the elder Elizabeth of York, had six sons: Lincoln; Edward, who died before 1485; Edmund; Humphrey, who became a priest and died in 1513; William; and Richard. Edmund succeeded to the dukedom on the death of his father in 1492, but almost immediately was forced to resign it on the grounds that with Lincoln's attainder and the loss of his share of family lands which his father had been permitted to retain only for his own lifetime, he did not have the resources to support it. He thereafter held only the earldom of Suffolk and probably resented the disparagement. Nevertheless he played his proper part in English life until 1501, when he left the country with his youngest brother, Richard, and joined Maximilian in the Tyrol, where he assumed the title of duke of Suffolk and was given the pseudonym of 'the White Rose'.

Maximilian chose only to give Suffolk covert assistance, since diplomacy at this point required him to stay on good terms with Henry. The king's reaction was first to confiscate the lands of the earldom and then in 1503 to attaint Suffolk and his brothers William and Richard for alleged projected rebellion. The unfortunate William, who was in England at the time, was committed to the Tower, and never again left it. Suffolk, who had spent two years at Aachen under Maximilian's protection, departed in an attempt to join the duke of Saxony in Friesland, leaving his brother Richard behind as a hostage to his creditors. Unfortunately for Suffolk, he fell into the hands of Archduke Philip of Burgundy, who eventually handed him over to Henry and he joined his brother William in the Tower in 1506. Richard took over the mantle of the White Rose, and even styled himself duke of Suffolk during his brother's lifetime. His claim to the throne of England was supported by France from about 1512. With England and France at war, Henry VIII seized the opportunity to execute Edmund for treason without further proceedings against him. Richard died unmarried fighting for France at the battle of Pavia in 1525. Although William was still a prisoner in the Tower, and remained so until his death in 1539, the legitimate Yorkist male line had come to an end. The female descendants of Richard, duke of York, however, were numerous; there still remained, apart from the queen and her sisters, Clarence's daughter Margaret, who was married in the early 1490s to a connection of the king's mother, Sir Richard Pole, considered a suitably safe match, Anne St Leger and the daughters of Elizabeth, duchess of Suffolk.

Elizabeth of York, Henry's queen, presumably watched the careers of her male relatives, real and pretended, with very mixed feelings. She can hardly have wanted their deaths, but they threatened the safety of her husband and the succession of her son. After Prince Arthur's birth in 1484, she had given Henry a second son, Henry, born in 1491, as well as two daughters, Margaret and Mary; several other children died in infancy, including a third son, Edmund, born in 1499, who lived for eighteen months. The names given to the children are not without significance. Arthur, as we have seen, was a link with the ancient British past; Henry was named both for his father and the last Lancastrian king, Henry VI, popularly regarded as a saint. Edmund was the name of Henry's own father. None of the boys had a name associated with the Yorkist regime. Of Henry and Elizabeth's daughters, the eldest was named for Henry's mother, the second for the Virgin, or even perhaps for Mary Bohun, wife of the first Lancastrian king; short-lived babies were baptized with the name of Elizabeth and Katherine, the first for the queen, the second perhaps for Katherine Swynford, ancestress of the Beaufort family. The country palace of Greenwich seems to have been one of the queen's favourite residences. Just as her father's younger siblings had been largely brought up there, so too were Elizabeth's younger children. In 1502 extensive improvements were carried out there, apparently based upon the queen's own plans. Despite Greenwich's popularity as a home for royal children, in February 1487 the town of Farnham proudly described itself as being 'where the king's first-born son is now being nursed' in its application for a licence to found a chantry.[9]

Henry VII's queen is often overlooked and dismissed as being under the thumb of her mother-in-law, but that is seriously to misjudge her position. It is true that she took no part in political affairs; that was not her role and would certainly not have been welcomed by anyone, but the success of her marriage suggests that any advice or influence she brought to bear behind the scenes may well have been effective. More importantly, she gave to Henry one priceless asset, namely popularity; for, unlike most foreign queens, Elizabeth of York was beloved by her husband's subjects. As well as bringing him her lineage, in her person she was lovely, gentle, pious and as good with people as her father. Her privy purse expenses for the last year of her life show a steady stream of gifts brought to her by poor people, as well as those from the great and the good. There was plenty of opportunity for them to see her, because she travelled frequently between the royal palaces up and down the Thames valley, from Greenwich to Windsor. No contemporary portrait of the queen survives and the effigy on her tomb, by the great Italian scultor, Pietro Torrigiano, is an idealized one created more than ten years after her death, but may be presumed to show a likeness of Elizabeth in her youth. Middle age and regular childbearing had altered her looks towards the end of her life. In May 1501, two years before her death and when the queen was in her mid thirties, the Portuguese ambassador wrote home to his master: 'There is no more news to write to your highness except that the queen was supposed to be with child; but her apothecary told me that a Genoese physician confirmed that she was pregnant, yet it is not so; she has much embonpoint and large breasts'.[10] Such honest and unflattering comments about queens are rare, but it must be balanced against an earlier description of the queen by an Italian visitor as 'a very handsome woman' and 'of great ability'.[11]

Although that particular pregnancy seems to have ended in a miscarriage, the queen's fertility was important, and despite the deaths of several babies, she provided a royal nursery of four children growing to adulthood; an heir and a spare, and two daughters for diplomatic purposes. The trouble for Henry and Elizabeth was that European rulers viewed the dynastic upheavals in England with suspicion and were initially not overly eager to match their children to the offspring of a usurper. As had been true under Edward IV, the states with which England was most concerned were France, Burgundy, Spain, Brittany and Scotland. For much of his reign, one of the central tenets of Henry's foreign policy was a marriage between his heir and a daughter of the Spanish monarchs, Ferdinand of Aragon and Isabella of Castile, a project which was first mooted in 1492. Despite the worrying activities of various Yorkist pretenders, the match between Arthur and the youngest daughter, Katherine, was agreed in 1496, though there was much bargaining over her dowry, and the treaty was not finally ratified until 1500. In the meantime Henry concluded a truce with James IV of Scotland in 1497, after James had abandoned Perkin Warbeck, and negotiations continued to turn it into a full peace treaty, to be cemented by his marriage to Henry's elder daughter, Margaret. Only after Warbeck's death were matters finally settled, but because of Margaret's youth, the marriage was delayed until the summer of 1503. The Infanta Katherine finally arrived in England in October 1501 and was married a few weeks later amid lavish celebrations and pageantry to Prince Arthur in person; they had previously been married by proxy. The young couple then travelled to Arthur's home in Ludlow to settle into married life.

Five months after his marriage, Prince Arthur died of tuberculosis. It was a devastating blow to Henry and Elizabeth, both personally and dynastically. An anonymous account of their behaviour when the news arrived at court gives a rare glimpse into their personal relationship. Henry sent for his wife immediately

saying that he and his Queene would take the painful sorrows together. After that she was come and sawe the King her Lord, and that naturall and painefull sorrowe, as I have heard saye, she with full great and constant comfortable words besought his Grace that he would first after God remember the weale of his own noble person, the comfort of his realme and of her. She then saied that my Ladye his mother had never no more children but him only, and that God by his Grace had ever preserved him, and brought him where he was. Over that, howe that God had left him yet a fayre Prince, two fayre princesses and that God is where he was, and we are both young ynoughe.

When she finally left him and returned to her own chambers, she collapsed with grief and her ladies sent for the king, who 'of true gentle and faithful love, in good hast came and relieved her'.[12] True to her words, within a few weeks of Arthur's death, Elizabeth was again pregnant, but the baby lived only long enough to be baptized Katherine. This was bad enough, but the queen then succumbed to puerperal fever and died a few days later, on her thirty-eighth birthday. The sorrowing Henry 'privily departed to a solitary place and would no man should resort to him'.[13] The queen's death 'was as heavy and dolorous to the king's highness as hath been seen or heard of, and also in like wise to all estates of this realm, as well citizens as commons, for she was one of the most gracious and best beloved Princesses in the world in her time being'.[14]

The Yorkist dynasty truly came to an end that day, 11 February 1503. It was left to her son Henry, then the ten-year-old duke of York and who grew up to look so like his grandfather, Edward IV, and to act as ruthlessly as his great uncle Richard III, finally to expunge the last embers of the Yorkist flame. During the course of his reign he executed Henry Courtenay, marquess of Exeter, Edmund de la Pole, duke of Suffolk, and most outrageously of all, Margaret Pole, countess of Salisbury, the aged daughter of Clarence, and her eldest son, Henry, Lord Montagu; only then did the Tudor dynasty finally feel itself secure. In an ironic twist of fate, it was the other Arthur, Edward IV's illegitimate son, who survived to die an old man in 1542, since bastard blood was irrelevant in dynastic power struggles. His mother, Elizabeth Waite, from a Hampshire gentry family, married a Lucy, and was a young widow when her relationship with the king began; we do not know exactly when that was but almost certainly before his marriage. Edward recognized his son, but made no settlement on him and the boy was largely brought up by his grandparents in Hampshire. He joined the household of his half-sister, the queen, in 1501 and on her death transferred to that of the king as a squire of the body to Henry VII. Despite the difference in their ages he became a favourite of his nephew, Henry VIII, receiving, among other offices, the governorship of Calais. His marriage in 1511, to Elizabeth, de jure baroness Lisle, brought him a title in her right, and three daughters but no male heir. He was imprisoned in the Tower in 1540 on suspicion of treason, but was too ill to take advantage of the king's order for his release and died there, one of the very few Yorkist males to die in his bed.

Conclusion

At the end of Shakespeare's *Richard III*, the victorious Henry Tudor proclaims his intention of ending the civil war by uniting the red and white roses. The white rose was one, though not the sole, badge of Richard, duke of York, but its importance is illustrated by the 'brooch of gold with a great point of diamond set upon a rose enamelled white', one of the most valuable pieces of jewellery known to have been owned by a noble in medieval England (it cost the duke more than £2500), which he pledged to Sir John Fastolf in return for a loan.[1] During his son's reign, Edward IV used the white rose widely, perhaps playing on his early nickname of the 'Rose of Rouen'. The red rose was not used as a badge by Henry VI. Shakespeare did not invent the symbolism, however, for Henry VII used it as a badge in his pageantry to show how his marriage to Elizabeth had united the two warring houses. The earliest reference to it comes in the Crowland Chronicle, written only a few months after Henry became king. The author includes some verse (not his own) comparing the three kings called Richard, in which Richard III's defeat at Bosworth is described thus: 'the tusks of the Boar [Richard's badge was a white boar] were blunted and the red rose, the avenger of the white, shines upon us'.[2] The poem also contains the first reference in English to Richard as the murderer of his nephews, since he is described as the suppressor of his brother's progeny.

Henry VII did not win the throne of England; the Yorkists lost it. In the quarter century of Yorkist rule, some of the underlying problems which had bedevilled their Lancastrian predecessors receded. The cost and difficulty of their rule in France had been eliminated by 1453, and Edward IV's concentration on improving the crown's finances and the conditions for foreign trade, particularly his pro-Burgundian policy, benefited the country generally and helped lift it out of recession. His policy of enforcing the law impartially and his reliance on powerful nobles for regional stability, although it did not solve the problem of lawlessness overnight, gradually enabled a much greater sense of peace and security to flourish. These improvements, however, did not happen overnight and it was the lack of perceived progress that permitted Warwick to stage his *coup d'etat*. Edward IV was, in the main, popular, his court splendid and his personal foibles regarded with an indulgent eye. Even his marriage was deplored more in court circles than in the country at large. In military terms, Edward's government had dealt with the final throes of Lancastrian resistance: if the threat to his throne in 1469 had been external, the king would undoubtedly have been able to handle it. It was the injured pride and ambition of one man, Warwick, and the selfish ambition of another, Clarence, which led to Edward's temporary downfall, and pointed the way to the ultimate defeat of the house of York from within. With a few ultra-loyal Lancastrian exceptions, England, or rather the upper reaches of society who determined such matters, had no wish to see the restoration of Henry VI, for the benefits of Yorkist rule were becoming apparent. Once he had regained his throne in 1471, Edward's hold on it was uncontestable. The very fact that he was able to twist the law of inheritance for the benefit of his brothers and his younger son illustrate the degree of authority he was able to exercise over his kingdom. It also enabled him to ignore any unrest felt over the peaceful outcome of the invasion of France, which had a beneficial effect on the royal finances and the advancement of his family on the European stage. In the negotiations over the matches for his children, however, Edward's increasing miserliness led him to overplay his hand diplomatically. He had nobody but himself to blame for the unravelling of his foreign policy at the end of his reign, though much credit has to go to Louis XI, whose cunning ran rings round Edward.

Edward had surmounted immense difficulties in becoming king and holding on to the throne, but some of those difficulties had been of his own making. If he seriously erred in not responding quickly enough to the disaffection of Warwick and Clarence, his single greatest mistake was his marriage. There is no doubt that Elizabeth performed her queenly duties admirably, but the clandestine nature of her wedding later allowed doubts to be cast on its legality. While her family became a singularly loyal group of royal servants, some of the manipulation of the inheritance laws was for their benefit. The unpopularity of the Woodvilles has tended to be exaggerated, and any closely knit group seen as having preferential access to the king would have aroused the same dislike among their competitors, but it was fear of their influence on the king's heir which allowed the usurpation of 1483 to take place. The supreme test of any dynasty, particularly a royal one, is its ability to pass the succession from father to son unchallenged. The Lancastrians passed it, both in 1413 and again in the far more difficult circumstances of 1422, when the heir was a baby. The Yorkists failed that test in 1483, but it was only a partial failure as it was due to a struggle within the dynasty itself. Nobody had expected Edward IV's premature death. If he had lived five years longer, until his heir was fully grown, the outcome would have been very different. The ruling class and the country at large accepted the accession of the young Edward V without hesitation. Only one man did not, but Richard of Gloucester had the power and the ruthlessness to depose his nephew. Whatever skill at ruling Richard displayed, however, he was never able to overcome the manner in which he achieved his crown.

Five times between 1399 and 1485 the reigning king was overthrown and three of those occasions were during the Yorkist period. The fifteenth century was a violent age and the house of York epitomizes that violence. Edward IV died in his bed, but his father, all three of his brothers, his two legitimate sons and various cousins and nephews were not so lucky. The only way to avoid such a fate, it seemed, was to avoid politics altogether. The most English of dynasties found it hardest to maintain itself on the throne, but the threat of its revival was to haunt the Tudors for decades. The Spanish ambassador wrote in 1500 that where there had been 'divers heirs of the kingdom and of such a quality that the matter could be disputed between the two sides. Now it has pleased God that all should be thoroughly and duly purged and cleansed, so that not a doubtful drop of royal blood remains in this kingdom, except the true blood of the king and queen'.[3] Henry VIII proved that De Puebla was wrong and it was not until the execution of Margaret, countess of Salisbury at the age of sixty-eight in 1541 that the last Yorkist outside the royal family was removed from the body politic.

Appendix 1

The Question of Edward IV's Legitimacy

Doubts were first cast on the legitimacy of Edward IV's birth during the earl of Warwick's propaganda campaign against him in 1469, when rumours that he was not a son of Richard, duke of York, spread on the continent. While noting them in passing, no historian had ever given them serious attention until Michael K. Jones found new evidence in 2002 which he claimed supported the illegitimacy theory. The evidence proved that the Pontoise campaign, which took York away from Rouen in the summer of 1441, was considerably longer than had previously been appreciated, making it unlikely that his wife could have conceived a child by him at a date which made Edward's birth the following April plausibly legitimate. Readers should, of course, study Dr Jones's arguments for themselves, but below are set out the arguments against the correctness of his premise.[1]

Edward was born on 28 April 1442 at Rouen in Normandy, where his father was governor. The previous summer York had been campaigning against the French king, Charles VII, which took him away from Rouen for five weeks from mid July, according to the reliable source used by Dr Jones. On 6 August he broke the siege of Pontoise for a second time, having already sent Charles fleeing back to Paris. He entered the town and spent a week there strengthening its defences before returning to Rouen. The standard gestation period is thirty-eight weeks (266 days), which leads to a likely conception date of the week beginning 4 August 1441. If Edward's birth was a couple of weeks early, it suggests conception in the week beginning 18 August when York returned to Rouen and his wife in triumph, a highly likely occasion for marital activity. While Dr Jones's evidence places York away from Rouen in the critical period, there is no evidence about the whereabouts of Duchess Cecily. She presumably remained in Rouen, but it is not impossible, even if it is unlikely, that she was with her husband at some point during the campaign. If Edward's birth was merely two or three weeks early, it is unlikely to have attracted any comment. Had he been very premature, it might have been noted, as was the birth of Prince Arthur in 1486, but when he was born a month early, Arthur was the anxiously awaited heir to the throne, while Edward was merely the son of a noble, born abroad. If Edward was indeed slightly premature, it might explain an early baptism in the castle chapel, which was in marked contrast to his younger brother Edmund's grand christening in Rouen cathedral, a point given considerable emphasis by Dr Jones.

In terms of the gestation period, York's absence is really too ambivalent to count as crucial evidence of Edward's illegitimacy. It is unlikely that those about Duchess Cecily had exact knowledge of the average gestation period, and there is no evidence whatsoever that questions were raised at the time. When the issue first surfaced a quarter of a century later, people close to the couple at the time of Edward's birth were unlikely to be able to remember exactly. The cathedral baptism for Edmund can at least in part be explained by what appears to be York's decision to make his second son heir to all his French possessions. What better way to begin than by impressing the Normans with such a magnificent ceremony? Despite his private baptism, one of Edward's godmothers was Elizabeth Boteler, sister of Lord Sudeley and married to Lord Say (and by a later marriage, the mother of Sir Thomas Montgomery, Edward's councillor). This is known from a later reference by the king himself, so it indicates that there was nothing out of the ordinary about his chapel baptism. His sister, Elizabeth, was also baptized in Rouen Cathedral in 1444, when her godparents included Lord Talbot and Jacquetta, duchess of Bedford, who presumably happened to be in Rouen at the time. Dr Jones also makes the point that on two separate occasions in 1459 and 1460 York kept his younger son with him while his heir travelled separately, suggesting that this was because York knew Edmund to be the true heir of his blood, but was this not really just the caution still practised today by the royal family in their travel arrangements?

In assessing the likelihood that Edward was illegitimate, psychological considerations should be taken into account. Duchess Cecily had given birth at Hatfield in the previous February, 1441, to her first son, Henry. There is no record of a grand baptism for the short-lived Henry either. He died as a baby and we have no clue as to when; he may either have gone with his parents to France in June, or been left behind at nurse, but it is probably safe to say that he died prior to their departure from England. Cecily therefore conceived again less than six months after the birth of her previous child, a pattern non-nursing aristocratic mothers could sustain, and indeed one that was to become a pattern in her own child-bearing. In that six month period, she and Duke Richard had to deal with the grief of their son and heir dying. Given the great stress that Dr Jones lays on Cecily's concern for the family honour, it seems unlikely that she would have agreed to a quick fling when her husband was only briefly away, when she was still recovering from parturition and grief, and when she had not yet borne her husband a healthy son. It is also doubtful whether someone who was in effect queen of English France would ever be unattended for long enough to have a liaison. Even if she did, rumours would almost certainly have circulated in Rouen.

There appear to have been absolutely no rumours questioning Edward's birth in England, Normandy or anywhere else until it suited Warwick politically. The earliest rumours appeared on the continent, where Warwick was held in high regard and where he had many connections. Any royal birth abroad was used to float such rumours, as John of Gaunt found when an attempt was made to undermine his power and influence at the court of the young Richard II. Henry V specifically made sure that his queen was in England in time for Henry VI to be born at Windsor. It is surely for this reason that one Yorkist chronicle specifically states that Edward was conceived at Hatfield, a statement easily disproved. The first contemporary record is a letter dated 8 August 1469 from Sforza de Bettini to the duke of Milan, saying that Warwick was spreading a rumour that Edward was a bastard and that George was therefore the rightful heir. Since the beneficiary of the rumour had just become his son-in-law, Warwick's motive was plain.

The earl had also been responsible earlier for rumours that Queen Margaret was an adulteress, thus casting doubts on the legitimacy of her son. He was, not surprisingly, using a similar tactic here. It was a particularly good one to use at this juncture, since the Woodville marriage had clearly not been appropriate behaviour for a king – something over which even his mother had quarrelled with Edward. Dr Jones regards Cecily's visit to Warwick and Clarence at Canterbury as a sign that she was privy to and approved of the plan to depose Edward on grounds of illegitimacy. But how do we know what her motive was? An attempt at reconciliation seems much more likely, since we know she and her daughters successfully engineered reconciliation with Clarence later. Thus the first bastardy stories did not appear on either side of the Channel until 1469, when they had a clear political purpose and look as though they emanated from someone with a specific political grudge and were timed for a specific purpose. Once in the public domain, of course, they were embroidered, like the one Dr Jones relates from Commynes about the identity of Cecily's putative lover being an archer called Blaybourne.

The key figure in all this is Duchess Cecily herself. What was her role? There can be little doubting the reports of her fury when she learned of Edward's unsuitable marriage. It was an astonishing action on the king's part and it can only be explained by the strength of his personal feelings for Elizabeth. Until then Cecily, as queen mother, had been the first lady in England and her influence on her son was judged to be considerable. In May 1463, in anticipation of any future marriage Edward might make, she had adopted a much grander seal than she had hitherto used, which declared her husband's right to the throne. While she would presumably have given way happily to a foreign princess, in the summer of 1464 she found she was supplanted by an Englishwoman of considerably lower status, and a widow with two small sons to boot. Both Warwick and Cecily were affronted on personal and political grounds. Warwick felt he had been made a fool of in diplomatic circles. Cecily, 'Proud Cis' as she was known, could not believe that any son of hers could act in a manner so contrary to family honour.

That there was a massive row between Edward and his mother is not really in doubt. While it is pure conjecture to suggest that in her rage Cecily could have used words such as 'you are no son of your father, no true son of York could ever have behaved this way' without meaning it literally, it is the sort of hurtful thing that gets said in family rows. Once said, it could not be unsaid, and could certainly be used for propaganda purposes in the future. Nor was there any way that Edward could really appease his mother. The marriage he had contracted, in however secret a manner, could not be undone, short of an annulment, which Edward would not consider. His mother was the only person who felt free to tell Edward exactly what she thought of his irresponsible behaviour, something for which Elizabeth Woodville probably never forgave her mother-in-law. A quarrel of this nature can be smoothed over, but never forgotten. Cecily had to live with the consequences. It was in direct response to Edward's choice of wife that she adopted the title 'queen by right'; she was going to allow Elizabeth Woodville as little precedence as she could.

The most graphic story of Cecily's rage comes from Thomas More and is a wonderful fictional account; Dr Jones cites Edward's mistress, Jane Shore, as More's source, but More himself gives no indication of his source, though he waxes eloquent about Jane Shore, who was still alive when he wrote. It is not impossible that she could have been the source of the story, but if Edward had ever told her of the quarrel himself, it is beyond belief that she could have given More the exact words used by her lover and his mother half a century earlier. The only contemporary source is Mancini, who says that Cecily 'fell into such a frenzy that she offered to submit to a public enquiry, and asserted that Edward was not the offspring of her husband the duke of York but was conceived in adultery and therefore in no wise worthy of the honour of kingship'.[2] Even Mancini was relying on gossip here, because the incident had occurred some twenty years before he arrived in England: 'the story runs …', he writes. Mancini himself takes it no further, and makes no mention of his source, of how widespread the story was, or what credence it was given. It is certainly possible from reading Mancini to accept that he himself thought it was just an idle rumour.

One of the most important factors in considering Edward's supposed bastardy is the regularity with which queens (and queen mothers) were charged with adultery. The Quinevere syndrome, as it has been dubbed, could have a number of different reasons: to challenge the king himself, to challenge the rights of her children, to enable a king to get rid of his wife, or for courtiers to advance themselves at her expense. The first is the most important and is the emblem of failed kingship. If the king could not control his wife and keep her faithful, the theory went, he could not rule the country. A queen was always in a vulnerable position. She was usually the only woman at the centre of a male power structure; and in most cases she was foreign, quite probably from an enemy country, and hence always under suspicion. Stories that John of Gaunt was not Edward III's son circulated at the height of his political power and hence unpopularity, though by this time his mother, the much loved Philippa of Hainault, was conveniently dead. Queen Margaret of Anjou had suffered in the same way. From 1453 people suggested that Prince Edward was not the king's son, undermining his legitimacy, and he was referred to as the queen's son. The point of the charge against Margaret was that, if she were adulterous, she was not fit to play a political role. With others, including Cecily, their lovers were asserted to be common men, the implication being that thus their children were even less fitted to rule. This also had the practical effect of making their supposed fathers untraceable. It is against this background that the charge against Cecily must be viewed.

Each time the story of Edward's bastardy was used, it was for political purposes. The rumour is said to have been started by Warwick in 1469, but it was only a justification for a change of ruler and not the reason for it. In 1475 when Commynes reported that Charles of Burgundy named the English archer, Blaybourne, as Edward's father, he was relating Duke Charles's fury at Edward's willingness to allow himself to be bought off by Louis XI under the terms of the treaty of Picquigny, an act he regarded as so dishonourable as to be unthinkable by anyone of noble blood. To resurrect the story of the king's base birth at this particular moment made perfect sense. In 1478, when the story was first mentioned officially by the king's lawyers as part of the evidence against Clarence, it was refuted by Edward in public, itself an indication of how much the king had been affected by his brother's use of it. In 1483 the charge was resurrected to support Richard III's claim to the throne, though Mancini is the only source to use the story. It was certainly not included in the king's own formal claim, which was based on his brother's precontract of marriage, not his bastardy. Even if Richard had encouraged the spreading of the rumour, he could hardly declare in a formal document that his mother was an adulteress who had foisted her bastard on the people of England as their king, thus making a mockery of the whole idea of a Yorkist dynasty. The story is, in fact, highly implausible. Cecily and her son Richard seem to have had a good relationship and it was from her house, Baynard's Castle, that he launched his bid for the throne, but she is hardly likely to have given him her authority to blacken her reputation by spreading rumours, even if she supported his bid to usurp her grandson and there is no evidence that she did.

Unlike Mancini, other sources only refer to the illegitimacy of the two princes and make no mention of their father. Polydore Vergil, writing much later, says that afterwards Cecily complained bitterly 'in sundry places to right many noble men, whereof some yet live' of the great injury which her son Richard had done her.[3] Tudor writers used it to show how bad Richard was, and to deflect attention from the pre-contract story, which, if true, made their queen, Elizabeth of York, illegitimate. Thus on each occasion that the charge against Cecily is made, there are cogent political reasons for its use; its truth was irrelevant, however hurtful Cecily herself may have found it. Neither contemporaries, nor subsequent historians, have ever given it serious consideration. While Dr Jones is to be congratulated on discovering a hitherto unused source, his use of it cannot reasonably be justified.

Perhaps it is fitting that the last word should go to Cecily herself. Years after the slander had ceased to have any political relevance, the duchess ordered the drawing up of her will in which she describes herself as 'wife unto the right noble prince Richard, late duke of York and father unto the most Christian prince my Lord and son King Edward the fourth', not only once, but twice.[4] It was an unequivocal statement at the time she was approaching her Maker.

Edward IV's Possible Pre-contract of Marriage

The claim that Edward was at some point contracted to Lady Eleanor Talbot, the widow of Sir Thomas Butler, heir of Ralph, lord Sudeley, needs to be looked at in the context of York's plans for his children. Eleanor was the daughter of John Talbot, first earl of Shrewsbury, the great military commander in France. She was born about 1436 and married Thomas Butler, who was about fifteen years her senior, in about 1450. Thomas died about ten years after the marriage in about 1460 and Eleanor herself died in 1468, having not remarried. If Edward was ever formally contracted to her, it was presumably before her marriage. There may have been discussions of a projected marriage between the duke of York and the earl of Shrewsbury, possibly while they were both serving in France. At this stage, however, York still had hopes of a French marriage for his eldest son. In addition, Talbot had only just been created an earl, though by inheritance and marriage he held baronies. He was a close colleague of York's and indeed had stood as godfather to the latter's daughter, Elizabeth, when she was christened in Rouen Cathedral, but it is doubtful whether York, so proud of his royal lineage, would have considered such an alliance for his eldest son at this stage, even if Eleanor had been Shrewsbury's heiress, which she was not. By the time Edward was seven, Eleanor, about eight years his senior, was already married to Butler, a respectable but not an outstanding match. If any contract for a marriage to Edward had been agreed, her marriage to Butler annulled it. Was such a marriage projected or resurrected in about 1460, when Eleanor was widowed? By this date, York regarded himself as rightful king of England. It seems hardly likely that he would have thrown away the marriage of his heir in such a way, and at that date the house of York had more pressing concerns on its collective mind.

If the precontract did exist, the most likely time for it to have been made was in the early years of Edward's reign and the supposition must be that the king gained the compliance of this widow by going through a form of pre-contract in a cynical move that foreshadowed his marriage to Dame Elizabeth Grey. If he did so, and Eleanor Butler regarded herself as contracted to him, why did she not protest when his marriage to Elizabeth was announced? It was hardly as if she did not have influential relatives; she was better born than Elizabeth Woodville, and had her husband's connections to call upon as well. When Richard III put forward her claim in the *Titulus Regius*, no comment either way is recorded as having been made by any of her family. If her family had known of the claim, and for some reason no action had been taken in 1464, it is rather surprising that they did not publicly endorse Richard's claim. If they knew nothing about the pre-contract, then Eleanor's death meant there was nothing they could say either way.

If Edward IV did go through some form of pre-contract with Eleanor, he was certainly not stupid enough to imagine that this could not affect the legitimacy of any children of his marriage. A discreet application to the pope to free him from any possible comeback would have been the action of any prudent king and his advisers. As far as we know, no such application was made.

Notes

Notes to Chapter 1: Richard of York

1   *Registrum Abbatiae Johannis Whethamstede*, i, ed. H. T. Riley (Rolls Series, 1872), p. 160.
2   Elizabeth Hallam, *Chronicles of the Wars of the Roses* (1988), pp. 194, 196.
3   Chancery memorandum, cited by B. Wilkinson, *Constitutional History of England in the Fifteenth Century* (1964), p. 128.
4   *England under the Lancastrians*, ed. J. Flemming (1921), p. 122.
5   *Rotuli Parliamentorum*, v, p. 255.
6   G. L. and M. A. Harriss, eds, 'John Benet's Chronicle for the Years 1400–1462', in *Camden Miscellany* 24 (1972), p. 212.
7   Ibid., p. 217.
8   P. A. Johnson, *Duke Richard of York, 1411–1460* (Oxford, 1988), p. 214.
9   Anne Crawford, *Letters of the Queens of England, 1100–1547*, (Stroud, 1994), p. 129.
10   *Rotuli Parliamentorum*, ed. J. Strachey and others, 6 vols (1767–77), v, p. 375.

Notes to Chapter 2: Edward IV's First Reign

1   Philippe de Commynes, *Mémoires*, ed. J. Calmette and G. Durville, 3 vols (Paris, 1923–25), i, pp. 180–1.
2   *Crowland Chronicle Continuations, 1459–1486*, ed. Nicholas Pronay and John Cox (1986), p. 115.
3   'Hearne's Fragment', in *Chronicles of the White Rose of York*, ed. J.A. Giles (1845), p. 23.
4   Calendars of State Papers, Milan, 1385–1618, ed. A.B. Hinds (1913), p. 132.
5   *Crowland Chronicle*, pp. 116–7.
6   CSP Milan, p. 140.
7   *Chronicles of the White Rose of York*, p. 239–40.
8   Warkworth's Chronicle in *Three Chronicles of the Reign of Edward IV* (Gloucester, 1988), p. 11
9   *Historie of the Arrivall of Edward IV in England*, ed. J. Bruce (Camden Society, 1838), p. 7
10   Warkworth's Chronicle, p. 16.
11   Ibid., p. 21.
12   *Political Poems and Songs Relating to English History*, ed. T. Wright, 2 vols (1859–61), ii, p. 274.

Notes to Chapter 3: Edward IV's Second Reign

1   See Chapter 7.
2   This and the succeeding paragraph are based on figures provided in Charles Ross, *Edward IV*, (1974), pp. 371–77.
3   *Crowland Chronicle*, p. 139
4   Ibid.
5   *Rotuli Parliamentorum*, v, pp. 572, 622; *The Paston Letters*, ed. J. Gairdner (reprinted Gloucester, 1983), no. 477.
6   *CSP Milan*, 1385–1618, pp. 197–98.
7   Commynes, *Mémoires*, p. 226.
8   Ibid., pp. 57–58.
9   *CSP Milan*, pp. 235–37.

Notes to Chapter 4: Edward the King

1   *CSP Milan*, p. 69.
2   'Gregory's Chronicle', in *Collections of a Citizen of London*, ed. J. Gairdner (Camden Society, 1876), p. 215.
3   See Appendix 1.
4   *Excerpta Historica*, ed. S. Bentley (1831), pp. 8–9.
5   Sir Thomas More, *The History of King Richard III*, ed. R.S. Sylvester (1963), pp. 4–5; Charles Ross, *Edward IV* (1974), pp. 86–87.
6   *Crowland Chronicle*, p. 153.
7   Dominic Mancini, *The Usurpation of Richard III*, ed. C. A. J. Armstrong (Oxford, 1969), p. 67.
8   Ibid., p. 69.
9   More, *Richard III*, pp. 55–56.
10 *Crowland Chronicle*, p. 149.
11 Ross, *Edward IV*, p. 258.
12 *The Travels of Leo of Rozmital*, ed. and trans. M. Letts, Hakluyt Soc., 2nd series, 108 (1957), pp. 46–47.
13 W. Blades, *The Life and Typography of William Caxton*, i (1861), p. 165; Ross, *Edward IV*, p. 267.
14 W. J. B. Crotch, *The Prologues and Epilogues of William Caxton*, EETS, Original series, 176 (1928), p. cix.

Notes to Chapter 5: The King's Mother and the Queen

1   *CSP, Milan*, pp. 65–66
2   Anne Crawford, *Letters of Medieval Women* (Stroud, 2002), p. 134.
3   *Rotuli Parliamentorum*, ed. J. Strachey and others, 6 vols (1767–77), vi, p. 141.

4   Anne Crawford, *Letters of the Queens of England, 1100–1547*, pp. 142–43.
5   Crawford, *Letters of Medieval Women*, p. 269.
6   R. Fabyan, *The New Chronicles of England and France*, ed. H. Ellis (1811), p. 654.
7   Jean de Waurin, *Historical Writing in England*, 2, ed. A. Gransden (1982), p. 293.
8   Sir Thomas More, *The History of King Richard III*, ed. R. S. Sylvester (1963), p. 64.
9   Crawford, *Letters of the Queens*, pp. 135–36.
10 Dominic Mancini, *The Usurpation of Richard III*, ed. C. A. J. Armstrong (Oxford, 1969), p. 61.

Notes to Chapter 6: Nevills and Woodvilles

1   *Chronicles of the Wars of the Roses*, ed. Elizabeth Hallam (1988), p. 244.
2   Antonia Gransden, *Historical Writing in England* (1982), ii, pp. 292–93.
3   'Annales rerum anglicarum' in *Letters and Papers Illustrative of the Wars of the English in France*, ed. J. Stevenson, 2 vols (Rolls Series, 1864), ii, p. 783.
4   Robert Fabyan, *The New Chronicles of England and France*, ed. H. Ellis (1811), p. 65.
5   'Warkworth's Chronicle', *Three Chronicles of the Reign of Edward IV*, ed. Keith Dockray (Gloucester, 1988), pp. 46–47.
6   *CSP Milan*, pp. 227–8.
7   Dominic Mancini, *The Usurpation of Richard III*, p. 69.
8   Ibid.

Notes to Chapter 7: The King's Brothers

1   *Crowland Chronicle*, p. 133.
2   *The Paston Letters*, ed. J. Gairdner (reprinted Gloucester, 1983), iii, p. 233.
3   John Rous, *The Rous Roll* (Gloucester, 1980), p. 59.
4   'Historie of the Arrivall of Edward IV', *Three Chronicles of the Reign of Edward IV*, p. 10.
5   *Crowland Chronicle*, p. 133.
6   TNA, KB 9/347/28; Michael Hicks, *False, Fleeting, Perjur'd Clarence* (Gloucester, 1980), p. 124.
7   *Crowland Chronicle*, p. 145.
8   Ibid.
9   Polydore Vergil, *Three Books of Polydore Vergil's English History*, ed. H. Ellis (Camden Society, 1844), p. 167.

Notes to Chapter 8: The King's Sisters

1   *Paston Letters*, iii, p. 296.
2   *Chronicles of London*, ed. C.L. Kingsford (1905; reprinted Gloucester, 1977), p. 164.
3   Warkworth's Chronicle, p. 17.

4   *Paston Letters*, v, pp. 30–32.

5   Crawford, *Letters of Medieval Women*, pp. 75–76.

6   Ibid., p. 184.

7   *Great Chronicle of London*, ed. A. H. Thomas and I. D. Thornley (1938; reprinted Gloucester, 1983), p. 204.

8   *Paston Letters*, iv, pp. 298–99.

9   Jean de Haynin, *Mémoires*, ed. D. D. Brouwers (Liege 1905–6), pp. 20–63.

10 Christine Weightman, *Margaret of York, Duchess of Burgundy, 1446–1503* (1989), p. 120.

11 Ibid., p. 121, quoting Plancher, *Histoire de Bourgogne*, iv, pp. 400–1.

12 Ibid., p. 120.

Notes to Chapter 9: Edward V

1   *Calendar of Patent Rolls, 1467–1477*, p. 414.

2   Ibid., p. 417.

3   Ibid.

4   *Crowland Chronicle*, p. 155.

5   Ibid.

6   Mancini, *Usurpation*, p. 75.

7   *Crowland Chronicle*, p. 159.

8   Ibid.

9   Mancini, *Usurpation*, p. 91.

10 Commynes, *Mémoires*, p. 353.

11 Mancini, *Usurpation*, p. 93.

Notes to Chapter 10: Richard III

1   *Crowland Chronicle*, p. 163.

2   TNA, C81/1392/6, quoted in Peter Hammond and Anne Sutton, *Richard III: The Road to Bosworth Field* (1985), p. 145.

3   *Crowland Chronicle*, p. 171.

4   Edward Hall, *Union of the Two Illustre Families of Lancaster and York*, ed. H. Ellis (1809), p. 398.

5   *Three Books of Polydore Vergil's English History*, ed. H. Ellis (Camden Society, 1844), pp. 207–8.

6   *Crowland Chronicle*, p. 171.

7   Ibid., p. 175.

8   *The Rous Roll*, p. 62.

9   *Crowland Chronicle*, p. 175.

10 Ibid., p. 183.

11 Ibid.

12 Charles Ross, *Richard III* (1981), pp. 131–32.

Notes to Chapter 11: Elizabeth of York and the Pretenders

1 *Calendar of Patent Rolls, 1494–1509*, p. 8.
2 *Materials for a History of the Reign of Henry VII*, ed. W. Campbell, 2 vols (1877), ii, p. 379.
3 Quoted in J.L. Laynesmith, *The Last Medieval Queens* (Oxford, 2004), p. 211.
4 Thomas Madox, *Formulare Anglicanum* (1702), pp. 109–10; *Privy Purse Expenses of Elizabeth of York*, ed. N. H. Nicolas (1830), pp. 9, 94.
5 *Calendar of State Papers, Spanish*, i, p. 176.
6 Polydore Vergil, *Anglica Historia, AD 1485–1537*, ed. Denys Hay (Camden Society, 1950), p. 19.
7 Ibid., p. 17.
8 Ibid., pp. 56–57.
9 *Materials for a History*, ii, p. 115.
10 *Letters and Papers Illustrative of the Reigns of Richard III and Henry VII*, ed. J. Gairdner, 2 vols (Rolls Series, 1861, 1863), ii, p. 102.
11 *Calendar of State Papers, Venetian*, i, pp. 754, 833.
12 Stanley Chrimes, *Henry VII* (1972), p. 303, quoting Leland and College of Arms MS.
13 R.L. Storey, *The Reign of Henry VII* (1968), p. 62.
14 *Privy Purse Expenses*, p. xcvii.

Notes to Conclusion

1 *Paston Letters*, p. 280.
2 *Crowland Chronicle*, p. 185.
3 *Letters & Papers*, i, pp. 113–19.

Notes to Appendix 1

1 Michael K. Jones, *Bosworth, 1485: Pyschology of a Battle* (Stroud, 2002).
2 Mancini, *Usurpation*, pp. 60–63.
3 Vergil, *Anglica Historia*, pp. 186–87.
4 *Wills from Doctors Commons*, ed. J. G. Nichols and J. Bruce (Camden Society, 1863), p. 1.

Select Bibliography

In compiling this bibliography, principally those primary sources which have provided quotations have been cited. As far as the secondary sources are concerned, the list is by no means exhaustive. The Journals and Bulletins of the Richard III Society also provide a treasure trove of information on their king and his times. The place of publication is London unless differently noted.

PRINTED PRIMARY SOURCES

British Library Harleian Manuscript 433, ed. Rosemary Horrox, 4 vols (The Richard III Society, 1979–83).

Calendars of Patent Rolls, 1461–1467 (1897), *1467–1477* (1899), *1476–1485* (1901).

Calendars of State Papers, Milan, i, *1385–1618* (1913).

Calendar of State Papers Spanish, i, *1485–1559* (1862).

Calendar of State Papers Venetian, i, *1202–1509* (1864).

Chronicles of London, ed. C. L. Kingsford (1905 reprinted Gloucester, 1977).

Chronicles of the Wars of the Roses, ed. E. Hallam (1988).

Commynes, Philippe de, *Mémoires*, ed. J. Calmette and G. Durville, 3 vols (Paris, 1923–25).

Crowland Chronicle Continuations, 1459–1486, ed. Nicholas Pronay and John Cox (1986).

Excerpta Historica, ed. S. Bentley (1831).

Fabyan, Robert, *The New Chronicles of England and France*, ed. H. Ellis (1811).

The Great Chronicle of London, ed. A. H. Thomas and I. D. Thornley (1938, reprinted Gloucester, 1983).

The Great Red Book of Bristol, ed. E. Veale (Bristol Record Society, 18, 1953).

'Gregory's Chronicle', in *Collections of a Citizen of London*, ed. J. Gairdner (Camden Society, 1876).

Hall, Edward, *Union of the Two Illustre Families of Lancaster and York*, ed. H. Ellis (1809).

Haynin, Jean de, *Mémoires*, ed. D. D. Brouwers (Liege 1905–6).

'Hearne's Fragment', in *Chronicles of the White Rose of York*, ed. J. A. Giles (1845).

Historie of the Arrivall of Edward IV in England, ed. J. Bruce (Camden Society, 1838).

'John Benet's Chronicle for the Years 1400–1462', ed. Harriss, G. L. and M. A., in *Camden Miscellany*, 24 (Camden Society, 1972).

Letters and Papers Illustrative of the Reigns of Richard III and Henry VII, ed. J. Gairdner, 2 vols (Rolls Series, 1861, 1863).

Madox, Thomas, *Formulare Anglicanum* (1702).

Mancini, Dominic, *The Usurpation of Richard III*, ed. C. A. J. Armstrong (Oxford, 1969).

Materials for a History of the Reign of Henry VII, ed. W. Campbell, 2 vols (1877).

More, Sir Thomas, *The History of King Richard III*, ed. R. S. Sylvester (1963).

The Paston Letters, ed. J. Gairdner (Gloucester, 1983).

Political Poems and Songs Relating to English History, ed. T. Wright, 2 vols (1859–61).

Privy Purse Expenses of Elizabeth of York, ed. N. H. Nicolas (1830).

Registrum Abbatiae Johannis Whethamstede, i, ed. H. T. Riley (Rolls Series, 1872).

Rotuli Parliamentorum, ed. J. Strachey et al., 6 vols (1767–77).

Rous, John, *The Rous Roll* (Gloucester, 1980).

Three Chronicles of the Reign of Edward IV (Gloucester, 1988).

The Travels of Leo of Rozmital, ed. and trans. M. Letts (Hakluyt Society, 2nd series, 108, 1957).

Vergil, Polydore, *Three Books of Polydore Vergil's English History*, ed. H. Ellis (Camden Society, 1844).

Vergil, Polydore, *Anglica Historia, AD 1485–1537*, ed. Denys Hay (Camden Society, 1950).

Waurin, Jean de, *Historical Writing in England*, ii, ed. A. Gransden, (1982).

SECONDARY SOURCES

Armstrong, C. A. J., 'The Piety of Cecily, Duchess of York: A Study in late Medieval Culture', in *England, France and Burgundy in the Fifteenth Century* (1983).

Arthurson, Ian, *The Perkin Warbeck Conspiracy, 1491–1499* (Stroud, 1994).

Baldwin, David, *Elizabeth Woodville* (Stroud, 2002).

Bennett, Michael, *Lambert Simnel and the Battle of Stoke* (Stroud, 1987).

Blades, W., *The Life and Typography of William Caxton*, i (1861).

Carpenter, Christine, *The Wars of the Roses* (Cambridge, 1997).

Castor, Helen, *Blood and Roses: The Paston Family in the Fifteenth Century* (2004).

Crawford, Anne, *Letters of the Queens of England, 1100–1547*, (Stroud, 1994).

Crawford, Anne, *Letters of Medieval Women* (Stroud, 2002).

Chrimes, Stanley, *Henry VII* (1972).

Crotch, W. J. B., *The Prologues and Epilogues of William Caxton* (EETS, original series, 176, 1928).

Dockray, Keith, *Henry VI, Margaret of Anjou and the Wars of the Roses: A Source Book* (Stroud, 2000).

Dockray, Keith, *Edward IV: A Source Book* (Stroud, 1999).

Dockray, Keith, *Richard III: A Source Book* (Stroud, 1997).

Flemming, J., ed., *England under the Lancastrians* (1921).

Gillingham, John, *The Wars of the Roses* (1981).

Gransden, Antonia, *Historical Writing in England*, 2 vols (1982).

Griffiths, Ralph A., and Thomas, Roger, *The Making of the Tudor Dynasty* (Gloucester, 1985).

Griffiths, Ralph A., *The Reign of King Henry VI* (2004 edn).

Griffiths, Ralph A., 'Local Rivalries and National Politics: The Percies, the Nevills and the Duke of Exeter, 1452–55', *Speculum*, 93 (1968).

Griffiths, Ralph A., 'Duke Richard of York's Intentions in 1450 and the Origins of the Wars of the Roses', *Journal of Medieval History*, 1 (1975).

Griffiths, Ralph A., 'The Sense of Dynasty in the Reign of Henry VI', *Patronage, Pedigree and Power*, ed. Charles Ross (Gloucester, 1979).

Griffiths, Ralph A., 'The King's Council and the First Protectorate of the Duke of York, 1453–4', *English Historical Review*, 99 (1984).

Hallam, Elizabeth, *Chronicles of the Wars of the Roses* (1988).

Hammond, Peter, and Sutton, Anne, *Richard III: The Road to Bosworth Field* (1985).

Harriss, G. L., 'The Struggle for Calais: An Aspect of the Rivalry between York and Lancaster', *English Historical Review*, 75 (1960).

Hicks, Michael, False, *Fleeting, Purjur'd Clarence* (Gloucester, 1980).

Hicks, Michael, *Richard III: The Man Behind the Myth* (1991).

Hicks, Michael, *Warwick the Kingmaker* (Oxford, 1998).

Hicks, Michael, *Edward V* (Stroud, 2003).

Hicks, Michael, *Edward IV* (2004).

Hicks, Michael, 'The Changing Role of the Wydevilles in Yorkist Politics to 1483', *Patronage, Pedigree and Power*, ed. Charles Ross (Gloucester, 1979).

Hicks, Michael, 'Cement or Solvent? Kinship and Politics in Late Medieval England: The Case of the Nevills', *History*, 83 (1998).

Horrox, Rosemary, *Richard III: A Study of Service* (Cambridge, 1989).

Horrox, Rosemary, ed., *Fifteenth-Century Attitudes* (Cambridge, 1994).

Hughes, Jonathan, *Arthurian Myths and Alchemy: The Kingship of Edward IV* (Stroud, 2002).

Ives, E., 'Andrew Dymmock and the Papers of Anthony, Earl Rivers', *Bulletin of the Institute of Historical Research*, 41 (1968).

Johnson, P. A., *Duke Richard of York, 1411–1460* (Oxford, 1988).

Jones, Michael K., *Bosworth, 1485: Psychology of a Battle* (Stroud, 2002).

Jones, Michael K., 'Edward IV, the Earl of Warwick and the Yorkist Claim to the Throne', *Historical Research*, 70 (1997).

Lander, J. R., 'Henry VI and the Duke of York's Second Protectorate, 1455–6', *Bulletin of the John Rylands Library*, 43 (1960–1).

Lander, J. R., 'Marriage and Politics in the Fifteenth Century: Nevills and Wydevilles', *Bulletin of the Institute of Historical Research*, 36 (1963).

Laynesmith, J. L., *The Last Medieval Queens* (Oxford, 2004).

Maurer, Helen, *Margaret of Anjou* (Woodbridge, 2003).

Petre, J., ed., *Richard III, Crown and People* (The Richard III Society, 1985).

Pollard, A. J., *Richard III and the Princes in the Tower* (Stroud, 1991).

Pollard, A. J., ed., *The Wars of the Roses* (1995).

Pollard, A. J., *The Worlds of Richard III* (Stroud, 2001).

Pugh, T. B., 'Richard Plantagenet, Duke of York as King's Lieutenant in France and Ireland', *Aspects of Late Medieval Government and Society*, ed. J.G. Rowe (1986).

Rosenthal, J. T., 'Fifteenth Century Baronial Incomes and Richard, Duke of York', *Bulletin of the Institute of Historical Research*, 37 (1964).

Ross, Charles, *Edward IV* (1974).

Ross, Charles, *The Wars of the Roses* (1976).

Ross, Charles, *Richard III* (1981).

Saul, Nigel, *The Three Richards* (2005).

Stansfield, M., 'John Holland and the Costs of War', *Profit, Piety and the Professions in Later Medieval England*, ed. Michael Hicks (Gloucester, 1990).

Storey, R. L., *The Reign of Henry VII* (1968).

Sutton, Anne F. and Visser-Fuchs, Livia, *The Reburial of Richard, Duke of York, 21–30 July 1476* (The Richard III Society, 1996).

Sutton, Anne F., and Visser-Fuchs, Livia, *The Royal Funerals of the House of York at Windsor* (The Richard III Society, 2005).

Thomson, John A. F., 'John de la Pole, Duke of Suffolk', *Speculum*, 44 (1979).

Watts, John, *Henry VI and the Politics of Kingship* (Cambridge, 1996).

Weightman, Christine, *Margaret of York, Duchess of Burgundy, 1446–1503* (1989).

Wilkinson, B., *Constitutional History of England in the Fifteenth Century* (1964).

Wroe, Ann, *Perkin: A Story of Deception* (2003).

Index

Members of the English royal family are indexed under their Christian names, members of the nobility by their surname.